Beyond the Darkness

DR. CHAD SCOTT

First published in 2025 by Dr. Chad Scott,
in partnership with Whitefox Publishing Ltd, London

www.drchadscott.com

www.wearewhitefox.com

Copyright © Dr. Chad Scott, 2025

ISBN 978-1-917523-00-4
Also available as an eBook
ISBN 978-1-917523-01-1

Dr. Chad Scott asserts the moral right to be identified as
the author of this work.

EU GPSR Authorised Representative
LOGOS EUROPE, 9 rue Nicolas Poussin, 17000, LA ROCHELLE, France
E-mail: Contact@logoseurope.eu

All rights reserved. No part of this publication may be reproduced, stored in a retrieval system or transmitted in any form or by any means, electronic, mechanical, photocopying, recording or otherwise, without prior written permission of the author.

While every effort has been made to trace the owners of copyright material reproduced herein, the author would like to apologise for any omissions and will be pleased to incorporate missing acknowledgements in any future editions.

All photographs in this book © Dr. Chad Scott,
unless otherwise stated in Picture Credits on p. 223

Designed and typeset by Typo•glyphix
Cover design by Chris Bentham
Project management by Whitefox Publishing

To those who pursued the greater good,
endured unimaginable trials, or sacrificed everything
for their beliefs—only to fade into history's shadows.
This book is dedicated to you.

Contents

	Foreword	vii
	Introduction	1
1.	The Making of a "Dark Tourist"	5
2.	America's Early Battlefields	22
3.	Historic Properties	40
4.	Places of Light and Darkness	56
5.	Medical and Macabre Museums	85
6.	Prison Tourism	102
7.	Wars and Battlefields	114
8.	Shadows of the Holocaust	134
9.	Legendary Legacies	152
10.	Historic Cemeteries and Graveyards	166
11.	Ghosts: Hauntings and Hunts	187
12.	A Journey's End	203
	To My Readers	213
	Bibliography	215
	Acknowledgments	222
	Picture Credits	223
	Index	225

> **Content Warning**
>
> This book explores themes of death, tragedy, and human suffering within historical and cultural contexts, including war, genocide, and personal loss. While written with reverence and thoughtfulness, some depictions of violence and trauma may be distressing.
> Reader discretion is advised.

Foreword

WE LIVE IN A DOMINION OF THE DEAD. We always have. Throughout history, the pact between the living and the dead has been one of mutual obligation. We ritualize the distinct dead, granting them a memorialized afterlife where they depend on the living to preserve their memory. In return, our significant dead guide us—to know ourselves, to structure our lives, to regulate our social relations, and to temper our reckless impulses. They sustain our cultural and social order, serving as our immortal custodians. We offer the discernible dead a commemorative future so that they may bestow upon us an honored past.

To that end, the world is now sadly filled with new dominions of death—places where contemporary rituals of memorialization are ever-present. Many such locations, often steeped in tragedy, have become sites of tourism, where the line between commemoration and commercialization grows increasingly blurred. These "dark tourism" sites, tied to fatality and historical moments of mortality, serve as reminders of our collective past and the significance we attach to those lives lost. The term "dark tourism" is an academic construct encompassing a diverse spectrum of visitor attractions, museums, and memorials that form part of the global visitor economy. Such sites engage with our difficult and often contested heritage, intertwining the politics of remembrance with cultural trauma. As a field of study, dark tourism has illuminated the thanatological condition of society, raising profound questions about how and why we remember our significant dead. It has also deepened our understanding of the emotional and ethical dimensions of tourism in spaces of suffering and places of "pain and shame."

We attach significance to certain kinds of death—those that unsettle the collective consciousness—making them spectacular and turning them into public spectacles. In our (secular) society of the spectacle, death that is deemed noteworthy becomes a "fatal attraction" within the touristic landscape. Yet, these sites of atrocity and adversity do more than highlight our painful pasts; they reframe historical calamities and provoke reflection. Dark tourism mediates mortality, offering both a commercialized experience and a profound contemplation of our shared, if not contested, history. In these spaces, the dead are selectively memorialized, and memories of trauma are curated within a visitor economy that trades on tragedy. The departed, resurrected through touristic narratives, return as spectral figures—reimagined "ghosts" that warn us of our past follies and misfortunes. In this way, dark tourism mirrors our own mortality, confronting us with the presence of absence.

In this book, Chad Scott invites us on a personal journey through dark tourism, exploring sites of pain and memory across the world. As we accompany Scott and his sightseeing in the mansions of the dead, we are drawn into the emotional weight of these experiences. There is, of course, no such thing as a "dark" tourist in the sense of moral deviance—only individuals, like Scott, navigating their own lifeworld, seeking meaning in places where tragedy lingers.

Scott's travels take him to former slavery plantations, battlefields, prisons, murder sites, cemeteries, and sites of the Holocaust. His reflections are not merely historical; they are deeply personal. Interwoven with his professional experience as a therapist and aviator, and his own struggles with marital challenges and health maladies, Scott's journey through these spaces of memory explores his own existence. Through dark tourism, he not only engages with the tragic past but also gains insight into himself and his loved ones. His touristic encounters with the commemorated dead serve as a memento mori—a reminder of life's impermanence, which haunts both him, and us as readers.

Dr. Chad Scott

Scott demonstrates how dark tourism is not simply passive observation but a complex immersive experience—one that elicits deep emotional responses and fosters personal transformation. Of course, any official interpretation of heritage is fraught with bias and dissonance; yet Scott reveals the power of dark tourism to challenge, provoke, and inspire. He confronts the uncomfortable truths of our tragic past, seeking meaning in places of cultural anguish, political remembrance, and selective recall. In doing so, Scott moves beyond the darkness of death and embraces the illumination of life. His journey through sites of human suffering is not one of despair but of understanding, connection, and, ultimately, renewal.

Dr Philip R. Stone
Director: Institute for Dark Tourism Research (iDTR)
University of Lancashire
United Kingdom

Introduction

AS I DESCENDED THE STEPS into Crematorium I at Auschwitz, the weight of history pressed heavily upon me. These were the same steps thousands of men, women, and children had walked, most unaware they were moving toward their deaths. Within minutes, they faced the horror of pellets releasing lethal gas into the crowded, suffocating chamber. Standing alone in that cold, silent basement, I felt the walls closing in around me, and the echoes of their suffering seemed almost tangible—a moment when the unspeakable pierced through time. In that instant, I realized I was standing in what might be the closest place to hell I will ever know.

In silent reflection, I envisioned the overwhelming panic of the victims as they realized there was no escape. The haunting image of them collapsing, one by one, onto the concrete floor consumed my thoughts. I suddenly became aware that my tour group had moved to the next room, and I couldn't understand how they could leave so quickly, as if the tragic significance of this room didn't demand more time. When I eventually followed, I imagined the dead being dragged along my route into the adjacent room, where small rail tracks carried the bodies to large brick ovens.

When I step into such dark, hallowed spaces, I feel the presence of both victims and, when they exist, survivors—not just through the physical memorials and guides but also within my own reflections. Fully immersing myself in these experiences, with a mindset rooted in remembrance and honor, has substantially transformed my perspective on the world—and myself.

This book isn't just about the sites I've visited over the course of more than two decades—it's about the way those visits have unexpectedly resurfaced in my life, transforming how I understand myself and the world around me. Through this personal lens, I want to share not only the transformative power of dark tourism but also the deeply human questions it evokes, in hopes that it resonates with others the way books like Viktor Frankl's *Man's Search for Meaning* or Jane Goodall's *Reason for Hope* have with me.

Most of us know the feeling of wanting to avoid uncomfortable truths. It's natural, isn't it? Many of us also shy away from situations that force us to confront pain. Historical sites can feel like open wounds, places where suffering lingers in the air. It's much like how someone might avoid therapy to escape painful triggers or hesitate to view an open casket at a funeral. But growth, both personal and societal, doesn't happen by turning away. It comes from facing what we fear or don't understand. Confronting grief, guilt, and anger allows us to process those emotions, reframe our fears, and open a path toward healing. From that process, something remarkable can emerge: meaning—a deeper understanding of ourselves, others, and the shared human experience.

When I explore these places and look deeply—beyond the layers of history and tragedy—I see more than just physical remnants. In the shadows of these sites, a mirror emerges, reflecting pieces of myself: my vulnerabilities, my strengths, and my own stories of loss and growth. These places transform from destinations into reflections of who I am and who I might become. But here's the thing—it only works if I approach them with an empathetic mindset, one focused on the lives and suffering of those I seek to honor with sincere reverence.

Visiting dark sites became a lifeline for me during my own struggles, offering both perspective and personal strength long after my visits. I didn't fully realize this until I found myself wandering through my second cemetery in as many days while in Los Angeles. I thought: "Of all the things to do here, why am I at a cemetery looking for the graves of celebrities?" Then it hit me—I was drawn to these places because, on a subconscious level, honoring and reflecting on the past was helping me find strength within myself. Paying tribute to celebrities with often complex legacies, whose fame revealed their successes, struggles, and the ways they strived to live, offered me a unique lens for understanding my own life.

This realization showed me how my interactions with history helped lift me out of the depths of sadness after my divorce. They also gave me the strength to endure a difficult illness and a liver transplant with a resilience I didn't know I had. The more I invested in honoring and learning from others, especially those who suffered, the more insight I gained into my own life. These kinds of experiences have proved to be priceless.

Journeys to sites of darkness, where death and tragedy have occurred, have come to be known as dark tourism. Coined by researchers in the 1990s, the term has gained popularity and become a well-established field of study. Dark tourism includes sites tied to wars, natural disasters, dark historical events, and infamous individuals. It also encompasses cemeteries and allegedly haunted places. Even locations with a more entertainment-focused appeal can fall under dark tourism, provided they maintain a dark edge. The varied motivations for visiting these sites can sometimes perplex those unfamiliar with the concept.

On one end of the spectrum are serious explorers of dark destinations—individuals with a deep interest in history and a respect for those whose lives were directly affected by these events. I normally count myself among this group. On the other end are those who seek the dark primarily for its sensationalistic appeal, though they might still learn important lessons in the process. These seekers of the macabre often view blood and guts as part of the fun. Many dark tourists begin in this latter group.

There usually isn't anything inherently wrong with the thrill-seeker group as long as they stick to entertainment-oriented attractions. The issue arises when thrill-seekers visit more serious sites with sensationalistic motivations, failing to respect the gravity of these locations. I've visited a variety of attractions and destinations that span the range of dark tourism, and ensuring my mindset aligns with the significance of each site is vital.

Places like the Catacombs of Paris, where tunnels lined with skulls and bones tell the story of lives lived and lost, serve as a stark reminder of our own mortality and the fragility of life. They compel us to live with love and intention. Gazing down at the main floor of the Roman Colosseum, I couldn't help but ponder what it must have been like to witness gladiators fighting for their lives, teetering on the edge of survival as if dancing on the blade of a sword. Even more haunting was imagining what it must have felt like to *be* a gladiator, often forced to entertain the masses with nothing less than their life. What did they feel? Was it fear, pride, or something deeper? Perhaps a resigned acceptance of their fate, or hope that their struggle might somehow endure beyond the roar of the crowd?

For centuries, people have been drawn to places marked by tragedy, suffering, and the macabre. In ancient Rome, the thrill of public spectacles like gladiator games and executions captured crowds. In medieval Europe, public hangings and witch trials were grimly popular events. Elsewhere, sites of reflection and commemoration emerged. The Battle of Marathon of 490 BCE, for example, became a lasting symbol of heroism and sacrifice in Greek culture. Centuries later, the ruins of Pompeii, unearthed after being buried by the eruption of Mount Vesuvius, stood as a grim reminder of nature's power. Even today, these places compel us to reflect on the legacies of the past, a testament to our amazing capacity for empathy and resilience.

I'm honored to have you join me on this journey into the often challenging, but highly transformative realm of dark tourism. Together, we'll explore places that range from intriguing curiosities to profoundly significant landmarks, all bound by a shared connection to darkness. Some of these sites invite quiet reflection and learning, while others bear the weight of humanity's most pivotal and painful moments, offering the rare privilege of standing where history was made. By the end of this book, I hope you'll gain a deeper understanding of suffering—both your own and that of others. My journey through these powerful places brought me resilience and clarity, and I hope that as you follow me beyond the darkness, you'll find that honoring the past can reveal a clearer sense of who you are and what truly gives your life meaning.

Chapter 1

The Making of a "Dark Tourist"

> "What you leave behind is not what is engraved in stone monuments, but what is woven into the lives of others."
>
> —Pericles

I'VE NEVER BEEN A FAN of the term "dark tourism" or "dark tourist." Sure, it's a convenient label, but it feels vague and a little too sensational. To me, a tourist is someone who's just checking off boxes on a list, while a traveler looks for something deeper—a real connection with the places they visit. The phrase "dark tourist" makes me picture someone skipping a beach day to indulge in a voyeuristic fascination with death and tragedy. That image couldn't be further from what I do.

Still, it's the term we have, so I'll wear the label—if only to help others see that exploring the shadows of history can be about more than the surface-level shock value. For me, it's about digging into the depth and history of a place, not just skimming over it. The reality is that not every so-called "dark" destination is that dark. Dark tourism is on a wide spectrum. A ghost tour can be good fun, and if enjoying a bit of campy storytelling makes me a "dark tourist," then I'll gladly take the hit.

But when I step onto hallowed ground—where the gravity of history is undeniable—I'm there to reflect, to learn, and to connect with the stories etched into those spaces.

So, how did I become someone who would rather stand in the shadow of history than ride a wave in Waikiki?

I wasn't a goth kid. I didn't listen to death metal, and I certainly wasn't examining dead animals on the side of the road. I was just a pretty average kid growing up on the rugged Iron Range of Northern Minnesota surrounded by taconite mines, lakes, and forests. School bored me, which made it tough to stay engaged, and I carried a quiet undercurrent of anxiety that I kept hidden from the world.

As a kid, I made my own fun and ran with a crew as wild as I was. I excelled in sports, drank far too much on weekends, and barely scraped by in school. Somehow, I always managed to get through, even if it wasn't pretty. Travel was a big deal in my family, and we often roamed the country to visit historical sites and connect with relatives.

College felt like a fresh start. With a clean slate and a newfound focus after discovering a love of the social sciences, I began to excel. Soon after graduating, I secured work in the mental health field while also teaching part-time at a university. This financial security became a lifeline because, at the age of 24, my relationship with my son's mom ended, and I became a single father. Being a single dad is, without a doubt, my proudest accomplishment.

Together, my son and I traveled extensively across the United States, and for the first time, I saw the real value of traveling as a form of education, something I had taken for granted as a child. I truly believe these trips had a deep influence on my son. He was exposed to different cultures, tasted new foods, and gained a level of wisdom beyond his years. Recently, he made history as one of the youngest mayors ever elected in Minnesota. Did our trips to places like Washington, D.C., Paris, and London—where we toured historical landmarks and government institutions—shape his path? I like to think they did.

One day, as I sat in my office, a slender, curly-haired woman about my age sank into the chair across from me, looking drained. She wore a

Rolling Stones T-shirt and introduced herself as Sarah, a social worker from St. Cloud—a city four hours to the south. Like me, she was a single parent, navigating the challenges of raising her own children. A month or two later, after mustering the courage and pushing past my fear of rejection, I finally asked her on a date. A few years later, we were married in a beautiful ceremony in Duluth, complete with a Frank Sinatra-style band.

Because we both had shared custody of our children, Sarah and I couldn't live together full-time. On the weeks I didn't have my son, I would drive 300 kilometers to her house—a routine we maintained for 11 years. This long-distance arrangement made vacations and travel a cornerstone of our relationship. Over time, I watched Sarah evolve from someone who would well up with tears and need a Xanax before boarding a plane into a confident and adventurous woman who fell in love with travel. It's yet another testament to travel's transformative power.

It was during these trips that we began venturing to off-the-beaten-path places. My first meaningful encounter with a cemetery happened in Key West and was a turning point in my dark tourism journey. Sarah and I were sitting at one of Ernest Hemingway's favorite bars, Sloppy Joe's, when a man wearing a Hawaiian shirt, straw hat, and flip-flops approached us. His casual demeanor epitomized the quirky charm of Key West, and I couldn't resist commenting on it. Eventually, the conversation turned to the Key West Cemetery, which he described as a must-see destination. Intrigued, we decided to check it out.

Upon arrival, we were greeted by tombstones with humorous and unconventional inscriptions like, "At least I know where he's sleeping tonight," "I told you I was sick," and my personal favorite, "Devoted fan of Julio Iglesias." Chickens roamed freely among the above-ground tombs, adding to the odd charm of the place. The cemetery's unique mix of cultures and its lighthearted take on life and death made it an unforgettable stop. This visit sparked a theme that blossomed on many of our subsequent trips: making it a point to visit a cemetery or two in most places we explored.

I'll admit, at the time, I loved exploring the taboo and didn't give much thought to the ethics of it all. However, I was always respectful and let common sense guide me. I also saw that it wasn't harming my son—in fact, it fostered his interests through experiential learning. Whenever we traveled, we often found ourselves on gangster or ghost tours or visiting museums with a dark edge. I think his fascination stemmed from his early teenage dream of becoming a detective. Right or wrong, I supported him in his interests. After all, what other teen spends their free time reading *Mindhunter*, the story of the FBI's profiling unit, or the *Encyclopedia of Serial Killers*?

For his high school graduation, we traveled to Paris and London, determined to explore every dark destination we could find: the Catacombs, the Panthéon, Napoleon's Tomb, the beaches of Normandy, the London Dungeon, the Tower of London, and the Churchill War Rooms—you name it. We even ventured into London's Whitechapel district for a Jack the Ripper tour. The variety of sites demanded different levels of reflection, and we always managed to adapt appropriately to the tone and seriousness each place required.

Years earlier, I first encountered the traveling anatomy exhibition *Body Worlds* with my son, when it came to St. Paul, Minnesota. That experience became another turning point for me. Initially, I wanted to see it out of a voyeuristic fascination with the taboo—real-life human bodies posed without their skin. I couldn't help but wonder: how on earth could something like this be considered acceptable, let alone appropriate for children? I had to find out. What we discovered was an extraordinarily tasteful and educational display of the human body, something my son would never experience inside a traditional classroom. Not only that: we learned about the process of plastination and how the bodies on display had been donated by individuals who had chosen to contribute to the exhibition.

I believe I subconsciously began seeking out these experiences with Sarah, my son, and even on my own during business trips. On one particularly memorable trip, we visited Ground Zero in New York, just before the museum opened. Standing before the monumental fountains where the towers once stood, I felt an instant connection to my loved ones. Seeing the names of the victims inscribed on the fountains' railings and reflecting on their lives and families, I couldn't help but think about how much I loved my own family. It was a powerful reminder of how precious every moment with them truly is and how deeply I never want to lose anyone I care about—not Sarah, not my son, not my stepdaughters, parents, or friends. Those in my inner circle were cherished beyond measure, whether they realized it or not.

Losing Altitude Fast

I have always strived to be the best I could be—or at least wanted to be. It was this mindset that allowed me to achieve success as a young adult. Yet, I had a couple of demons living inside me. One was called anxiety, and the other was a love of alcohol. Alcohol helped with anxiety—a lot. For non-work-related events that were difficult, just have a few beers and power through it. No problem!

As a therapist, I worked with hundreds of people struggling with alcohol and drug addictions. I also encountered anxiety on a daily basis in my clients. Yet, these struggles didn't seem to reflect my own—or so I thought. I never avoided going places because of anxiety, never missed a shift due to a hangover, and certainly never drank at work. Those were behaviors I often saw in my clients, not myself. I knew what an alcoholic was, and I didn't fit the strict criteria set forth in the diagnostic manual I frequently used as a therapist. But just because I didn't regularly drink to the point of stupor, get into trouble, or miss work didn't mean I wasn't suffering from an addiction. It simply meant I was a functioning alcoholic.

While I was still unaware of my struggles with alcohol, a new and unexpected health crisis began to unfold. While attending the Oshkosh Airshow in Wisconsin with Sarah, I noticed a few red bumps and an itch on my leg that gradually worsened. After several trips to the doctor, they determined it wasn't a simple rash—it was vasculitis. A disease in the same category that claimed the life of *Ghostbusters* actor Harold Ramis.

The pain of my symptoms steadily became more excruciating, and I was warned it could be a life-threatening type, though it was a matter of waiting to see how it progressed.

Over the next several months, I became consumed with my lab results, checking them obsessively throughout the day and even waking in the middle of the night to do the same. If a troubling thought crossed my mind while driving, I'd pull off the road to Google my fears, only to further stoke the flames of my anxiety. The worry that had haunted me as a child and resurfaced periodically as an adult returned with hurricane force.

During this time, Sarah was going through her own difficult period. The combination of my vasculitis and her mounting stressors began to strain our marriage. My anxiety spiraled out of control, but when she suggested I seek help, I refused. I dismissed her concerns as dramatic and worried about jeopardizing my pilot's license. Not long after, we received an early morning call: my dad had fallen gravely ill with sepsis while on a trip to Arizona with my mom. The doctor described his chances of survival as a "coin flip."

While in Arizona, I began experiencing a nagging stomach ache. "It's just anxiety," I told myself. Even after my dad recovered, the pain worsened, and I soon started having frequent bouts of bloody stool. My anxiety skyrocketed to an all-time high, yet I still convinced myself that seeking help wasn't the answer.

In my insecurity, I began saying things that made Sarah feel uncertain, and I often couldn't even recall the words I spoke during my moments of panic. Eventually, Sarah had had enough and asked for a divorce. It was the kind of loss that left me feeling like a shell of my former self—a version I could barely recognize.

During this time, I embarked on several adventure-based trips, including hiking through Costa Rica's vibrant tropical rainforests and assisting medical staff at a refuge in Colorado pull alligators out of swamps by their tails. In Florida, I attended a venomous snake-handling class and dove with sharks in the Keys. Each evening, I ended the day in the local pub, talking with locals and other travelers about the day's adventures. It was exhilarating to experience life again after my divorce. While some might view these activities as a mid-life crisis, they were remarkably effective in helping me regain focus and reduce my level of anxiety.

I've always been a strong advocate for stepping outside of comfort zones, a practice well supported by psychological literature for its transformative benefits. I often tell my clients in therapy, "Comfort zones are for couch potatoes"—a saying I strive to live by.

What I didn't realize during these travels was that I had a series of underlying genetic and autoimmune liver diseases, which, when combined with alcohol, pushed me into end-stage liver disease. What I dismissed as the natural aging process was actually my liver crying out for help. I always believed I'd quit drinking if I were ever diagnosed with a serious health problem that called for it—and I would have. But when I was finally diagnosed, it was too late. I quit drinking immediately and without issue, but the damage was already done.

Meaning Through Dark Tourism

A few years before learning of my liver disease, I read *Man's Search for Meaning* by Viktor Frankl. At the time, it was a deeply impactful read that helped me counsel others more effectively. But it wasn't until my diagnosis and the health struggles that followed that I realized how deeply relevant it was to my own life. No longer did I seek the temporary highs of adventure travel; even if I had wanted to, my illness would have made many of those pursuits difficult. Instead, I embarked on a series of journeys to dark destinations—local, national, and international—to find meaning. These travels also became a way to see as many places as I could while I still had the health to do so—and, frankly, in case I didn't survive.

The most meaningful dark destinations I've visited stemmed from a sincere desire to honor and pay respect to the victims of unspeakable tragedies. My deep interest in history also drew me to these places—sites I had long wanted to visit, not just to witness their history but to learn from them, in whatever form that learning took. Most of these places welcome visitors as a way to reflect on the tragedies and remember those who endured them—not as a way to make a buck. In a parallel to Frankl's book, I found myself searching for my own meaning and discovered it through my visits to the shadows of history.

During my visits to these places, I discovered that approaching them with genuine humility and wholehearted respect offers something in return—insights into our own lives. This is not to trivialize the suffering tied to these places but to acknowledge how it can transform us. For me, these journeys revealed meaning in my own life. No, I have never been a victim of an inconceivable traumatic event and may never truly know what it feels like to endure such a situation. But through the stories these places told—through witnessing, reflecting, and honoring—I gained a deep understanding of resilience, humanity, and purpose.

What began as an innocent curiosity about the underworld transformed into a profound journey through darkness that reshaped every aspect of my life. These experiences not only helped me endure the challenges of divorce and illness but also empowered me to emerge stronger and more resilient. I evolved from an anxious and uncertain person to someone with remarkable control over anxiety and a renewed sense of purpose. This transformation gave me the strength to face my eventual liver transplant with the mindset of a survivor.

But these are not just my stories—they are the stories of those who lived, suffered, and persevered in the places I visited. By exploring beyond the darkness, I often uncovered meaning in their struggles and, through them, discovered my best self. It's a reminder that even in life's darkest moments, there is often a path to growth, strength, and hope.

Shades of Darkness

Is it wrong to get into dark tourism as a way to be entertained? The simple answer is no—not if you started the way I did, with visits to lighthearted attractions. Take the London or Berlin Dungeons, for example; these are immersive exhibitions, often brought to life through theatrical performances that lean toward comedy, recounting tales from centuries past. They transport you to a time when killers lurked along cobblestone streets, witches were tried by being dunked in water until they confessed, torture chambers were a common form of punishment, and the chaos of the plague created mass hysteria.

Then there are ghost tours, available in just about any major city, which guide you through streets and buildings where alleged ghosts are said to wander in search of their final rest. Some of these tours take a more serious tone, while others are purely entertainment. At their core, though, there is always at least some darkness, as they are based—mostly—on actual events. Often, however, these events no longer feel deeply personal due to the passage of time. I place these experiences squarely in the edutainment category: places where you can have fun, reflect a little, and learn something at the same time. Personally, I've gained a lot from these attractions, which—unknowingly at the time—became my launching pad into the more serious aspects of dark tourism. Now, take a ghost tour at the home of someone who was just recently murdered, and it becomes a much more sensitive—and undeniably sour—subject.

When visiting sites of significant historical trauma, carrying a mindset of mere entertainment—or failing to approach the site with the reverence it demands—not only risks appearing insensitive but can also cause harm to others. I liken the approach required for dark tourism to my career as a therapist. People come to me with stories of substantial trauma, and if I were to treat those stories lightly, it would come across as judgmental and deeply hurtful. Therapists are trained to listen with empathy and non-judgment, reflecting on their clients' experiences, to help them process their emotions and situations. Similarly, dark tourism requires an empathetic mindset—one that seeks to grow and understand, not to be entertained by the tragedies of others.

Then there are moderate-intensity sites that are not as black and white. In fact, I feel that most dark tourism destinations fall into this category. These are places that demand greater respect and reflection, such as cemeteries, battlefields from past generations, and museums with exhibits related to darker subjects and death. While these places may not always be where the events themselves occurred, they serve as spaces for remembering and honoring the people and histories tied to them. Approaching these sites with respect allows us to reflect on the weight of what they represent.

Historic estates tied to dark pasts are a good example of middle-ground sites. I live near the Glensheen Mansion in Duluth, Minnesota, nestled on the shores of Lake Superior. This turn-of-the-century estate, built for the Congdon family, is famous for the industrial and philanthropic legacy of its patriarch, Chester Congdon. I've been visiting the mansion since the 1980s, not long after it was opened to the public for tours. It had been donated to the University of Minnesota Duluth to operate tours after the death of its last remaining tenant, Chester Congdon's daughter.

In 1977, Elisabeth Congdon, 83 years old and in declining health, was found murdered in her bed. Her nurse, Velma Pietila, was also killed, bludgeoned with a candlestick on the grand staircase. When tours began in 1979, they avoided going into the room where Elisabeth was killed and made no mention of the murders or the investigation. I remember being about seven or eight years old, looking for bloodstains on the floor and trying to figure out which room the murder took place in.

Fast-forward a couple of decades: the mansion now occasionally offers ghost tours, and guides are allowed to answer questions about the murders. Depending on the tour, visitors may pass through the room where Elisabeth's death occurred—a significant shift in policy from the early years after it opened. While the murders are not part of the official tour narrative, their acknowledgment reflects how time can change the shades of darkness at sites of tragedy.

Museums are another fascinating subject, as many blend seriousness with playfulness. The Spy Museum in Washington, D.C. is a great example. It showcases the critical and often dangerous work of real-world espionage, with exhibits highlighting how spies gather intelligence to protect nations from threats, such as terrorism or the smuggling of dangerous materials. At the same time, the museum embraces the pop-culture fascination with spies, offering interactive displays and areas designed for families, such as tunnels kids can crawl through for a sense of adventure. It also appeals to James Bond enthusiasts with exhibits featuring iconic spy gadgets and vehicles.

These museums cater to a wide audience and offer a mix of education and entertainment. While they are for-profit institutions, they can serve as an excellent gateway for aspiring dark tourists, blending intrigue with history. After all, few things are darker than the shadowy world of espionage and the looming threats it seeks to prevent.

As a pilot, I'm fascinated by the history of aviation and the story behind every plane I see at aviation museums. Any museum with war-related artifacts could be considered part of dark tourism. One such aviation museum is the United States Air Force Museum in Dayton, Ohio. Like most people, I feel pride in our military and honor those who have helped preserve our way of life. Yet, I often feel conflicted because I realize that on the other side of the gun barrel are people also fighting for their way of life. Even in cases where the opponents are led by dictators or fascists, the soldiers are often individuals forced by their governments to fight.

These middle-ground sites are fascinating because they embody both shades of gray and moments of distinct black-and-white clarity. I have a picture of my young son and me, smiling broadly in front of a B-29 Superfortress called "Bockscar." This is the very plane that dropped the bomb on Nagasaki—a bomb so devastating it had its own name: "Fat Man." I hate this picture. In the moment, I was caught up in the excitement and forgot about who was on the other side of that bomb—forgot about the lives it took, the trauma it created for generations, and the precedent it set for nuclear war.

At the time, I saw it as a famous plane that ended the greatest war—one that my grandfather fought in. I didn't see it as a symbol of something my country did that killed thousands of civilians and forever altered history. Now, that picture serves as a reminder of how I need to approach these sites—with empathy and a full awareness of the human cost, ensuring I never lose sight of the complexity behind the history.

Even cemeteries and graveyards can fall into gray areas. To me, all cemeteries are worthy of dark tourism because of their intrinsic connection to death. Some cemeteries carry an air of mystery and eeriness, such as London's Highgate Cemetery, which is Gothic and overgrown yet famous for its notable inhabitants, like Karl Marx. Others are well maintained and serve as final resting places for individuals who fought wars, led nations, or became heroes of civil rights—places of deep reverence.

Some cemeteries might even evoke nostalgia. Visiting the grave of a favorite entertainer and reflecting on their legacy can be a meaningful experience. Who knows—maybe it's meaningful for those you visit, too. I'd like to think that might be the case.

Yet, all cemeteries demand respect. Even when I've visited the graves of individuals I strongly disliked or whose actions I do not respect, I still honor the institution of burial and memorialization. The reflections I have at such sites may trigger different emotions, but there's a significant difference between how we feel internally and how we act.

We must always act in accordance with local customs, at the very least. "Spitting on someone's grave" should remain just an expression. When it comes to selfies, it might be appropriate to pose alongside a personal hero's headstone, but it certainly wouldn't be wise—or respectful—to do so at the grave of someone responsible for the slaughter of thousands.

The final category of dark tourism includes places tied to more recent tragedies, many of which remain sensitive topics for those affected. Take, for example, the Whitney Plantation near New Orleans, a site with a horrific history of slavery, torture, and death. Unlike most plantation tours, Whitney Plantation tells the story from the perspective of the enslaved, making it a place of substantial reverence and reflection.

When I was in the hospital with a severe case of hepatic encephalopathy, a condition that caused extreme cognitive challenges, I had an African American lab technician draw my blood. She had been temporarily assigned to the hospital from New Orleans. I mentioned to her that I had recently visited New Orleans and toured a plantation. Struggling with my condition, I couldn't fully articulate the significance of the visit or explain that the plantation focused on the history of slavery. She likely would have appreciated hearing that. Instead, she expressed disappointment, saying, "Why would anyone want to go to a place like that?"

That was the end of our conversation, and I just lay there, saddened for unintentionally causing her pain. The memory still upsets me. It serves as a stark reminder of how deeply personal and sensitive these sites can be and the importance of considering how we talk about them with others.

These most serious dark tourism sites demand the utmost respect. When I visit them, I feel as if I were attending the funeral of a close relative. Anything less would feel superficial and sensationalistic to me. Yes, I go there to learn and reflect, but my primary objective is always to honor the memory of those who suffered with as much reverence and dignity as I can give.

Many of these sites are places where recent genocide or other deaths occurred. Nazi death camps, the killing fields of Cambodia, and the Kigali Genocide Memorial in Rwanda are among those where unthinkable atrocities took place. Lives and families were destroyed, and the effects still significantly impact survivors and their loved ones to this day. The same applies to many battlefields and other sites of disaster or tragedy. These are places where we must act with respect—where children should be kept in check, and photos carefully considered before being taken. For example, a posed photo at one site might strike an entirely different tone and risk coming across as deeply insensitive at another.

The ways in which we engage with history must be tailored to the specific context of each location, as the events of the past continue to shape the present in subtle but significant ways. This lingering impact ties into the concept of historical trauma, where the effects of traumatic experiences are passed down through generations. I see this firsthand in my work with the Native American population during the two days I spend each week on a local reservation, providing therapy at a clinic. These experiences have deepened my understanding of how trauma resonates across time. In fact, there is a Native American belief that trauma is passed down for seven generations before it is resolved. I don't disagree. Even science, through the study of epigenetics, has shown that traumatic experiences can alter the way DNA is expressed, which is then passed down through generations. This intersection of cultural wisdom and scientific research underscores the importance of approaching history—both personal and collective—with intention and sensitivity.

Stepping into the Shadows

Preparing to visit places of tragedy is less about logistics and more about mental and emotional readiness. For lower-level sites or tours, preparation might not extend beyond the logistical details. But stepping into spaces tied to death or significant historical tragedy requires a deeper sense of purpose, respect, and reflection. I always ask myself: am I free enough from my own personal stressors to truly engage with this place? If not, I know to wait, and there have been times when I've chosen to visit on a different day.

Still, there are moments when entering dark spaces during personal distress can help us honor victims and find deeper meaning. This contradiction is something I've wrestled with, particularly when visiting sites of death during my own illness. At that point in my life, I found I could reflect more deeply and connect meaningfully with those who had suffered. It reminded me of my work as a therapist: the more life experience we have, the better we can empathize with others and help them heal.

That said, timing remains important. If I'm dealing with something urgent—like the frustration of a fraudulent charge on my credit card—I might need to wait until I've regained my focus. Entering these spaces with the right mindset is crucial to honoring them fully and engaging with the gravity they hold.

These places demand more than simply showing up—they require intentionality and reverence. Without the right mindset, I risk becoming numb to tragedy, which can erode empathy for the suffering of others. To truly confront the dark, I must approach it with a readiness to honor the victims and fully understand the gravity of what happened there. I must be in a place where I can reflect. But, what does reflection actually mean? In dark tourism, I see reflection as a thoughtful consideration of the experiences, emotions, and historical or cultural significance of the places visited. For me, reflection comprises these four basic areas:

Understanding and Cultivating Empathy

I immerse myself in the perspective of those who lived through these events, imagining their struggles, emotions, and the weight of their experiences. While I can never fully know how they felt, I try to connect with their humanity and place myself in their position. In doing so, I seek to feel with them, even if only briefly, to gain a deeper understanding of their reality.

Recognizing Shared Humanity

I reflect on how their suffering fits into the larger human story. Their pain, resilience, and hope serve as reminders of the threads that connect us all, transcending time, place, and individual circumstances.

Evaluating My Role

I consider what my visit means. Am I honoring their memory in the right way? How can I ensure that my actions respect their stories and preserve the lessons they teach? These questions guide my intentions and actions.

Finding Meaning or Insight

I search for the lessons this experience holds—about resilience, justice, and the strength and fragility of the human spirit. These reflections shape my understanding of the world and influence how I move forward in it.

Not every dark site is meant for the consumption of outsiders, even if visiting is technically legal. Consider the case of United Airlines Flight 93 that went down in Pennsylvania during the September 11th terrorist attacks. The landowner initially charged visitors a fee to access the crash site. This sparked significant public debate about the ethics of viewing such a site, especially when someone profits from it or when families might feel it's still too soon. The backlash led to federal intervention, and, eventually, the National Park Service acquired the land, transforming it into the Flight 93 National Memorial—a place of remembrance and reflection.

Would I have visited when the farmer owned it? Absolutely not. But now, as a place designed for honoring and reflection, I would. To me, there's usually a clear line between gawking and visiting with respect. This line is often defined by the time since the incident and the views of the victims, survivors, and their families. If there's controversy about a site, I simply don't go.

Some places exist in ethical gray areas, like Aokigahara Forest in Japan, known as the "Suicide Forest." While the Japanese government promotes its natural beauty and unique features, they actively discourage visits for problematic reasons, such as suicide or searching for victims out of curiosity. Widely criticized incidents like YouTuber Logan Paul's 2017 video—where he filmed and posed near a hanging corpse as if it were left there for his own amusement—highlight the disrespect and harm that can arise from treating places of tragedy insensitively.

I chose to visit Aokigahara with significant reverence for the individuals who lost their lives there, approaching it from the perspective of someone who works closely with clients facing suicidal ideation. Walking through the forest offered me a rare glimpse into the mindset of a suicidal person outside the confines of my office. Following their path allowed me to better understand their struggles in a more tangible way, transforming the experience. When you step into another person's perspective, even briefly, you expand not only your capacity for empathy but also your ability to honor their pain and humanity.

Some believe that traveling to places marked by poverty or war qualifies as dark tourism. For me, intent is everything. If someone enters a war zone purely for the adrenaline rush, they aren't engaging in dark tourism—they're chasing a void that no destination can fill. I've had my share of thrill-seeking adventures with alligators and snakes, but dark tourism is fundamentally different. That's not to say everyone who visits war zones or disaster-stricken areas is thrill-seeking. Those who enter such spaces to help others or support a cause are acting with purpose, not as tourists.

While traditional learning sharpens my mind, it's the experiences that engage my heart that have truly transformed me. They reshape not only how I understand the past but also how I see the present and future.

I often think back to a moment in Oslo, lying in my hotel room thousands of miles from my loved ones, feeling sick with what I knew was the end of my liver's ability to sustain life. I understood what was happening, but it didn't worry me much. My former self would have been nearly paralyzed with anxiety.

Lying in that tiny room in Norway, I came across an article about visiting sites of death and tragedy. It described two types of visitors: those who sought these places for the thrill, and those—like me—driven by a need to honor, reflect, and learn. In that moment, I recognized and accepted something about myself: I was a dark tourist. Shortly after returning home, I was placed on the transplant list, facing the uncertainties of survival. Yet, despite everything I had endured, I felt stronger than ever.

In the chapters ahead, I'll take you to the places that have shaped me, sharing the stories and lessons I've learned along the way. My hope is that through these journeys, you'll honor these places alongside me, find reflections of your own, and perhaps discover the courage to see yourself and the world a little differently.

After all, dark tourism, at its core, is a journey into humanity's collective reminder of mortality—what the ancients called "memento mori." It's not about dwelling on death but about using its inevitability as a call to live more fully and meaningfully.

Chapter 2

America's Early Battlefields

> "The world will little note, nor long remember what we say here, but it can never forget what they did here."
>
> —Abraham Lincoln, Gettysburg Address

I BEGIN MY STORY of dark tourism in my homeland—a place where my life started and, in all likelihood, where it will one day end. Every nation has its story, a tapestry woven with struggles, triumphs, and, often, bloodshed. Some nations came into being through war and rebellion, while others emerged through diplomacy.

It's natural for people to be curious about their origins, including their culture and nation. These origins are often filled with dynamic tales of heroism, resilience, and, at times, state-sanctioned violence and oppression. The United States is no exception. As a child, I visited many American historical sites and felt immense pride in my country, rarely questioning the stories I was told. However, seeing these places through adult eyes has given me a more nuanced perspective. While it's important to celebrate our nation's rise, it's equally vital to confront the darker chapters that shaped it—chapters that include the forced displacement of Native Americans and the horrors of slavery.

My story picks up after the Americas were discovered by the European world—a time when the British ruled over this new land. Like many countries, America's early history is marked by conflict and conquest. This isn't unique to us. South Africa, for instance, endured colonial domination under the Dutch and the British, leaving behind a legacy of systemic exploitation and apartheid—a system of institutionalized racial segregation and discrimination. Similarly, Australia began as a British penal colony, its history darkened by the displacement, violence, and systemic oppression of its Aboriginal peoples, which some historians argue amounted to genocide.

These shared histories reveal a far-reaching truth: the foundations of nations are often built on both light and shadow. Understanding both is essential—not to diminish our pride, but to deepen our perspective. It is through this lens that I begin my exploration of dark tourism, a journey into the past that at times can mirror the struggles and triumphs of our own lives.

The building of a nation is not only reflected in the details that shape its foundation but also in the growing pains it endures after its establishment. America serves as an excellent example of a country with a deeply dark history, marked by slavery, a full-scale civil war, and the attempted eradication of its Indigenous population. This is why we must not ban books or whitewash our history—it is essential to confront and learn from the past to grow as a nation. That doesn't mean I lack national pride; on the contrary, I believe acknowledging our history makes us stronger and more unified.

Boston and the Fight for Independence

When I think of Boston, I picture America's historic journey to independence unfolding against the backdrop of a vibrant, modern metropolis. It's a city where passionate citizens and iconic landmarks coexist, and historic buildings that shaped the nation's birth stand proudly amid the bustling energy of contemporary life. With its walkable streets and easy-to-navigate transit system, the "T," Boston has become one of my favorite places to explore—a city where the past and present blend seamlessly.

A great place to start a walk through America's formation is by walking the four-kilometer Freedom Trail. It's easy to navigate thanks to its famous red line that points the way. All I needed to do was follow the red bricks, and I would encounter several historically significant sites—some dark, some not so much, but all undeniably important. The darker sites along the trail offered opportunities to stand in history, reflect on the founding of a nation, and contemplate the immense struggles faced by the inhabitants of the American colonies.

My first stop was the Granary Burying Ground. Among the weathered tombstones lie the eternal resting places of several true patriots. Here, I discovered the graves of legends like Paul Revere, Samuel Adams, and John Hancock—men who were instrumental in the founding of America as a nation. This tiny cemetery also includes victims of the Boston Massacre of 1770, marked by thin headstones, many adorned with the "soul effigy" engraved at the top—a skull with wings, symbolizing the journey to heaven.

Moving along the trail, I eventually came to a brick building with large arched windows topped with an elegant steeple. This is the Old South Meeting House, which was once the largest building in Boston. This is where colonists gathered to protest the Tea Act. After passionate debate, the assembly here moved on to Griffin's Wharf, where the infamous Boston Tea Party took place. This decision to protest in a non-violent but impactful manner led to the destruction of a significant amount of tea in the harbor—approximately $2 million in today's money—all due to their frustration with "no taxation without representation."

Just a five-minute walk away stood another historic brick building, the Old State House, guarded by an ornate golden lion and unicorn—a relic of British monarchy. Ironically, from the balcony of this very building the Declaration of Independence was read to the citizens for the first time, in 1776. But six years earlier, this spot witnessed the Boston Massacre, where British soldiers opened fire on a crowd of colonists, killing five and wounding several others. It was a powder keg of escalating tensions and confusion, with one shot triggering a deadly chain reaction. As I looked closer, I noticed a circular pattern of cobblestones in front of the building, marking the exact spot of the massacre.

Despite the differing theories, most believe the massacre was a mistake, a tragic product of immense tension and fear. I could imagine the charged atmosphere between the crown's soldiers and the patriots. The soldiers were likely terrified, thinking they were about to be attacked by the mob. A misunderstanding of an order, or perhaps just pure panic may have led to that first shot being fired by an itchy-fingered soldier full of fear.

Fear, adrenaline, and confusion can drive us to actions we later regret. In the case of the Boston Massacre, these emotions led to a tragic and deadly mistake that altered the course of history. Sometimes, we can anticipate challenges and use tools like deep breathing or positive self-talk to stay grounded. Other times, we don't have that luxury and must act immediately. That's why it's so important to prepare by taking care of ourselves and planning for different scenarios—these practices help us respond more effectively when stress strikes. This idea wasn't lost on me as I reflected on the reckless shot that ignited the tragedy.

Just as important is expanding our comfort zones by deliberately putting ourselves in high-stress situations. It's a way to train ourselves not to panic but to react calmly with intention. I once had a flight instructor who used to say that the first thing to do in an emergency was to not panic. What if that soldier hadn't panicked and shot? What would that have done to the course of American history? Maybe things happen for a reason, and he was meant to shoot. Although, I'm not sure the loved ones of those who died would have agreed.

Walking the red line, I stopped at Faneuil Hall. Known as the "Cradle of Liberty," it has been a gathering place for citizens since the mid-1700s. This grand colonial building still serves as a meeting spot, now nestled alongside the bustling Quincy Market. It's a place I've visited every time I've walked the trail—whether to grab a snack or sit down for a meal. In my drinking days, it was also a great spot for a Boston Lager and good conversation.

The next few stops on the walk highlight a notable figure: Paul Revere, a skilled silversmith and a member of the "Sons of Liberty," a secret organization formed to oppose British rule. He is best known for his midnight ride to warn the colonists of the advancing British troops.

His home, the oldest building in downtown Boston, is able to be toured. The dark-brown gabled, wood-frame house stands out among the more modern-looking brick buildings of its neighborhood. The rooms are restored to their 18th-century appearance, complete with period furniture. Here, I examined artifacts related to his silversmith trade as well as some of his personal belongings, such as cookware, tools, and documents.

On a brisk spring night in 1775, Paul Revere got the word from Dr. Joseph Warren that the British were coming in by sea. This news triggered a pre-set plan devised by the Sons of Liberty to alert the patriots of the troop movements. Revere didn't waste a second. He coordinated for an associate to hang two lanterns in the steeple of the Old North Church—the next stop on my walk. The signal blazed out across the night, "One if by land, two if by sea." With that, Revere mounted his horse and rode into the dark, heading toward Lexington and Concord to spread the alarm.

The Old North Church, with its towering white steeple, is a sight to behold—not just for its remarkable craftsmanship but for what it represents. Imagining the light from the lanterns shining from this steeple serves as a poignant reminder that the revolution was sparked here. The mix of emotions the townspeople and patriots must have felt upon seeing that light must have been overwhelming. Urgency, fear, resolve, and hope likely surged through them, not unlike what troops might feel as they approach their destinations before mounting an offensive—the weight of knowing that a battle is imminent.

Next, I made my way to the USS *Constitution*, affectionately known as "Old Ironsides." This black-and-white painted ship earned its nickname because cannonballs fired at her formidable wooden hull seemed to bounce off harmlessly. Launched in 1797, after the Revolutionary War, the ship saw its share of action during the Quasi-War with France and the Barbary Wars. Later, she was a key player in the War of 1812 and fought valiantly against pirates.

Climbing aboard this floating piece of American history, I could almost feel the wind filling the sails, hear the crack of the cannons, and smell the salty sea air. The ship's towering masts and intricate rigging transported me back to an era when naval warfare was fought with grit, and wooden ships ruled the seas. I then stepped onto the weathered decks, where sailors once scrambled, and imagined the life of those who called this ship home. It's a raw, visceral connection to the past, a testament of the rugged bravery of the men.

My next stop on the Freedom Trail was Bunker Hill. While much of the fighting actually took place on nearby Breed's Hill, the site is commemorated with a 67-meter-tall obelisk that challenged me with 294 steps to the top. Once there, I was rewarded with a stunning panoramic view of the city—a perfect spot to reflect on the journey I had just made.

Descending from the monument, I was able to learn more about the history of this site. This is where the Battle of Bunker Hill took place—a significant clash during the Revolutionary War. Though the British technically won, the heavy casualties they suffered turned the tide, fueling the revolutionary fire and optimism among the colonists.

Lexington and Concord

I then took a short 25-minute drive to Lexington's Buckman Tavern and caught back up with Paul Revere on his midnight ride. Revere arrived at the tavern, which was a bustling meeting place for the local militia, and burst through the door, delivering the urgent news of British movement. The atmosphere was electric with urgency and resolve as the militia prepared to face the impending threat.

Revere then mounted his horse again and headed toward Concord, only to be captured by a British patrol. Ever the quick thinker, he spun a tale of an approaching mob of colonists, convincing the patrol to release him. They hastily let him go and fled the area, fearing an ambush. It's a moment of quick wit and daring that underscores the intensity and improvisational spirit of the revolution. His ride a major success.

Back at the Buckman Tavern I walked around the historic building, its wooden floor creaking with each step. The tavern now stands as a museum, where I learned about the Battle of Lexington and the lives of those who fought for independence.

The morning Revere arrived, the small militia left the tavern and came face-to-face with the British troops. Then it happened: "the shot heard 'round the world." No one knows who fired the first shot, but with it the war had begun. I stood on the spot where that shot was fired and tried to imagine the courage it must have taken to face the British troops, outnumbered by tenfold. In the aftermath, eight colonists were killed, and 10 were injured. On the British side, only one soldier was wounded. Undeterred, the British continued their march to Concord.

I then drove alongside the route the British troops took to Concord. My mission, however, is one of learning rather than fighting. In Concord, I walked across the Old North Bridge, the site of the first major resistance where militiamen fired upon British soldiers. This iconic spot echoes with the courage and determination of those early revolutionaries. This small New England gem is surrounded by beautiful landscapes and dense hardwood forests, creating a serene escape. History pulses through the streets, blending seamlessly with modern life.

As I wrapped up my day in and around Boston, traversing the grounds where the American story took root, I was reminded of the early struggles, the sacrifices, and the ultimate resilience that defined my nation. I thought about the shot heard 'round the world. This single shot, even though they may have known it was coming, must still have been a shock. We've all had those moments in our lives—events we knew would change everything forever. Reflecting on what the soldiers thought and felt in the moments after that shot can give us perspective on our own life-altering experiences.

I've had a few "shot heard 'round the world" moments myself. There was the call from a doctor when I thought I had a minor problem with bloating. "Chad, I looked at the images of your ultrasound and your liver appears very cirrhotic." I laid on the couch in my office for an hour or more, staring at the ceiling in shock. Then there was the early morning phone call from my mom, telling me to get to Arizona because my dad had sepsis, and they were giving him a 50/50 chance of making it. Luckily, he began to recover after a few days in a severe state, but it was a long road to full health.

My biggest "shot heard 'round the world" moment came with another call. It was during the most significant rough patch in our marriage—a time when both Sarah and I were grappling with our own difficulties. I was battling a potentially deadly autoimmune disease, and she was dealing with her own set of hardships and stressors. Up until that point, we had always been able to pull each other out of our struggles. But this time was different—this time, we were both struggling at the same time.

Rather than communicating openly about our challenges, I took her distancing personally instead of recognizing it as her needing time and space to deal with her own struggles. In my hurt, I chased after her and made anxious comments, which only pushed her further away. The pattern snowballed. Just before the call, we had attended a couples' counseling session together, and I was looking forward to another. I felt cautiously optimistic.

"Hello, how's it going?" "Good." "I want a divorce."

BANG! There it was—the shot that changed my life forever.

Devastation and heartbreak consumed me, and I turned to drinking more heavily than I ever had before. In the months that followed, I gave everything I had to work on myself and fought fiercely to save our relationship—everything except cutting back on drinking. I also respected her request for space, though it felt like an impossible ask at the time.

Every moment of every day, it was as if a poet lived in my head, endlessly reciting the saddest poem ever written—a poem about the greatest love I had ever lost. Oddly enough, I thought about the men on Bunker Hill, standing firm in what they believed in, fighting with unshakable conviction for what they thought was right. But, like that battle, my efforts weren't enough. Despite giving it my all, I lost. A few months later, we were divorced.

What the colonists went through was obviously much darker than my divorce, but this was my reality. Their resolve, however, inspired me, even years after my last visit to Bunker Hill.

While I didn't win Sarah back, I came to realize that the real battle I needed to fight was within myself. In the depths of loneliness and solitude, I discovered something unexpected: I didn't need Sarah to feel whole. Through the pain, I uncovered my inner strength and emerged as a renewed, stronger version of myself, filled with resilience and purpose. A site that resonates with me in a similar way is the Alamo, a place that symbolizes perseverance and the fight for something greater than oneself.

The Alamo

In the decade before Texas became the 28th state, it fought fiercely for its independence from the Mexican government. Standing outside the iconic Tex-Mex façade of the Alamo, often called the Bunker Hill of Texas, I found it hard to imagine what the defenders must have endured. Originally built as a walled Spanish mission to serve as a safe haven for the faithful in their efforts to convert Indigenous people to Catholicism, it had become a fortress in San Antonio—a city that was Mexican but heavily contested at the time. The defenders, numbering only a couple hundred, were more ethnically and culturally diverse than I had expected. Yet, despite their differences, they united for a common cause. Among them were legendary figures like Jim Bowie, William Travis, and Davy Crockett.

The battle raged for 13 days as General Santa Anna's troops relentlessly bombarded the defenders within the compound. At dawn on 6 March 1836, a Mexican force 10 times their size launched a final assault. The Texans fought valiantly, but the overwhelming numbers and firepower of Santa Anna's troops proved too much. The compound's walls were breached, and brutal hand-to-hand combat followed. Nearly every defender perished, with only a handful spared—mostly noncombatants.

Much like the Battle of Bunker Hill, this loss became a catalyst for the Texans to fight even harder. As Colonel William Travis wrote before the battle: "Victory or Death." While the forces at the Alamo perished, the rallying cry "Remember the Alamo" lived on. It galvanized the Texans, who eventually won their war for independence.

Stepping inside the modest stone chapel, I felt a deep sense of respect for the bravery and sacrifice of the defenders. Moving through the dimly lit space, illuminated by simple chandeliers, I noticed plaques bearing the names of those who fought. On the last plaque, however, it read: "In Honor of Those Alamo Heroes Whose Names History Did Not Record." Despite their tragic fate, their courageous fight continues to inspire.

I then walked into the Long Barrack Museum, one of the oldest buildings in Texas, which now houses exhibits on the Alamo and the Texas Revolution. The museum doesn't take long to tour, but the insights gained from reflecting on what this place stands for today reinforced an important lesson: some causes are so valuable, so deeply believed in that people are willing to give their lives for them. This building symbolizes sacrifice, a reminder that their deaths were not in vain.

My visit left me pondering, as it still does today: what causes would I be willing to die for? Two easily come to mind—my family and those I consider family, and the protection of my homeland from existential threats. Could I *really* die for a cause? I'd like to think so, but it's easy to say from the comfort of an armchair. The men at the Alamo were tested, and they proved their resolve through their actions, as many men and women throughout history have in the name of a cause.

The Alamo also saw use during the Confederacy's occupation during the Civil War—a cause that, thankfully, did not overshadow its earlier legacy of resilience and sacrifice. It stands as a powerful "first-shot" symbol, representing the fight for something greater than oneself and the unyielding courage that continues to inspire nearly two centuries later. When I'm up against something difficult, I have a little saying I use with myself: I whisper, "Remember the Alamo." It's a self-talk technique, a personal rallying cry that reminds me to face my fears and stand strong, no matter the odds.

The Battle of Gettysburg

There are numerous Civil War sites that demand reflection and honor for the sacrifices made. By the war's end, America remained united, and the evil of slavery was finally abolished. But this came at a tremendous cost—the Civil War remains the deadliest conflict in American history. Approximately 700,000 lives were lost in just four years, a number nearly equal to half of all American deaths in other conflicts combined.

The turning point of the war came when General Robert E. Lee suffered his first major defeat at the Battle of Gettysburg. Fought from 1–3 July 1863, the engagement left up to 8,000 dead on the battlefield, with many more later succumbing to their injuries. Despite its small population of 2,500, Gettysburg was a key crossroads where several major roads converged. This quaint, quiet town would host the bloodiest battle in American history, where over 160,000 soldiers fought.

I began my exploration of Gettysburg at the Welcome Center, located near the National Cemetery. The Welcome Center features an impressive museum filled with artifacts and information about the Civil War. It is also home to the Cyclorama, a light and sound show centered around a massive circular painting of the battle, viewed from within its panoramic radius. The most fascinating aspect is that it has captivated visitors since the 1800s. Experiencing the Cyclorama when it was first unveiled would likely have been as awe-inspiring as visiting a modern marvel like the Sphere in Las Vegas today.

I visited the cemetery next. It put the loss of life into perspective and allowed me to spend time with the soldiers from my home state of Minnesota—a small volunteer brigade that played a crucial role in defending against Pickett's Charge, which ultimately sealed the Confederacy's fate.

The cemetery is also where a prominent speaker, akin to the Oprah of the 1800s, Edward Everett, gave a nearly two-hour speech. He was the headliner, but it was the speech that followed, delivered by Abraham Lincoln, that became one of the most famous in American history—the two-minute, 272-word Gettysburg Address. I took a moment to pause at the memorial dedicated to Lincoln and his speech, and reflected on the words that not only honored the fallen soldiers but also reinforced the cause of the United States, igniting pride and hope. While the exact spot of Lincoln's address is not precisely marked, the Soldiers' National Monument stands nearby, about 110 meters north of the Lincoln Speech Memorial.

Early the next morning, I took a guided bus tour of the battlefield and later returned in my car to visit sites the tour didn't stop at. The battlefield features 16 official stops along the 38-kilometer drive, each marked with informational signs detailing the landscape and the events that unfolded there nearly 160 years ago. Standing at the various vantage points, I could almost envision the men and horses charging toward each other across the fields.

In total, there are nearly 1,400 monuments and statues at the Gettysburg National Military Park dedicated to the soldiers who fought and fell here. As I moved from stop to stop, I traced the course of the battle. One of the first stops is at McPherson Ridge, where I found the marker for the first shot of the battle. A short but bloody skirmish here saw the Confederates push back the Union line, forcing them to retreat to more defensible positions. At the next stop, atop a small hill, I encountered the towering Eternal Light Peace Memorial—a powerful tribute to the unity and sacrifice of those who fought here.

As I drove around the battlefield, I passed fields, trees, and hills—a landscape much like it was during the battle. Remarkably, about 60 percent of the buildings that stood during the battle are still standing today. While it would be nearly impossible to stop at each monument, I took several short walks at the recommended stops to view the information signs and learn more about the battle. I made a point to follow the Minnesota troops because of my connection, and it made me even more proud to be a Minnesotan. The 1st Minnesota Infantry Regiment was credited as being "saviors of our country" by General Hancock, who ordered the 262 men to charge a much larger Confederate force. The charge resulted in 215 casualties within minutes, a sacrifice that helped hold the Union line at a critical moment in the Battle of Gettysburg.

Continuing my exploration, I saw how the battle unfolded at each stop. It was much like a game of chess, except the pieces shot back. The generals, atop their horses, appeared confident as they raised their pistols and voices, directing the next moves. When I reached the rocky hill called Little Round Top, I stood where Union forces once watched over the battlefield. Looking down at the monuments, each one stands as a testament to bravery or sacrifice. This is where Union forces, low on ammunition, charged the approaching Confederate troops, preventing them from gaining the high ground—a crucial advantage that could have changed the outcome of the battle.

Before leaving the battlefield, I made sure to visit Cemetery Ridge, the site of the climax of the battle—Pickett's Charge. Looking across the field, I noticed the large Codori Family Barn, a spot where many Confederate troops gathered and perished. The National Park Service preserves this field to look much like it did on 3 July 1863. It was here that approximately 12,500 Confederate soldiers, under the command of George Pickett, advanced across open ground. Their goal was to reach a small cluster of trees, now known as the "Copse of Trees." This spot marks the farthest point the Confederates reached, often referred to as the "High Water Mark of the Confederacy."

A granite monument marks the site, featuring a bronze open book engraved with the names of the units that fought there. The monument is surrounded by cannonballs and flanked by cannons, a solemn tribute to the pivotal moment in American history that unfolded here.

After a long day of touring the battlefield, I took some time to explore the quaint, historic town of Gettysburg. While walking through town, I found myself at the Jennie Wade House. Wade was the only civilian casualty of the battle, struck down by a bullet while in the kitchen of her sister's home, baking bread for Union soldiers.

As I left the Jennie Wade House, I walked just two blocks to a restaurant called the Farnsworth House Inn. This building is believed to be where a Confederate sharpshooter fired the shot that killed Jennie Wade, mistaking her sister's home for a Union headquarters. The historic brick walls outside bear the scars of war, with white patches marking the bullet holes left behind.

Upstairs, it's easy to picture the chaos that led to that fatal shot—a sobering reminder of the harsh realities of war and the so-called "collateral damage" too often justified by those far removed from the suffering. Jennie was only 20 years old—a daughter, a sister, and a fiancée—tragically caught in the crossfire of the Battle of Gettysburg.

Confederate White House

While Gettysburg reflected the bloody consequences of the Civil War and marked a major Union victory, another site associated with the war showcased the political and ideological center of the Confederacy. When I toured the Confederate White House in Richmond, Virginia, the contrast between its plain exterior and the elegance within was striking. Once the executive home of Jefferson Davis, president of the Confederacy, the mansion carried a palpable weight of history. As I walked through its halls, I noticed paintings of George Washington, and the irony was hard to ignore. Both the Union and the Confederacy claimed Washington's legacy—one as a symbol of unity and the Constitution, the other as a justification for rebellion against perceived tyranny.

In the dining room, where Confederate strategies were discussed, a large portrait of Washington hung prominently. It was striking to see the image of a man who had fought to create the United States in a house dedicated to dividing it. Washington, a slave owner who later freed his enslaved people in his will, became a complex figure in the ideological battle over slavery. The Union pointed to his final actions as a step toward freedom and unity, while the Confederacy used his lifelong ownership of slaves to defend their cause. This portrait was a reminder of how history's icons are reshaped to fit the needs of the moment.

As I walked through the house where Jefferson Davis once lived, I was struck by how much it revealed his human side. The nursery room where his children played and the quiet spot where he worked without distraction painted a picture of a father and a leader fighting for a belief he held dear. For a fleeting moment, I felt guilty for almost understanding him. It was uncomfortable to glimpse the person behind the cause. But I quickly pulled myself out of that thought, remembering exactly what he was fighting for—a system built on the enslavement of others.

Standing in the same space where Davis lived, I reflected on how, just a day after he fled Richmond, Abraham Lincoln walked through this very house. The juxtaposition of these two leaders—Davis clinging to a fractured Confederacy, Lincoln steering a wounded nation—was a stark reminder of the swift collapse of the Confederacy and the opposing visions that defined the Civil War.

Touring the house, I couldn't ignore how Davis's legacy became intertwined with some of the darkest chapters of American history. He was a family man and, in many ways, unremarkable—yet he was a man with the potential to alter not only the course of American history, but world history. It raises a sobering question: had the cause he led won, would there still be slaves?

This is why we need to preserve places like this. They offer us more than just a glimpse into history; they remind us of the complexities of human nature and the consequences of the causes we choose to fight for.

Ford's Theatre

Less than two years after the Battle of Gettysburg, and less than a week after Lee's surrender at Appomattox Court House ended the Civil War, one of America's most horrifyingly consequential moments took place. I can hardly imagine what it must have been like to sit in Ford's Theatre in Washington, D.C., enjoying the popular play *Our American Cousin*. The audience was laughing along as the comedy unfolded when suddenly, during one of the show's funniest lines, a loud bang shattered the moment. As confusion set in, a man leapt from the balcony onto the stage, shouting, "*Sic semper tyrannis*"—Latin for "Thus always to tyrants." Chaos erupted as he rushed offstage, and the crowd scrambled toward the presidential box, where Abraham Lincoln and his wife, Mary Todd, were seated. It soon became clear that the bang was an assassin's bullet.

Lincoln was quickly carried across the street to a boarding house, which became his makeshift hospital room. The first doctor to attend to him, Charles Leale, worked tirelessly to save the president, clearing blood clots to relieve pressure from the wound. Despite their efforts, Lincoln died about nine hours later, cementing the legacy of arguably the greatest and most celebrated American president. His body was taken by train to Springfield, Illinois, Lincoln's hometown, in a funeral procession that became one of the most widely attended and mourned events in American history. He now rests there in a tomb at the Oak Ridge Cemetery.

When I visited Ford's Theatre and sat in a chair on the main floor, I looked up to the right and saw the white balcony draped in American flags, marking the spot where Lincoln was seated when John Wilkes Booth fired that infamous shot with a small Derringer pistol. In the museum portion of the theatre, I stood face-to-face with that tiny gun—an object that caused one of the largest impacts in history. Across the street, I entered the Petersen House and stood in the room where Lincoln was attended to and ultimately died. A small plaque on the dresser solemnly commemorates this moment, marking the place where Lincoln took his final breath at 7:22 a.m.

As for Booth, he broke his leg while jumping to the stage but managed to escape. He sought help from a doctor who set his broken leg. Although the doctor claimed he did not know about the assassination, he was later implicated in the conspiracy. Booth was found 12 days after the assassination, hiding in a tobacco barn near Port Royal, Virginia. Surrounded by Union troops and refusing to surrender, the barn was set on fire to force him out. Booth was shot in the neck and died from his injury a few hours later.

The Battle of Little Bighorn

Not all of America's founding stories are meant for fireworks and celebration. Some, at least for me, need to be mourned. Lincoln himself is not without controversy, as he presided over not only Reconstruction but also Western expansion—a time marked by violent clashes between American settlers and Native tribes. In my home state of Minnesota, following the U.S.-Dakota War of 1862, 38 Dakota men were executed in the largest mass execution in U.S. history in the town of Mankato. While Lincoln commuted the sentences of 265 others, his decision to allow these executions remains deeply controversial.

The tensions between Native tribes and the U.S. government didn't end there. One of the Union's prominent Civil War leaders, George Armstrong Custer, was renowned for his fearless confidence. At the Battle of Gettysburg, Custer commanded the Michigan Cavalry Brigade and led a daring charge against the Confederates at East Cavalry Field. His bold action prevented Major General J.E.B. Stuart from outflanking the Union Army and disrupting its rear during Pickett's Charge, playing a crucial role in securing the Union's defensive position. Custer's actions in Gettysburg solidified his reputation as a Union hero.

As I stood on the vast field marking the site of the Battle of Little Bighorn, gazing at the small tombstones for both U.S. soldiers and Native warriors, I was filled with a great sense of loss. It wasn't just the lives lost—it was sorrow for what came afterward. Custer, a man who had once fought to preserve the Union, now led forces into Indian territory to take land and strip Native people of their culture and identity.

Having worked as a therapist with an Ojibwe tribe for several years, I have witnessed the ongoing effects of historical trauma. I see the persistent challenges faced by a community still grappling with the repercussions of systemic racism and cultural suppression. Yet, their resilience shines through in their storytelling, customs, and spiritual connection to the world, which I find enduringly beautiful and profoundly moving.

During this era, many viewed Native people as dangerous and in need of "civilizing." Boarding schools were established, and children were forcibly taken from their homes. Native families that spoke their ancestral language or practiced their spirituality faced severe punishment. The saying "kill the Indian, save the man" reflected the dehumanizing mindset behind these policies. This mentality persisted well into the 20th century, as a woman once shared with me. Her mother, raised in boarding schools, taught her children to hide whenever a well-dressed white woman came to the house, fearing a social worker might come to take them away.

The battlefield itself is a place of quiet reflection. Rolling hills stretch to the horizon, blending with the wide, open sky. Each white headstone marks a life lost following orders from a misguided government, while each red marker honors a life lost in defense of land, culture, and identity. At battle's end, over 260 U.S. soldiers and up to 100 Native warriors lay dead.

The victory by the Sioux and Cheyenne warriors was guided by Chief Sitting Bull's spiritual visions and led by War Chief Crazy Horse, with tactical support from Chief Gall. It was a rare triumph, but it could not stop the tide of U.S. expansion.

Standing on Last Stand Hill, where Custer and his men made their final stand, I was reminded that building a nation comes with enormous costs. It's a sobering reality that we must honor not only those who gave their lives for our country but also the lives and cultures lost in its creation. I take pride in being an American, but I carry an awareness of the heavy price paid by so many. This is a truth we must never forget, for if we do, history has a way of repeating itself—a warning echoed by so many of the dark destinations I have visited.

Chapter 3

Historic Properties

"Places of grandeur often cast the longest shadows."

—Unknown

HISTORIC PROPERTIES AND ESTATES around the globe often fall under the umbrella of dark tourism. While some are infamous for tragedies, natural disasters, or scandals, others carry a darker history that has shaped their legacy, even if they aren't traditionally considered "dark destinations." These places—whether mansions, castles, or hotels—have witnessed moments of both light and shadow, their stories often tarnished to some degree by tragedy and death. From globally renowned landmarks to mysterious houses with dark pasts in our own hometowns, these places invite reflection on the events that made them historic and, in some cases, infamous. Exploring the stories of some of the world's most fascinating properties, where history and myth intertwine, offers valuable lessons from the past.

One remarkable estate that blurs the lines between myth and legend is Bran Castle, famously associated with Count Dracula and often linked to Vlad the Impaler. Interestingly, when Bram Stoker wrote *Dracula*, he had never visited Romania, where Bran Castle is located. However, speculation suggests he may have drawn inspiration from descriptions or sketches he encountered, as the novel describes a castle that bears a striking resemblance to Bran Castle. It's worth noting that while Vlad the Impaler may have served as a minor inspiration for the character of Dracula, there is no substantial evidence to connect Bran Castle to Vlad beyond speculative associations. In fact, it's unclear whether Vlad ever even visited the castle.

Despite Bran Castle being a popular dark tourism destination, I tend to focus on places grounded more in fact than fiction. Not that I would pass up a stay in Transylvania or a tour of Bran Castle—it's undeniably fascinating—but it doesn't quite align with the brand of dark tourism that sparks my personal interests.

Another site worth mentioning that blurs the line between myth and legend is the Stanley Hotel. I visited this estate during a trip to the Rocky Mountains in Colorado. In 1974, Stephen King stayed there alongside his wife, Tabitha. They were the only guests in the hotel just prior to its closing for the season. The hotel's haunted reputation, alongside the long empty corridors and canned orchestral music in the bar, inspired King to write *The Shining*. He later revealed that he went to bed that night with the story mostly formed in his mind but had a vivid nightmare about his son being chased by a demonic presence, waking up in a sweaty panic. That terrifying dream gave him another key piece of the story.

Despite its history of hauntings, the Stanley Hotel didn't become the popular tourist attraction it is today until King's novel brought it into the spotlight. With its early 1900s grandeur, originally a playground for the wealthy, it's a place where your imagination can easily take over. Visitors can stay in room 217, the same room where King and his wife stayed, and experience the eerie atmosphere that inspired one of the most iconic horror stories of all time.

While Bran Castle and the Stanley Hotel have an undeniable allure, the estates I chose for this chapter stand apart for their ability to act as windows into events grounded in history, not myth. I will explore properties where royalty ruled but faced tragedy, as well as places where ordinary people—often denied a fair chance at life—struggled for survival to amuse others. Immersing ourselves in the stories of these estates allows us to connect with the lives once lived there. It challenges us to imagine the weight of their struggles and the consequences of their choices.

Tower of London

After crossing the River Thames via Tower Bridge, with its twin Gothic-style towers, I approach the Tower of London on the northern bank. Its fortress-like exterior and thick stone walls, crowned with turrets, exude an air of military might and defense. Today, the Tower is surrounded by the bustling cityscape of modern London, but during its heyday, it would have been flanked by humble timber-framed buildings, winding streets, and farmland stretching into the distance. One feature that has vanished over time is the moat, which once encircled the Tower. Originally filled with water from the Thames, the moat measured 15 to 30 meters wide and about three meters deep. As London expanded, however, the moat became polluted and sewer-infested, leading to its permanent drainage in the mid-19th century.

A visit to the Tower of London offers a long-exposure snapshot into the workings of one of the most famous places on Earth. It is home to the Royal Family's Crown Jewels, which is the highlight for many visitors. However, I skipped the Crown Jewels line and headed for the real history, its former role as a fortress, palace, and prison.

The focal point of the Tower of London is the White Tower. Built by William the Conqueror in the 11th century, it is a massive four-story stone structure with small windows and a tower at each corner. Once the residence of kings and queens, the White Tower now houses a museum dedicated to the armor and weapons of previous generations, including the oversized battle armor of Henry VIII. Inside, the small Chapel of St. John has witnessed many royal and religious ceremonies.

As I continued to walk around the grounds, I noticed the Yeoman Warders, better known as the Beefeaters, leading tour groups. This legendary group of British armed forces retirees wear distinguished dark blue robes and round, flat-brimmed hats adorned with red trimmings and gold accents. I also saw the King's Guard (or Queen's Guard), recognizable by their iconic red coats and tall bearskin caps, standing guard in front of the entrance to the Crown Jewels and other locations around the grounds.

The Tower of London has a dark history steeped in imprisonment, torture, and executions. The site has also seen murder. In 1483, two child princes, Edward V and his brother Richard, were placed in the Tower by their uncle, Richard, Duke of Gloucester, who took guardianship after the death of their father, King Edward IV. The princes were never seen again, and their possible remains were discovered under a set of stairs in the Tower in 1674. Richard III rose to capture the crown, but he was widely suspected of having ordered their murder to secure his claim.

Hearing the story of the princes was upsetting. I hadn't known about it before. How could anyone kill just to gain power, especially their own blood? As I reflected on the many ruthless dictators and fascists who have plagued the highest levels of government throughout history, it became easier to understand. Some people rise to the top because they genuinely want to help, while others seek power for its own sake. I believe that many of history's most notorious leaders may have started with good intentions but were ultimately corrupted by the power they gained.

This belief stems from my conviction that no one is born evil—individuals are shaped by their experiences and choices. As a therapist, I have embraced this philosophy to help anyone who walks through my door. While debates about the origins of human behavior persist, my experience has yet to disprove this perspective. Reflecting on history, it makes me wonder how Richard III's upbringing may have influenced his alleged decision to kill his nephews. Born in 1452, Richard grew up during the Wars of the Roses—a period of political chaos and violent rivalry between the House of York and the House of Lancaster. His father, Richard, Duke of York, and his brother, Edmund, Earl of Rutland, were both killed during the conflict, likely shaping his understanding of power and survival in a deeply unstable world.

Two other well-known deaths driven by political ambition were the executions of Anne Boleyn and Lady Jane Grey. Both were beheaded within the Tower of London, on the northeast side, in an area known as Tower Green. Their tragic ends serve as powerful reminders of the ruthless nature of power struggles during their time.

Anne Boleyn was the second wife of Henry VIII. Due to her inability to produce a male heir, and growing political pressures, she was accused of treason, adultery, and incest—charges widely believed to have been fabricated. On 19 May 1536, she was executed by an expert swordsman, a method chosen by Henry as an act of "mercy." This spared her the slower and often more brutal fate of execution by axe, which was the more common method for high treason.

Eighteen years after Anne Boleyn's death, another young queen met a similar fate. Lady Jane Grey, just 16 or 17 years old, was beheaded as a result of political maneuvering. Protestant nobles had placed her on the throne to prevent the Catholic Mary Tudor from claiming it. After only nine days as queen, Jane was imprisoned in the Tower of London. Mary Tudor, later known as Bloody Mary, reclaimed her rightful place on the throne. Seven months later, following a failed rebellion to restore Jane to power, Mary reluctantly ordered her execution at Tower Green, the same site where Anne Boleyn had been put to death.

There is a circular glass memorial dedicated to the 10 individuals executed at this spot, including Boleyn and Grey. At its center, a glass pedestal supports a glass pillow, symbolizing a place for their heads to rest. This memorial serves as a sobering reminder of the ruthless Machiavellianism that can infect nations when authority goes unchecked.

Despite the many executions, imprisonments, and acts of torture within the Tower of London, another story stands out to me. Thomas More was one of Henry VIII's closest advisers, but their relationship deteriorated when More refused to endorse the crown's separation from the Catholic Church. Henry VIII sought a divorce from his first wife, Catherine of Aragon, because she could not produce a male heir. When More objected to the King's authority over the Church, Henry VIII had him beheaded on Tower Hill, just outside the palace walls, in a public spectacle. More was buried in the Chapel of St. Peter ad Vincula inside the Tower, alongside others who had been executed there. In the years that followed, Anne Boleyn and Lady Jane Grey were also interred in the chapel. The Catholic Church later canonized More for his martyrdom.

In the end, despite Henry VIII's quest for a male heir, it was his daughter with Anne Boleyn who secured the Tudor legacy by becoming the iconic Queen Elizabeth I. The Elizabethan Era was marked by cultural flourishing, global expansion, and the solidification of England as a major power. The daughter Henry once dismissed due to her gender became one of the greatest monarchs in British history.

Palace of Versailles

The Palace of Versailles is one of the most stunning palaces in world history, but it also holds a place in dark tourism due to its role in the French Revolution, the occupation of Versailles, and its association with the opulent lifestyle of the monarchy. From 1682 until 1789, the French monarchy resided here, a period marked by widespread poverty and growing resentment among the French people.

The beauty of Versailles remains nearly unchanged since the time of French royalty. Built during the reign of Louis XIV, the Sun King, as a symbol of absolute power, the palace stands as a testament to that era. Versailles witnessed an extraordinary chapter in French history, encompassing the rise and fall of a monarchy and leaving behind stories of both grandeur and tragedy.

As I walked toward the entrance of the gold-trimmed three-story palace, I found myself on an expansive cobblestone courtyard, flanked on three sides by the palace and its wings. An imposing fence encloses this grand space, featuring a magnificent, ornate golden gateway.

As I got closer to the entrance of the palace, the sheer size of the building became more striking, with massive windows that beautifully reflected the sunlight. Surrounding the light-colored limestone and reddish façade are elegant sculptures and statues, adding to the grandeur. The symmetrical design of the building drew my eye to the main entrance, positioned under an enormous clock in the center.

Born in Vienna, Marie Antoinette was married off to the future King Louis XVI at 14 as a token of friendship between Austria and France. She moved to Versailles in 1770 and became queen four years later when her husband ascended to the throne. In the public eye, she was an extravagant indulger of fashion and the arts. In her private life, she often retreated to the more secluded Petit Trianon on the palace grounds, where she embraced an idealized version of rural life, away from the formalities of the court.

Over time, Marie Antoinette became a major symbol of the crown's perceived entitlement, which led to significant public resentment. She was the subject of many rumors, including infidelity and alleged lesbian relationships. Much like the misattribution of the famous saying, "Let them eat cake," there was little evidence to support these rumors. During the French Revolution, the monarchy was driven out of Versailles and moved to nearby Paris. A couple of years later, she was caught trying to flee France with the royal family. After the abolition of the French monarchy, she was imprisoned.

In my opinion, Marie Antoinette was a victim of her time. As a foreign-born queen trapped in a forced and unhappy marriage, she became an easy scapegoat for the monarchy's failings, leading to a distorted and often unfair public perception. Even her attempts to live a simpler life at the Petit Trianon were viewed as treasonous by the same French people who condemned her for her extravagance. It reminds me of modern politics—whether it's a politician or their spouse, there's always someone ready to criticize and call their actions awful.

Her imprisonment was harsh, and her trial was a sham. Convicted of treason, among other crimes—including a fictitious charge of incest with her son—she was sentenced to death. She was bound by her hands and paraded through the streets of Paris to the jeers of the crowds. Throughout the ordeal, she maintained her dignity, even famously apologizing to the executioner for accidentally stepping on his foot. Her life ended with the drop of the guillotine, but her legacy lives on well into the present day.

Throughout history, countless people have been labeled as villains in their time, often unfairly. Some, like Marie Antoinette, were persecuted or even killed for lives that were misunderstood. Historic figures such as Socrates, Joan of Arc, and Galileo Galilei are prime examples of this. Everyone has experienced being misunderstood at some point—whether in very public ways or in more intimate, personal moments. Yet, when misunderstandings are treated as factual judgments, they become not only unfair but potentially deadly. Rumors have led to death sentences, suicides, divorces, and countless other devastating outcomes.

Moving from the courtyard into the Palace of Versailles, the principal residence of French royalty, including Queen Marie Antoinette and King Louis XVI, I arrived at the Royal Chapel. This chapel, a site for daily Mass, also hosted Marie Antoinette and Louis XVI's wedding. Its most striking features include a magnificent organ and lavish decorations, with the intricately painted ceiling serving as the room's crowning highlight.

The King and Queen's apartments were in separate parts of the palace. Intimate encounters often took place in the Queen's apartment after the King entered through secret passageways. These meetings were usually planned in advance. The different apartments in the palace were similar in grandeur and elegance. In reality, nearly every square meter of the palace exudes historic opulent beauty. As I passed through each space, I saw lavish furniture, golden accents, crystal chandeliers, and scenes painted on the ceilings. Compared to the living conditions of the poor citizens at the time, it's easy to understand why they resented the monarchy's extravagant spending.

Connecting the King and Queen's apartments is the famous Hall of Mirrors. This centerpiece of Versailles features 357 large mirrors and 17 windows. It often hosted receptions, balls, and other state events. The most famous event to ever take place in this room happened long after the monarchy used the palace. The Treaty of Versailles was signed here in 1919, officially ending the Great War, World War I. The treaty imposed severe restrictions on Germany, including heavy reparations and territorial losses. These harsh terms contributed to economic hardship and political instability in Germany, which, along with other factors, eventually led to the rise of the Nazi Party and the outbreak of

World War II—another reason why touring Versailles is darker than the average person often realizes.

The palace itself is almost overwhelming due to its grandeur, making it a relief to step outside into the "backyard." Much like the palace itself, the Gardens of Versailles are no less breathtaking. Majestic fountains, statues, plants, flowers, and expansive green spaces create a stunning landscape. Tall walls of trees guided me through the gardens, giving them an enchanted forest feeling as the sun set. The experience is less of a sensory overload than the palace, thanks to the wide-open spaces.

I found a quiet corner in the garden, a perfect spot to reflect on the lives of the French monarchy and the splendor of the palace complex, as well as its impact on the French people. As I sat there, I asked myself: where in my life have I judged someone harshly without knowing the whole story? When have I felt unfairly judged? The truth is this happens all the time, and it's something we need to be more aware of. I could only imagine what it would be like to live in a world where judgment is grounded solely in the whole truth—nothing less.

Roman Colosseum

The Flavian Emperors built the Colosseum in the first century CE as a gift to the Roman people. This massive four-story elliptical amphitheater, made of stone and concrete, could seat over 50,000 spectators and served as the entertainment hub of Rome. The seating was arranged in tiers, similar to modern stadiums, providing clear views of the arena floor. The wooden floor, covered with sand, concealed the hypogeum—an underground area where animals and gladiators prepared for battle. Trap doors and lifts were incorporated into the hypogeum's tunnels, adding to the dramatic effect of the shows. While the wooden floor has long since disappeared, the tunnels are now visible from above. Over the nearly 400 years that the Colosseum was in use, more than one million animals and 400,000 people died for the entertainment of its spectators.

I've been to several of the most famous stadiums in the world, and they all evoke a sense of history and nostalgia tied to modern sports and entertainment. The Roman Colosseum, likely the world's most famous stadium in all of history, has a completely different feel, even after accounting for its ancient origins. Standing in that vast space, imagining the crowds cheering as people fought and died in gladiator battles, is surreal. In ancient times, across many cultures, death was a form of entertainment—death as sport. I've attended several sporting events and witnessed cheap shots at their worst, often thinking it couldn't get any worse. But standing in the Colosseum puts that all into a stark perspective.

During its inaugural games in 80 CE, which lasted 100 days, it is estimated that 9,000 animals were killed during the "hunts." Additionally, up to 5,000 human deaths occurred through public executions and brutal combat. These games included not only gladiatorial fights and animal hunts but also mock naval battles. To stage these battles, the arena floor was flooded, creating a small lake where ships engaged in dramatic displays of combat.

I've seen many reenactments during my travels—gunfights between cowboys, or pirates clashing with swords—but those were, of course, staged, with participants pretending to be hurt or killed. At the Colosseum, however, these "reenactments" were horrifyingly real. Men actually died, turning entertainment into a deadly spectacle.

Events at the Colosseum often lasted an entire day and could result in as many as 100 deaths. During special occasions, these events might stretch on for days or even weeks. In the morning, spectators might watch as men hunted exotic animals brought in from Africa and other distant lands. It was kill or be killed—facing bears, tigers, and lions with nothing but a spear, sword, or bow. With trap doors to fall through and animals lifted onto the arena floor from the hypogeum, it must have been a spectacle beyond imagination.

After a quick lunch, spectators would return for the midday event, where they might witness prisoner executions. These executions served both as punishment and entertainment. Prisoners of war, Christians, and criminals were thrown into the arena to be mauled by whatever animal was chosen, or they were simply beheaded. Others might have faced crucifixion or been burned at the stake. These more brutal deaths were often used as a warning to the masses not to cross Roman authority.

Then, upon the afternoon's main event, the horns blared and the parade of armored gladiators, swords and shields in hand, made their way into the arena below. They would give a salute to the emperor or another high official overseeing the games. It was a well-organized spectacle, something akin to an evening watching professional boxing. The combat began with lesser-known fighters, but as the afternoon wore on, the most highly skilled warriors would face off, bringing the crowd to the edge of their seats.

Whether it was a one-on-one or group fight, it was always a fight to the death—though not every match ended that way. The emperor decided whether a gladiator would need to deliver the fatal blow to his unfortunate opponent. The crowd was intense, cheering at every move the gladiators made. They often bet on their favorite fighters, and as they dispersed, they had stories to tell for days about how they won or lost their money.

Visiting the Colosseum over a thousand years after the last gladiator fell is still an intense experience. How did the spectators feel watching someone get mauled by a lion? How could they cheer for one human to kill another? It was a sign of the times—they didn't know any different. Or did they? Much like dark tourism today, there were likely a variety of motivations.

Death in ancient Rome wasn't seen as it is in most parts of the world today. Some spectators likely viewed it with a mix of fascination and detachment. Others saw it as a spectacle of combat and skill, a demonstration of bravery and stoicism, or even a symbol of Roman superiority. Whatever their reasons, it's clear that death and the games were deeply woven into Roman culture for hundreds of years.

Why do we find it so difficult to accept death as a natural part of life? The Romans saw death, whether natural or in the brutal spectacle of the Colosseum, as an inevitable part of life and embraced it with a sense of acceptance rather than fear. This perspective resonated with me during my illness and inspired me to adopt a more healthy and Stoic mindset—a philosophy deeply rooted in Roman culture. It wasn't that I wanted to die, but I realized that my fear of death and the thought of leaving things behind didn't have to paralyze me. In the months following my diagnosis and leading up to my transplant, I began to see it as a journey—one where I focused on what I could control, and surrendered the rest to fate. I developed a deepening acceptance of my circumstances, even while fully grasping what the outcome might be.

I also started to find peace in knowing that my family would be okay, no matter what happened. I knew that my love for them and the fact that I had lived a fairly virtuous life would endure in my absence. I found comfort in a thought I often shared with my clients, and reminded myself: I would always be with them in some way. Rather than consuming myself with worries about death and how they would manage after I was gone, I refused to waste time on those thoughts. Instead, I focused on passing as much love and wisdom to them as I could while I was still here. This reflection has stayed with me, and grown stronger as I have explored other places marked by suffering and resilience.

Whitney Plantation

When I was in New Orleans, I saw several advertisements for plantation tours and thought, "How odd." Sure, I'm all about facing dark places to honor and reflect, but these tours seemed to be glorifying the beauty of the plantations and the mansions where wealthy families lived—at the expense of the lives of the human beings they kept as slaves. There was no way I was going to visit a place that glosses over the tragedy to focus on the charm. Then I came across a brochure for the Whitney Plantation. It promised to show something horrifying, yet necessary—the life of the slaves from their point of view. I was skeptical, but the potential to see the unvarnished truth was too much to resist. So, I bought a ticket for my son and me for the 60-kilometer ride to the plantation from the French Quarter.

Upon entering the visitor's center at the plantation, I felt a wave of relief as I noticed numerous books for sale: most focused on the ills of slavery, alongside detailed displays on the transatlantic slave trade. This wasn't going to be just another sugarcoated tour but an opportunity to learn and pay respect to the families who endured such unimaginable horror. This horror felt personal. I've visited hundreds of historically dark places, but this was one of the most emotional sites I've ever experienced—and it was on my homeland's soil. We can no longer whitewash our American history. This happened here, and we must fight prejudice and racism at every turn, or risk returning to those darker times.

Working in mental health, I frequently witness the prejudice my clients face. Sometimes it's blatant racism; other times, it's more covert—like subconsciously passing over a job application because of the ethnic sound of someone's name. Regardless of the form it takes, prejudice always causes harm. Addressing it can sometimes be as simple as educating people about the impact of their behaviors. Other times, it requires significant action. In some cases, it might call for marches and protests—and in the case of slavery, it even called for war.

Walking through the average plantation, it would be easy to overlook its hidden history if one were caught up in the beauty and elegance of its southern charm. However, at the Whitney Plantation, there's no sugarcoating the reality of life there. Numerous memorials stand as testaments to the lives of those who endured the unspeakable cruelties of slavery. The main house, though grand in structure, feels more like a passthrough—arguably the least impactful part of the tour.

For me, the most haunting moment came when I saw the statue of a slave boy in overalls, gazing down the brick path toward the main house. It was a deeply moving moment that underscored the suffering endured by so many. What that boy must have witnessed is incomprehensible, and if he was one of the few fortunate enough to survive, the stories and trauma he carried with him are almost beyond understanding.

The slave quarters stand in sheer contrast to the nearby mansion. The simple, poorly constructed wooden shacks reveal the crude and crowded conditions the enslaved were forced to endure. Small statues of children sit on the porch, serving as another poignant reminder of the children and families so often overlooked in the narrative of slavery. Across the small field stands the overseer's house, a looming presence that likely served as a constant reminder that any behavior deemed out of line could result in the crack of a whip. Nearby is the jail—a chilling symbol of both punishment and humiliation. The large rusty outdoor cages there reflect conditions so inhumane that most people today would be horrified to see even an animal confined in such a way.

Like many, I find it especially difficult to reflect on the cruelties of history when children are involved. The innocence of childhood was torn from them, no matter how much love and reassurance their families tried to provide. At the Whitney Plantation, reminders of children are everywhere. It felt deeply personal as I walked through the Field of Angels, where the names of over 2,200 enslaved children are inscribed on plaques and stones. At the center of this solemn field stands a statue of an African American angel with wings, cradling a child as if offering comfort. The names I saw belonged to children who lived and died on Louisiana plantations—a haunting reminder of their stolen lives.

Not only did I feel emotional during my visit about the enslaved children, but I also couldn't help thinking about some of the children I've worked with over the years. Many grew up in harsh conditions, with parents who didn't provide proper care and, in some cases, lacked the capacity to show love. Some endured abuse, while others witnessed their parents fighting or saw their mothers bloodied and crying because of an abusive partner. These children were often punished for normal behaviors—crying when hungry or being irritable with an earache. Despite this, people still expect these children to perform well in school and eventually grow into healthy adults.

While some, by the grace of God, manage to grow into relatively well-adjusted adults, far fewer are able to do so. Most carry deep psychological scars, which often manifests as mental health symptoms, while others externalize their pain, struggling to control their own behavior. This trauma ripples into their future relationships and even their own parenting, creating cycles that can be difficult to break.

Reflecting on the enslaved children not only angered and saddened me but also renewed my commitment to helping today's children, regardless of their background or the color of their skin. If we can support children, perhaps we can shift their trajectory just enough to give them a chance to gain traction in their lives, despite difficult beginnings. Tragically, the children whose names are engraved in the Field of Angels never had that chance.

One of the most gruesome yet deeply emotional memorials I've ever encountered is the tribute to the enslaved people who lost their lives during the largest slave revolt in American history. The rebellion took place along the German Coast of the Mississippi River, where 500 enslaved individuals from two Baptist parishes organized a revolt. During the uprising, they damaged several plantations and killed two white men. Sadly, they were caught and brutally punished as a warning to others who might dare to resist. Dozens of enslaved people were executed by beheading, and their heads were placed on poles along the Mississippi—a grim display of power and control.

The memorial at Whitney Plantation features lifelike ceramic heads of 63 enslaved individuals mounted on steel rods, a visceral representation of their fate. At the end of the memorial stands a striking figure—a large statue of an enslaved person with arms raised and shackles broken, symbolizing that death, tragically, was one of the few ways they could attain freedom. This powerful reminder captures both the brutality of their punishment and the enduring spirit of resistance.

Another touching memorial at the plantation honors the enslaved workers themselves. It includes a plaque listing the names of those who were forced to live and work there, along with a few pictures and quotes attributed to them. One particularly haunting quote reads: "The folks died in piles and de coffins was piled as high as a house. They buried them in trenches, and later they dug graves and buried them. When they go to looking into the coffins, they discovered some had turned over in dey coffins and some had clawed dey eyes out and some had gnawed holes in dey hands. Dey was buried alive."

On the bus ride back, we passed many other plantations. As I looked out at the fields, I couldn't help but imagine the enslaved people who once worked them. Why are so many content to erase the greatest tragedy on America's soil?

The visit to Whitney Plantation was nothing less than disturbing, but that is the point—disturbing in a way that brought me closer to the truth of history. Standing on the very soil where it happened and experiencing it from this unique perspective, rather than just being told, elevates empathy, leaving lasting marks. I felt fortunate to honor the victims, leaving with a renewed commitment to never forget and to strive for a nation and world where human rights are held in equal regard for all.

Chapter 4

Places of Light and Darkness

"The light shines in the darkness,
and the darkness has not overcome it."

—John 1:5

LOCATIONS STEEPED IN DARK and complex pasts often take on a life of their own, their legends blending fact and fiction. The real events behind these stories—witch trials, executions, or hauntings—captivate us, yet they're often tangled with myth and lore. A good historian peels back those layers of exaggeration to uncover the true stories, which are often more fascinating and haunting than the legends themselves.

Three cities stand out to me for their dark histories that intertwine rich folklore: Salem, Massachusetts; New Orleans, Louisiana; and Edinburgh, Scotland. These locations share a common thread of fear, persecution, and injustice, yet they've also transformed their histories into symbols of resilience.

In Salem, the infamous witch trials left a lasting legacy, casting a shadow that lingers centuries later. During a walking tour around the city, my heart sank as I learned about Tituba, an enslaved Indigenous woman from South America. Forced into confessing to witchcraft—likely under duress—after being scapegoated by young girls who accused her of causing strange behavior in town, Tituba admitted to causing various supernatural phenomena, details she may not have fully understood.

Tituba's coerced confession fueled the hysteria and sparked the pandemonium that led to the execution of 19 people—14 women and five men—by hanging, as well as the pressing to death of Giles Corey under a pile of rocks. Giles, a successful farmer, drew suspicion after his wife publicly criticized the witch trials. He refused to give a plea in court, and the pressing was an attempt to force him to comply. However, he refused, allegedly saying, "More weight." Additionally, five more individuals died while incarcerated in dark, windowless jail cells, with barely enough room to stand or lie down.

As for Tituba, after spending a year in jail, an anonymous person paid her bail, and she disappeared from recorded history, her ultimate fate remaining a mystery.

Meanwhile, in Edinburgh, underground spaces such as Mary King's Close, originally built for commercial storage, became shelters for the city's poorest residents in the late 18th and early 19th centuries. Today, these spaces are infamous for their ghostly legends.

By the 1800s, Edinburgh had become a leading center for medical advancement, with a high demand for anatomical specimens—a practice that took a macabre turn during the Burke and Hare murders of 1827–8. These men killed 16 people and sold their bodies for dissection, leaving behind a chilling legacy. Part of Burke's sentence two centuries ago required that his remains be publicly dissected. Visitors can still view a book bound in Burke's skin, and skeletal remains at Edinburgh museums.

Edinburgh's grim history extends beyond its underground spaces and tales of murder. The towering Edinburgh Castle, a symbol of the city's turbulent past, witnessed numerous executions, including those of accused witches during the 16th and 17th centuries. Its dungeons held prisoners of war and political dissidents, and it remains steeped in eerie tales. Stories of public hangings in the Grassmarket and other hauntings only add to the city's enduringly dark allure.

When it comes to tourism, I don't usually like to pick favorites since every destination is unique and special in its own right. However, in the U.S., my top choice for dark tourism is easy: New Orleans. The city's above-ground cemeteries, voodoo culture, and tragic past make it a magnet for those drawn to the darker side of history. Yet beyond its haunted legacy, New Orleans is a vibrant city, alive with jazz, French and Spanish-inspired architecture, and some of the best food in the country. Savoring its gumbo and jambalaya or sipping coffee with a powdered beignet, there's something truly one-of-a-kind about this place.

What really sets New Orleans apart for me, though, are the sites that offer more than just a spooky experience. The National WWII Museum provides a powerful insight into one of the darkest periods in modern history, while the infamous LaLaurie Mansion, known for its horrifying stories of torture, and the nearby Whitney Plantation—which I explored in the previous chapter—serve as profound reminders of the city's complicated past. Additionally, the Battle of New Orleans, fought in 1815 during the War of 1812, left its own dark mark. The battle, despite occurring after the war had technically ended, was a bloody confrontation that saw General Andrew Jackson defeat the British. At the Chalmette Battlefield, where this pivotal conflict took place, I lay in the grass, reflecting on the senselessness of war and the sacrifices made, as the tour guide spat out facts faster than the musket shots likely did.

This chapter highlights a few of the world's most poignant places that have helped me reflect on the relationship between darkness and light. I begin with a visit—one of the most meaningful journeys I have ever taken—to a place not often considered dark. Yet, upon closer inspection, it reveals itself to be deeply shadowed by history and human experience. A shadow that still casts heavily to this day. Because of that connection, it earns its place as a site of dark tourism.

Old City of Jerusalem

A little over a year after learning of my liver disease, I had a strong desire to go to Israel. I can't pinpoint exactly why I went there, but it probably had something to do with feeling the need to be closer to God. Maybe learning about my diagnosis and its possible outcome gave me the push I needed. This need to get as close to God and as fast as I could reminded me of the cramming needed for exams in college after putting off studying for too long.

I've always felt better during the times in my life when my faith was stronger. Growing up Catholic, faith was serious business in my family but, like many young adults, I drifted away from it. I found myself believing again after getting married and attending church more regularly. However, after our divorce, I think I became angry with God and apathetic toward religion. That is, until my diagnosis—then it became a bit of an existential crisis.

Several years ago, I worked with a lawyer who had a saying, "There are no atheists in foxholes." I'm sure it originated from actual soldiers rather than someone armed with only a briefcase. Regardless, it resonated with me, and I think between remembering that saying and receiving the grim diagnosis, I boarded a plane, destination Jerusalem.

Arriving at the Old City of Jerusalem through the giant arch of Jaffa Gate is a bit like stepping into a time machine set to 2,000 years ago. Instantly, my eyes were pulled to the imposing fortress on the right—the Tower of David. This ancient brick compound, which was built by King Herod the Great, was part of Jerusalem's defenses. Named during the Byzantine period after the legendary King David, who famously took down Goliath, the tower stands as a testament to the Old City's dark and storied past.

Jerusalem is dark, very dark, but it is also light, very light. This is the one spot on Earth where good and evil collide with the greatest intensity. The spiritual war has been brewing here for millennia, often triggering real wars with real death. Throughout history, countless people have fought and died in the name of God, making it one of the most contentious and blood-soaked causes. The Old City of Jerusalem is ground zero. And I haven't even begun to talk about the actual events that occurred in this small, walled-off section of Jerusalem, flanked by the Mount of Olives, Mount Zion, and the rest of the city of Jerusalem.

The Old City of Jerusalem is small, relatively speaking—about one-fourth the size of Central Park or roughly the same size as Paris's Louvre

Museum complex. It's divided into four distinct quarters: Jewish, Muslim, Christian, and Armenian. Getting lost in the maze of tiny cobblestone streets is an unforgettable experience.

It seemed relatively safe during the day, but if there had been clashes or a major war in the area, I might have reconsidered my plans and done my soul-searching at the nearest Catholic church instead. In fact, only a few months later, tensions in the region escalated again, leading to violent clashes that are part of a conflict with roots stretching back centuries.

As I walked around, I encountered many sites tied to the three major religions that call this place home. The people here are welcoming, and there are relatively few restrictions on where you can go, especially as a Christian. That said, during times of heightened tension, boundaries can become much stricter, particularly for young Muslim men.

My own experience with restrictions came when I tried to approach the Dome of the Rock, with its iconic golden dome, and the adjacent Al-Aqsa Mosque, in an area known as the Temple Mount. Security officers carrying machine guns stopped me and firmly stated, "Muslims only." Non-Muslims are not allowed inside these buildings, so I respected the rule. I tend to heed instructions from people carrying machine guns, even though I would have liked to visit the spot where the Prophet Muhammad is believed to have ascended to heaven during the Night Journey.

The Temple Mount holds profound significance in Christian, Jewish, and Islamic traditions. For Jews, it is believed to be the rock that served as the foundation of the world and the site of the First and Second Temples, where the divine presence of God resided in the Holy of Holies. It is also considered the place where Abraham prepared to sacrifice his son—a story shared across Judaism, Christianity, and Islam, though Islamic tradition places this event in Mecca.

At the heart of the Temple Mount lies a single rock beneath the golden dome—the Foundation Stone. Measuring roughly 13 meters by 17 meters, its physical dimensions are modest. However, its spiritual and historical weight is immeasurable, making it a focal point for thousands of years and billions of people.

Throughout history, the Temple Mount has been a flashpoint for conflict. From the Crusades to modern disputes between Israelis and Palestinians, it has often stood at the intersection of religion and politics. Today, the site is overseen by the Islamic Waqf, while Israel maintains security control under a fragile status quo. Control over the Temple Mount symbolizes not just religious identity but also political sovereignty, cementing its status as one of the most contested places in the world.

Standing here, it's impossible not to feel both the historical importance and tension of the present. The Temple Mount is a powerful symbol of both unity and division. It underscores the complexities of coexistence and the challenges of shared heritage. Yet, it also offers a unique opportunity for reflection. Here, the intertwined histories of Judaism, Christianity, and Islam converge, providing hope that understanding and reconciliation are possible even in the face of enduring conflict.

As I continued to traverse the sacred city, the magnitude of its history settled in even more. From my first step inside the walls, I felt it, and the more time I spent there, the deeper it resonated. For the faithful, it's a surreal and deeply moving experience—like walking through a living Quran, Torah, or Bible. For me, caught in the depths of existential thought, it certainly felt as if it had the potential to penetrate even deeper into my soul. But would it? Would I find the answers to the questions my soul was asking, hidden just beyond the surface of my conscious mind?

Upon waking from my first night in the Old City, I ventured outside the southern walls to the nearby Mount Zion and visited the Tomb of King David. I donned a yarmulke to pay my respects to a figure of immense importance in both Jewish and Christian traditions. King David is also a significant figure in Islam, though access to the tomb is more challenging for Muslims. Just across the path is the Cenacle, the Room of the Last Supper. Standing in this room offered a powerful, tangible connection to the Passover meal Jesus shared with his disciples, an event that became the foundation of the Eucharist.

In the same building complex, I found the room where the Israeli command, including Prime Minister Levi Eshkol and Chief of Staff Yitzhak Rabin, was set up during the Six-Day War in 1967—a war between Israel and its Arab neighbors, primarily over land, borders, and resources, but with religious significance woven into its historical context. It felt paradoxical that this was part of the site tied to one of the most significant events in religious history.

Returning to the Old City of Jerusalem, I navigated through the well-maintained Jewish Quarter, an area that was largely destroyed during the 1948 Arab-Israeli War, placed under Jordanian control for nearly two decades, and reclaimed by Israel after the Six-Day War. The Quarter has since been beautifully restored, blending its historical significance with a sense of resilience and continuity.

Before long, I found myself at one of the holiest sites in Judaism, the Western Wall, also known historically as the Wailing Wall. It is a remnant of the retaining wall that once surrounded the courtyard of the Second Temple, which was destroyed by the Romans in 70 CE. The wall is the closest spot from which Jews can access the most sacred area of the temple, believed to lie under what is now the Muslim-controlled Dome of the Rock. Here, the devout can quite literally deliver notes and letters to God by placing them in the crevices of the ancient limestone.

Seeing the 19-meter-high wall is impressive, but witnessing the deep reverence it inspires in the faithful feels surreal. The area in front of the Wall is alive with the devotion of Orthodox Jews in their iconic black hats and coats, their side curls gently swaying as they rock back and forth in prayer. Others stand with their hands pressed against the Wall, tears streaming down their faces, lost in intimate conversation with the divine.

For me, the atmosphere transcends religious differences, bringing everyone into a shared experience of deep spirituality. Sitting down, I found myself meditating on my own life. The act of writing a heartfelt letter to God and placing it in a crack of the Wall brought tears to my eyes as well. The experience was both inspiring and transformative. Nearly every president in my lifetime has visited the site as a way to bring our nations together. I wonder if it resonated with them as much as it did with me.

Away from the quiet streets and alleyways of the Jewish Quarter, I started to notice changes that indicated I was in a very different place.

The atmosphere became livelier, with the pleasant aroma of spices, grilled meats, and perfumes filling the air. I had entered the Muslim Quarter. This sensory-rich area is lined with small open storefronts packed along narrow roads, where bargaining with shopkeepers is the norm. As a lover of street food and vibrant culture, this quarter felt like an oasis, a striking contrast to the familiar Western vibe I am used to.

Leaving the Muslim Quarter, I made my way toward the Lion's Gate, and passed the Church of St. Anne near the Pool of Bethesda, where it's said Jesus healed a paralyzed man. The church, named after Jesus's grandmother Anne, is a sacred piece of history. There's no record of Jesus visiting his grandparents, but if he did, this would have been Grandma and Grandpa's place. Just like heading over to our own grandparents' house, the cave gives a comforting feeling, a sense of familial warmth mixed with ancient reverence. I could almost picture young Jesus running around, perhaps being chased by Mary and his grandparents. Not much is known about Jesus during his early years, but when you are here, you might be standing in one of the most important places the Gospels do not mention.

The real allure lies in the belief that this is the birthplace of the Virgin Mary. I headed down the stairway upon entering, descending into the very room where she was allegedly born. As a Catholic, standing in the cave's room, I couldn't resist pulling off a few "Hail Marys" before heading back up. Mission accomplished.

Moving out through Lion's Gate toward the Mount of Olives, I came to another famous church, this one marking the final phase of Mary's life: her death and burial. I descended a wide, ancient staircase, its steps worn smooth by centuries of pilgrims, into a tomb area rich with Eastern Orthodox style. Icons, mosaics, and paintings of the Virgin Mary surrounded me, creating a space that felt both reverent and steeped in history. Inside the small tomb, I paid my respects to history's most famous young mom, shooting off one of the quickest Hail Marys I've ever said, mindful of the small group of pilgrims waiting their turn. I couldn't help but wonder if Mary might be okay with the "quantity over quality" approach.

I then took the short walk toward the Garden of Gethsemane and arrived at the Church of All Nations. It is impossible to miss, with its large mosaic on the façade depicting Jesus in deep conversation with God. Inside the church, I was met with a haunting feeling, created by the dim lighting and dark colors, symbolizing the night of agony. I gazed upon the short wrought-iron gate, adorned as if it were a crown of roses, which surrounded the rock where Jesus is said to have prayed to God the night before his arrest.

Next, I made my way up the Mount of Olives. About halfway up, I started feeling dizzy and tired, unsure of where I was heading and mindful of conserving my energy—something I now always have to consider due to the effects of my liver disease. Finding a good vantage point, I leaned against some ancient stones and took in the breathtaking beauty of the Old City of Jerusalem. The panoramic view was perfect for capturing a few stunning photos, with the large wall and the Temple Mount as focal points. As it turned out, I was standing next to what might be the most historic cemetery in the world. I took a walk through it on my way back to the Old City. This cemetery, over 3,000 years old, holds the remains of significant religious and political leaders, scholars, and martyrs. It's considered prime real estate because, in Jewish tradition, those buried on the Mount of Olives will be the first to be resurrected when the Messiah returns.

I headed back to the Lion's Gate and walked up to the Prison of Christ, a cave where Jesus may have been held after his arrest in the Garden of Gethsemane. I say "may" because there are at least five different claimed locations for the prison. Regardless of whether this was the exact site, it provides a powerful glimpse into what life was like for a prisoner in antiquity.

Following the signs pointing to the cell deep within the cave, I could almost feel the horror a prisoner must have experienced—something akin to the dread evoked when reading Edgar Allan Poe's *The Pit and the Pendulum*. The cell itself features a stone bench with two holes in it. A picture nearby illustrates their purpose: they were used to shackle the prisoner's legs. As I exited, I stopped by the cells of the two thieves who were crucified on either side of Jesus.

I was fortunate because my stay allowed me to be in the holy city on a Friday, which felt especially meaningful as a Christian. That afternoon, I met up with the Franciscan friars for a solemn religious procession that meets at an Islamic school just inside Lion's Gate. The friars have been caretakers of the most sacred sites here since the 13th century. The gathering traditionally takes place at 3:00 p.m., the time believed to be when Jesus died on the cross.

The courtyard of the school is thought to be where Pontius Pilate oversaw the trial of Jesus. Under political pressure and with the crowd demanding crucifixion, Pilate, despite his reluctance and declaration of innocence, condemned Jesus to death. This marks the site of the first station of the cross. I've heard the story countless times in church, as priests recount Jesus's walk toward his crucifixion. But following the friars along the same path as Jesus, listening to their chants, songs, and prayers at each station, is almost indescribable.

Across the street from the school is a small chapel called the Church of the Flagellation. This is where Jesus was beaten, whipped, and crowned with thorns. It's recognizable by its large bronze double doors, adorned with panels depicting a whip, crown of thorns, and nails. Once inside, I looked up to the golden dome above the altar and saw a large, vivid crown of thorns—a striking and powerful image.

The story of Jesus is not just one of faith, as it's well established that he once lived and was crucified here. This is what's known as the historical Jesus. The Christ of faith is another matter, with much debate surrounding his divinity. Regardless of whether he was just a man or the Son of God, reflecting on his suffering in the Church of the Flagellation was deeply meaningful. Being able to meditate and pray in this sacred space provided a powerful opportunity for reflection. If someone were to have visions of his suffering, this chapel feels like one of the most likely places it could happen. Did I have visions? No, but that didn't take away from the thoughts and emotions that came instead.

I then followed the procession of friars along the narrow road called the Via Dolorosa, passing churches and shops. The procession made nine stops before we finally reached the Church of the Holy Sepulchre.

Inside are the holiest sites in the Christian faith and the remaining stations of the cross. We entered through the large wooden doorway and immediately turned to go upstairs. By this time, dozens of people were following us. Many had joined our small group of about a dozen as we passed by them along the route.

Here, with the faithful, I stood at the very spot believed to be where the cross was placed during the crucifixion. After hours of being mocked, beaten, and bleeding from head to toe, Jesus spoke his final words, "Father, into your hands I commit my spirit," and died.

I thought back to my Sunday school days, hearing about the earthquake that struck at the exact moment of Christ's death. Next to where the cross once stood is a large rock with a noticeable crack, one that bears the classic signs of an earthquake. To me, it felt like more than just a story—it was something I could see with my own eyes, a bit of evidence that made faith feel more real. It spoke directly to my need to see evidence—a need deeply instilled in me as a social scientist.

By this time, the crowd following our procession had grown so large that I couldn't keep up with the friars leading the way. I descended the same steps and made my way toward the tomb on the opposite side of the church. Along the way, I came across a reddish-brown rectangular stone made into a shrine, with golden lanterns hanging above it. It was unmistakable, and a painting on the wall nearby confirmed what I suspected. Placing my hand on the stone, I could feel the oils left behind by countless pilgrims before me. This is the stone where Jesus's body is believed to have been cleaned and anointed with oils after his death.

I then caught back up with the friars as we reached the final stop on the Passion Walk—the tomb of Christ. Most Christians know the story: three days after Jesus died, Mary Magdalene came to the tomb and found it empty. His apparition appeared to her outside the tomb and later to others before his ascension to heaven.

With so many people crowded around, combined with the steady flow of tour groups, I decided not to step into the tomb of Jesus, which is enclosed within a small chapel-like structure called the Aedicule. The line stretched endlessly and, unfortunately, this isn't the kind of place that hands out fast passes like an amusement park. It reminded me of the cave in Bethlehem where Jesus is said to have been born—you wait in line for what feels like forever, only to be rushed through the moment you arrive. It's hard to fully take in the significance of such a sacred place when you're being shuffled along so quickly. I thought: a reason to go back should I survive my liver disease.

My time in Jerusalem's Old City was life-changing, but it didn't turn me into a sweater-wearing churchgoer. It did, however, make me more spiritual, less fearful, and, yes, a bit more religious, too. What struck me most about the Old City wasn't just the sites but the people. Witnessing how much this small patch of land means to so many touched me in a way that penetrated deeper than the history or the landmarks.

The religions here, though diverse, felt more peaceful and intertwined than divided—something that will likely be tested time and time again. Still, in any of the quarters of the holy city, I never really felt out of place—I was accepted with little exception. Only a small fraction of the people here harbor hate for one another, and I didn't encounter any of it. Yes, the Old City has its darkness, but after spending time here, I felt the brightness of the light truly overcame it.

Even though it felt like I was cramming for an exam, I passed. I walked away feeling closer to God—not just in a Christian sense but in a way that felt deeply human. While the Old City holds all the hallmarks of a dark tourism destination, its light shines brighter, reminding me that hope and goodness can prevail.

Lying in my bed on my final evening in the Old City, I thought about the meaning of the sites I had seen and the stories they held. I also thought about the devout people of the three major religions that inhabit the area. I realized in that quiet moment, regardless of whether my life ended soon or stretched into old age, I would be okay. My family would be too. For the first time since my diagnosis, I gave myself permission to release the suffocating fear of death and embrace life's uncertainty. It was a perspective I hadn't known to this degree since the reckless invincibility of my naïve youth, but now it came to me in a healthy, grounded, and deeply realistic way. One that sticks with me to this day.

Ancient Egypt

Seeing the Pyramids of Giza often tops the bucket list of many travelers. But would the experience be everything one might imagine? During the hour-long cab ride from Cairo's airport to Giza, several things stood out. The traffic was intense, with vehicles weaving through the chaos like a mass of slithering snakes, their incessant honking creating a constant noise. Signs bearing President Sisi's image seemed to be everywhere I looked, making me wonder if there was a touch of insecurity behind such omnipresence.

The streets were littered with trash swirling in the wind, while wild dogs darted fearlessly between cars, adding to the already frenetic atmosphere. Somehow, I made it in one piece to my very modest three-room hotel, which overlooked the Great Pyramid and the Sphinx—a last-minute booking I had miraculously managed to snag at the airport just before taking off for Egypt.

The poverty here is impossible to ignore, with vendors trying to sell you something at nearly every corner. I felt genuine sympathy for the people, though I have to admit it was a bit overwhelming to navigate all the "helpful" offers. Yet, despite the obvious hardships, the people were some of the friendliest I've encountered in all my travels. I met individuals whose kindness truly stood out. The only time I was knowingly targeted for a scam was, surprisingly, by a child. While using an ATM just outside the gates of the Great Pyramid complex, a boy waited nearby, watching me conduct my transaction. In the most authoritative tone a 10-year-old could manage, he declared, "The machine is broken, go over there," gesturing down the road. It didn't take long for me to realize his plan—to grab the money before I did. I calmly waited for my cash to dispense, then turned to him and said, with a mix of sarcasm and firmness, "Nice try, kid."

On my first night, I stepped onto my hotel balcony to find myself with a front-row seat to the Pyramids and the Sphinx. As the starry night gave way to the glow of the Giza Sound and Light Show, the pyramids came alive, illuminated in vibrant colors. The ancient stones seemed to speak, their tale interwoven with the narrated legacy of the pharaohs. Oddly, I realized I had heard it before, and then it clicked. The spectacle has remained virtually unchanged since Roger Moore's James Bond witnessed it in *The Spy Who Loved Me* back in 1977. Yet, standing there under the same vast night sky, with history's echoes all around, it felt as though the story was being told just for me.

After enjoying a small feast for breakfast on the balcony, I climbed into a simple horse carriage with Omar, a middle-aged Egyptian man whose sun-weathered skin told the story of a life spent under the blazing desert sky. Omar, who has been giving tours of the Giza Pyramids with the same horse for over 20 years, guided me down the long path to the largest pyramid in the complex—the Great Pyramid, where the tomb of the pharaoh Khufu is located. Standing nearly 150 meters tall, it is every bit as mesmerizing as its reputation suggests—a true historic icon and the only remaining wonder of the ancient world.

It's humbling to imagine the ingenuity and labor that went into building it 4,500 years ago—unless, of course, one subscribes to the conspiracy theories claiming alien civilizations intervened to gift humanity a pyramid. Personally, I do not. Scholars have also discredited the outdated belief that slaves built the pyramids, adding even more depth to their incredible story. In reality, it was likely a workforce of over 20,000 engineers, skilled craftsmen, and laborers who created the pyramids over just a 20-year period. It's not unlike how major buildings are constructed today, just with more manpower to compensate for the lack of heavy equipment.

The Great Pyramid is one of the few ancient pyramids that still allows explorers to enter its sacred passageways. As I ducked through the threshold, stepping from the modern world into the ancient, the air grew thick with the faint, earthy smell of stone. The farther I ventured into the narrow corridors, the more oppressive the air became. The massive limestone blocks seemed to press in around me, and a creeping sense of claustrophobia began to take hold. Navigating the next stage proved challenging, and I saw several people abandon their attempt to reach the inner chamber.

I was determined to press on despite my own struggles with increasing panic and health concerns. For those who struggle with a combination of claustrophobia and poor physical health, it must be nearly impossible. A simple reminder that the pyramid was never built with tourists in mind made the journey feel all the more like an authentic adventure.

To reach the inner chamber, I climbed several steps in an even smaller, more confined space. One particularly tight section lacked steps entirely due to its narrow enclosure. Here, the confined space forced me to squat down and ascend a long ramp, unable to take full strides, shuffling forward on my feet. The combination of physical exertion and the constricting environment made for an intense and unforgettable experience.

About midway through the passage, a bottleneck occurred, bringing the line of people heading to the chamber to a standstill. An older woman a few people ahead needed to pause and catch her breath. I glanced behind me to see a line of people stretching back into the darkness. That's when my claustrophobia fully kicked in. I've endured MRI machines and cramped cockpits before, but this felt different—this time, I panicked. Suddenly, I was back to the feeling of being on the playground as a child, stuck in that cursed covered corkscrew slide.

This time, instead of screaming, crying, and kicking my way out, I closed my eyes, told myself not to panic, assured myself I would be all right, and took a few deep breaths. Moments later, the line began to move again. Eventually, I made it into the king's inner chamber—a small, simple room, but a welcome sight after the confines of those tight passageways. As I walked around the sarcophagus, I paused to reflect on exactly where I was and everything in my life that had led me to this moment.

After spending a couple of hours exploring the complex, I was ready to move on. Before leaving, Omar took some time to wander around the majestic Great Sphinx. Carved by the ancient Egyptians from one massive piece of limestone, the lion with a human head likely symbolized royal power and protection. While I was there, a small pack of wild dog puppies roamed nearby. They seemed as curious about me as I was about them, and we cautiously approached the edge of each other's comfort zones. They reminded me of the cats in the Old City of Jerusalem. Did they know they were guardians of some of the world's most historic places? Probably not, but I like to think they did.

A couple of days later, I took a plane that followed the Nile down to Luxor, an ancient city about 640 kilometers south of Cairo. Situated along the Nile's shores, Luxor is often called the "world's greatest open-air museum," celebrated for its sprawling necropolises and grand temples. Among its many treasures are two of Egypt's most significant sites: the Luxor and Karnak temples. Since I didn't know the first thing about hieroglyphics and the symbolism of the various ruins, I decided to hire a guide who could deepen my understanding of the culture and history of this ancient civilization.

For a few brief hours, I had the privilege of employing Samir, an Egyptologist whose silk scarf draped effortlessly around his neck, accentuating the dark Egyptian skin of his ancestors. With an unmistakable charisma reminiscent of Anthony Bourdain, Samir's resemblance to the famed traveler went beyond appearances. Like Bourdain, his passion for storytelling was clear as he effortlessly weaved tales of ancient wonders with a depth of knowledge that captivated.

Samir guided me through the Luxor and Karnak temples, which are connected by a 2.5-kilometer road lined with sphinx statues. The ancient Egyptians dedicated both temples to honor Amun-Ra, a deity formed by merging Amun, a local Theban god of creation, and Ra, the sun god. Despite Egypt's polytheistic religious system, Amun-Ra was one of the most powerful and revered gods, particularly during the New Kingdom period.

The Temple of Karnak, one of the largest religious structures in the world, was absolutely mesmerizing. I've seen Egyptian hieroglyphs and statues in museums, but experiencing them in their original setting was on a completely different level—especially with Samir interpreting the meanings behind what I was seeing. Though much of the temple is in ruins, the remaining walls, statues, and obelisks made it easy to imagine what it might have looked like thousands of years ago. I could almost picture the kings riding in on their chariots, surrounded by the bustling life of ancient times. Just as I was lost in this daydream, the sound of blaring horns jolted me back to reality—wait, am I really hearing horns? No, that was just my imagination too.

The Temple of Luxor, though smaller in size compared to other temples, feels grander due to its architectural beauty and immense cultural significance. Construction began during the reign of Pharaoh Amenhotep III, which started around 1390 BCE, and continued for over 200 years. Significant additions were made during the reign of Ramses II, also known as Ramses the Great, in the 13th century BCE. Entering through the towering gateway flanked by two colossal statues of Ramses II was an experience that truly put the temple's proportions into perspective.

As I walked down the long corridor, I passed massive columns, their surfaces adorned with intricate hieroglyphics and carvings, framed by towering walls. Reaching the back of the temple, I noticed something unexpected—vividly colorful paintings. Upon closer inspection, I realized these weren't hieroglyphics at all but Roman-era artworks painted directly onto the walls. Added centuries later, during Roman control, these paintings offer a fascinating layer of history, showcasing how the temple evolved over time while maintaining its significance through different eras.

In Luxor, high priests performed rituals intended to communicate with the spirits of past pharaohs buried nearby. Once a year, during the New Kingdom period (*c.*1550–1070 BCE) and lasting nearly a month, the Opet Festival took place to honor the reigning pharaoh, who was believed to be the living embodiment of Amun-Ra. Being part of such a vibrant and spiritual celebration must have been exhilarating. I imagined the vivid colors of the decorations and costumes, the echoing sounds of joyful music and chants, the scent of incense filling the air, and the palpable feeling of excitement and unity among the participants, creating an electrifying atmosphere that would have left a lasting impression on everyone involved.

For me, the Karnak and Luxor temples were more than just an extravagant field trip; they were a journey into the heart of ancient Egypt that stirred something deep within me. Their towering columns and intricately carved hieroglyphs left an indelible mark, showcasing the enduring power of human creativity and spirituality. Yet, they also reminded me of the human cost behind their creation, as laborers endured grueling conditions. These temples stand as monuments to the brilliance and complexity of ancient civilizations, offering lessons in both their achievements and their contradictions.

After exploring the temples, I found myself seated with Samir in a cozy tea shop, its walls adorned with vibrant Egyptian wool and every tiny table accompanied by a hookah. The atmosphere was thick with the scent of flavored tobacco, and as the smoke curled lazily through the air, our conversation flowed just as easily. We delved into discussions about our families, the politics of the day, and everything in between. I shared my thoughts on Sisi, and he countered with his own insights on Trump. It was in these moments, connecting with people like Samir, that the true essence of travel once again revealed itself. I wasn't just collecting experiences; I was gaining an understanding, a deeper sense of what life is like in faraway lands.

Before leaving Egypt, I crossed the Nile to the nearby Valley of the Kings with my taxi driver turned makeshift guide. I had met him earlier at the airport and appreciated his blunt yet insightful cultural depictions during the drive to my hotel, so I decided to reach out to him again.

The Valley of the Kings carries a sense of darkness—not the frightening kind, but the quiet, contemplative feeling of walking through a strange yet magnificent graveyard. Many people assume the ancient Egyptians were obsessed with death and, in some ways, they were. But their true focus was on life and the afterlife. This is evident in their practices like mummification and their belief in the *Book of the Dead*, a guide meant to help the deceased overcome the challenges of the afterlife and achieve eternal rebirth.

The ancient Egyptians' obsession with life after death is best exemplified by their burial practices. They believed that the tombs of kings were portals to the afterlife, and the construction of these tombs often spanned the entire reign of a pharaoh. In the Valley of the Kings, I was able to step inside these elaborate tombs.

Beyond the Darkness

As I walked down the dusty path into the valley I was surrounded by the barren limestone cliffs. Modest structures built into the ground and cliffs come into view, each with a door leading to one of the over 60 tombs.

The most famous tomb in the Valley of the Kings belongs to the boy king, Tutankhamun. He ascended to the throne of both Upper and Lower Egypt around the age of nine. Born of incest between two royal siblings, Tutankhamun's reign was neither eventful nor impactful. His death, approximately 10 years later, likely came abruptly, as evidenced by the relatively small and less elaborate tomb compared to others of his stature. He likely died of illness or injury, and there is even speculation that he may have been murdered.

Why is King Tutankhamun so famous if he didn't rule long and nothing significant happened during his reign? His young age may have contributed to his notoriety, but other young leaders have existed, like Henry VI of England, who was crowned at nine months and also ruled over France. The main reason for Tutankhamun's legendary status is that his tomb, despite being smaller and more modest than others, was discovered in exceptional condition. Grave robbers had looted the other tombs, taking nearly all the valuable riches within, but while King Tut's tomb was thought to have been robbed twice in antiquity, only a small portion of the treasures were taken, preserving a wealth of artifacts that offer a glimpse into ancient Egyptian life and culture.

In 1922, after years of searching, archaeologist Howard Carter, employed by the aristocrat Lord Carnarvon, discovered the tomb of Tutankhamun. The find revealed an astonishing array of riches, including a solid gold funerary mask, intricately crafted jewelry, and elaborate burial items. Carter famously said that he was met with "wonderful things" upon entering the crypt. These treasures are now housed between the Egyptian Museum in Cairo and the Grand Egyptian Museum in Giza.

I imagined being in Howard Carter's shoes as I descend into the ancient burial site. Tutankhamun's tomb, known simply as KV62, remains full of wonder. The short corridor to the burial chamber may seem unremarkable unless one knew about the theory of the hurried burial. I then entered the Antechamber, which was once filled with the now-removed treasures. Despite the quick burial and unremarkable tomb, the treasures within were once fit for a king.

Looking to the left in the Antechamber, I saw one of the most historic finds in history: the boy king himself, King Tutankhamun. He lies under a protective, climate-controlled glass casing that allowed me to examine him up close. His body is covered by a white loincloth, but his face and feet are exposed.

Despite the millennia that have passed, seeing him feels like encountering a distant relative at a wake—someone I never knew personally, or, in Tut's case, not at all. Yet, I've heard fascinating stories and rumors about him. Now, here I am, face-to-face with his remains—a lifeless shell of someone whose life, though brief and thought to have been full of health challenges, left an enduring legacy. I often think, "If these walls could talk." But looking at Tut, I found myself pondering a similar question: what would he say?

The years of decay, combined with the mummification process, have left Tut's skin dark and leathery, stretched tightly over bone. Small fragments of cloth cling to his bony feet, with toenails that look unusually long due to decomposition. After viewing him, I stepped aside and watched others in awe of their own encounter with the boy king—someone who has captivated the world thousands of years after his heart took its last beat.

On the opposite side of the Antechamber, there's a smaller room that holds an enormous sarcophagus. Inside, Howard Carter discovered three nested coffins, which ultimately revealed the mummy of King Tut. What Carter found resting on Tut's head was one of the most priceless artifacts in world history, rivaled only by the Rosetta Stone and the *Mona Lisa*. The mask of King Tutankhamun, crafted from solid gold and adorned with stunning gemstones, is a breathtaking testament to ancient Egyptian artistry.

The scenes painted on the walls surrounding the sarcophagus are from religious texts and the *Book of the Dead*. Each painted scene offers thought-provoking insight into ancient Egyptian beliefs about death. One such scene depicts Tutankhamun's highest official, Ay, performing the "Opening of the Mouth" ceremony on the pharaoh's mummy. This ritual was believed to restore the deceased's ability to eat, breathe, and speak in the afterlife. Following Tutankhamun's death, Ay ascended to the throne, despite not being related by blood to the boy king—indicative of the significant influence he wielded during Tutankhamun's reign.

Another scene within the tomb is from the *Amduat*, a funerary text that details the journey to the next world. It is depicted by 12 baboons, symbolizing the beginning of the sun god Ra's voyage through the underworld, where he navigated past obstacles, spells, gods, and creatures. Egyptians believed this journey ensured the sun's rise each morning.

When I entered the tomb of Tutankhamun, I gave little thought to the myths of protective curses. Many of those who entered the tomb in the days following its discovery died within weeks, including Lord Carnarvon himself. Despite these stories, there are no known spells or curses depicted in the tomb. Howard Carter, who lived for two decades after the tomb's discovery, never believed in a curse, attributing the deaths to coincidence. Yet, there's one artifact that makes the myth a bit more intriguing. The statue of Anubis, the jackal-headed god of the dead, greeted Carter when he first entered the tomb, standing guard at the burial chamber—likely placed there to ward off potential grave robbers.

I then moved beyond Tut's tomb and explored others in the valley. Each tomb, like Tut's, features a descending corridor (long hallway), an antechamber (small entrance room), and a burial chamber. The walls are adorned with depictions from the *Book of the Dead* and the *Amduat*. Because these tombs have been sheltered from sunlight for millennia, the pictures and hieroglyphics remain remarkably well preserved, as if time has barely touched them. Many showcase elaborate, beautiful, and vividly colorful scenes, yet each tomb varies in size and detail depending on the significance of the person buried there and the time they had to prepare it. A long-serving and respected king, like Ramses II, was honored with a grand and elaborate tomb.

Reflecting on the differing sizes and artwork of the tombs, I thought about the vast majority of people who didn't even have the opportunity to have a tomb. I found that they were usually buried in simple graves, and if they were lucky, they were mummified, often with amulets and spell inscriptions. It's not unlike today's common practice of embalming and placing a Bible in the coffin.

In many of the tombs, I saw depictions of people working—laborers and servants of the pharaohs. These are often mistaken for slaves, but that's a modern misunderstanding. These figures were included because they were believed to be useful to the pharaoh in the afterlife. Then there were depictions of men bound with their hands behind their backs, marching. Many people also misinterpret these images as slaves, but they actually represent captives. These scenes were meant to highlight the pharaoh's victories in war, showcasing the groups of people he had captured. Through their art and rituals, the Egyptians sought to overcome the darkness of death, a timeless effort that reflects the struggles of those battling despair and seeking hope in their darkest moments today.

Golden Gate Bridge and Aokigahara Forest

The Golden Gate Bridge and Aokigahara Forest, though separated by an ocean, share a deep historical significance that transcends their outward beauty. The Golden Gate Bridge, an architectural marvel completed in 1937, symbolizes human ingenuity and resilience. Its striking Art Deco design and sweeping red arches connect San Francisco to Marin County, a testament to perseverance during the Great Depression—a time of immense hardship. The bridge's construction offered hope to a recovering nation.

On the other side of the Pacific, at the foothills of the majestic Mt. Fuji, lies Aokigahara Forest, a place steeped in Japanese folklore. Known as the Sea of Trees, its quiet mystical beauty was shaped by ancient volcanic eruptions and centuries of cultural reverence. Both the Golden Gate Bridge and Aokigahara Forest are awe-inspiring, blending natural and man-made wonders. Yet, each harbors a darker history.

On average, someone in the world dies by suicide every minute. Despite the fleeting nature of suicidal thoughts, the act is a permanent decision—the ultimate expression of hopelessness. As a therapist, conversations about suicide are part of my daily work. Knowing I've helped people find enough hope to choose life brings me immense fulfillment.

One of my most memorable experiences happened early in my career at a residential treatment facility. I caught a person on suicide watch sneaking out of our unlocked building. When I tried to coax him back, he bolted into the woods. I pursued him, with no one else witnessing the drama unfolding. About 100 meters in, I found him standing on a rock, noose in hand, ready to end his life. I reached him just as he was placing his head into the loop, tackling him to the ground as the branch holding the rope broke. After a brief struggle, he agreed to come back with me, and he received the help he needed in a hospital.

Over the years, I would see him from time to time. With a dark sense of humor, he sarcastically "blamed" me for saving his life. He didn't realize it, but I took satisfaction in that acknowledgment. He was still here, still alive, and that moment had made a difference.

A few years into my relationship with Sarah, our travels brought us to San Francisco. We rented bikes and pedaled our way across the Golden Gate Bridge, heading toward the charming hillside town of Sausalito. Originally, I had planned to propose to Sarah on the bridge—a big, romantic gesture—but after a conversation with a family member regarding its timing, I decided against it.

As we stopped mid-span to take in the view, I thought briefly about the plan I'd abandoned. Then something else caught my eye: a small blue sign attached to one of the towering red pillars. It read, "There is hope. Make the call. The consequences of jumping from this bridge are fatal and tragic." Just beneath the sign was a crisis phone.

At the time, I didn't know much about the bridge's dark history. Later, I learned how the strong winds and height often cause those who jump to hit the water at a fatal angle. Combined with its iconic symbolism and accessibility, these factors made it a frequent site for those seeking to end their lives. Even for the occasional survivor of the jump, the harbor's unforgiving currents claim most before rescue teams can reach them.

My decision not to propose that day marked a turning point in my feelings about the future of our relationship. I began to feel uncertain about its viability and grew somewhat hopeless about its potential, which eventually contributed to our breakup, despite my deep love for Sarah and my desire to stay together. After much reflection and effort, we found our way back to each other and eventually married. For those who jump from the bridge, however, their decision is tragically final, leaving no chance for reconciliation or second chances.

The real tragedy—and hope—lies in the stories of those who survive the leap to death. Of the thousands who have jumped, fewer than two percent have lived to tell their stories. Many survivors report feeling instant regret as they leapt. Remarkably, most who survive do not go on to die by suicide. Studies show a striking pattern: those stopped or who survive rarely attempt suicide again.

What changes? It's the help they receive. Many are committed to treatment, while others seek help voluntarily. At their most vulnerable, they realize—often within themselves—that their life is worth living. That moment becomes a turning point, offering new meaning to their suffering. Many survivors now advocate for mental health awareness and suicide prevention, sharing their stories to inspire hope.

The Golden Gate Bridge is the site of nearly 2,000 documented suicides, making it the world's most notorious location for suicides. Across the Pacific, Aokigahara Forest, often called the "Suicide Forest," holds the second-highest number of suicides. Set against the backdrop of Mt. Fuji, the forest is a serene yet tragic place. The silence of Aokigahara is palpable—lava-formed caverns and moss-covered trees create an eerie calm. Yet, this beauty is shadowed by the knowledge that many who enter do not return.

In Japan, suicide carries a complex cultural history, shaped by notions of honor, sacrifice, and the societal challenges surrounding mental illness. From the ancient tradition of *seppuku*, where samurai would ritually disembowel themselves as an act of honor or atonement, to the intense pressures of modern life, suicide in Japan has not always been viewed the same way as it is in the West. In recent years, however, Japan has made notable progress in promoting mental health awareness. Yet, Aokigahara remains a somber reminder of the ongoing challenges in addressing this issue.

Hiking through Aokigahara evokes a range of emotions. Rays of sunlight piercing the dense canopy above illuminate bursts of red and yellow from spiders, birds, and mushrooms, standing out against the dark greens and browns of the forest. The forest itself serves as a powerful metaphor. Those who wander off the paths often become lost and require rescue. In the same way, people lost in the darkness of their minds need intervention to prevent tragedy. Just as hikers can be guided back to safety, those who struggle can be led back to hope.

After nearly 30 years in mental health, I've learned that even the smallest spark of hope can save lives. Sometimes, all it takes is a compassionate ear and genuine care. I've seen many new therapists struggle when a client mentions suicide, often leading to unnecessary hospitalizations, but I know what truly matters in those moments is listening. I've also realized you don't need to be a therapist to offer support to someone struggling with serious thoughts. When I take the time to truly listen, I create space for them to express their pain, and in that moment of being heard clarity and connection often emerge. Much like those on the Golden Gate Bridge who are pulled back from the edge, I've seen how people can be brought back from the brink through nonjudgmental human connection and empathy. It's in those moments that they uncover that their story isn't over, and there's still a path ahead.

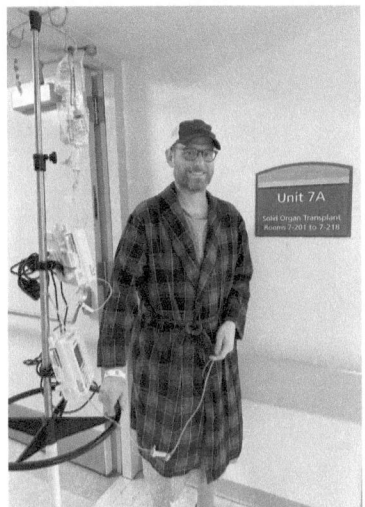

Chapter 5

Medical and Macabre Museums

What lingers longer after a museum visit: the knowledge it imparts or the emotions it stirs?

WHEN MOST PEOPLE think about dark tourism, the medical field isn't the first thing that comes to mind. However, exploring the history of disease, injury, and treatment uncovers a narrative that is both sobering and compelling. The progress we've made, though, is undeniable. Since 1900, the average lifespan in the developed world has increased by about 30 years, and many people enjoy a quality of life that was once unimaginable. Yet, it's important to remember the human suffering that paved the way for these advancements. Visiting medical sites offers a fascinating and sometimes unsettling look at how far we've come and the often difficult origins of modern medicine.

Two key areas have dramatically extended human life: breakthroughs in medical technology and the rise of evidence-based medicine. On the technological front, antibiotics, vaccines, and diagnostic imaging stand out as lifesaving miracles. Evidence-based medicine, meanwhile, has standardized protocols and improved treatments through systematic research. The field never stops evolving. We're now on the brink of new eras in genetics and stem cell research. But to understand where we're headed, we have to appreciate where we've been. There are many museums dedicated to medical history—places that have helped to shape the way I see life, the medical field, and even death. In this chapter, I explore a few of these remarkable places.

I can't overstate how grateful I am for modern medicine. At 46, I'm alive and writing this because of a donated liver from a selfless person I'll never get to thank. Not long ago, a diagnosis like mine would have been a death sentence. My end-stage liver disease was diagnosed three years ago. At the time, my doctors gave me a 50 percent chance of surviving two years without a transplant. The first ever liver transplant took place in 1967. Before then, even reaching that two-year mark would've been a miracle. Today, transplant recipients like me can have normal lifespans as long as we stick to our antirejection meds and regular checkups.

It's humbling to think that, just a century ago, my condition would've been a death sentence. The same is true for so many other diseases. Several museums I've visited have highlighted the often dark but significant history of medical progress. And then there are those that focus entirely on the final stage of life: death. All of these fall under the umbrella of dark tourism because of their connection to the fragility of life, human suffering, and mortality.

Mütter Museum

The Mütter Museum in Philadelphia is an unforgettable destination for anyone interested in medical history. It houses a remarkable collection of anatomical specimens, medical tools, and pathology exhibits. Founded in 1858 by Dr. Thomas Dent Mütter, a renowned surgeon, the museum began with his extensive personal collection, which he donated to the College of Physicians of Philadelphia. Established to educate both medical professionals and the public, it succeeds in being both fascinating and educational. It's a place that not only teaches about the medical field but also invites visitors to explore and learn from both common and rare diseases. Despite its sincere efforts, some exhibits may not always feel entirely respectful. This is likely a reflection of its 19th-century origins.

When I walked up to the museum for the first time, I was struck by the stately historic building—another reflection of its origins. Stepping inside, I felt transported in time. The first room's historical ambience, with its wood-paneled glass cabinets and carefully arranged artifacts, immediately captivated me.

One of the first displays I came across was the Soap Lady, a real-life specimen whose body underwent a rare biological process called saponification, where body fat transformed into a soap-like substance. Her body appeared impacted with dirt and soap, her mouth frozen open as though she had been yelling at the moment of her death. Initially, it was believed she died in the 1700s, possibly of yellow fever, based on her missing teeth—a condition often linked to the illness. However, further analysis in the 1980s determined her death likely occurred decades later, and she was much younger than originally thought, likely in her 20s.

Moving deeper inside the museum, I came across something I never expected—fragments of Albert Einstein's brain, mounted on glass slides for close examination. At first glance, they looked like any other brain specimen. But then it hit me: this was the brain of arguably the greatest thinker in human history. Standing there, I thought about how this very brain had conceived the theory of relativity, which changed our understanding of time and space and paved the way for technologies like GPS and nuclear energy. It was humbling to be in the presence of something so monumental, a testament to the immense potential of the human mind.

Not far from Einstein's brain was the Hyrtl Skull Collection—a haunting display of 139 human skulls. Each skull told a story of disease, trauma, and the lives these individuals once lived. The collection offered a glimpse into 19th-century Europe and the toll that life and death took on those on display. Hyrtl originally compiled the skulls to counter the pseudoscience of phrenology, challenging the notion that skull shape could determine intelligence or character. I doubt any of the individuals represented knew their skulls would one day be featured as part of a macabre-like medical exhibit, no matter how respectfully it is presented. The ethics of this display add another layer to the medical practices of the 19th century, a time when marginalized groups such as criminals, as well as unclaimed bodies, were often used to advance medicine without their consent. Is it ethical to continue displaying them?

Descending the stairs, I found myself face-to-face with the giant megacolon. This specimen was caused by Hirschsprung's disease, a severe disorder in which the absence of nerve cells leads to chronic constipation and significant bowel dilation. It was unsettling yet oddly mesmerizing, a vivid reminder of the genetic conditions that can afflict the human body. Nearby, another giant caught my attention: this time, a complete human skeleton standing at 7 feet 6 inches tall. It belonged to one of the tallest humans ever recorded, a striking reminder of the extremes of human biology.

As I wandered through the museum, I couldn't stop thinking about the lives behind the exhibits. There were displays of conjoined twins, giant tumors, mutated fetuses, early medical equipment, and various anatomical specimens. What kind of lives did these individuals lead? How did their extraordinary biological traits shape their experiences? These questions lingered with me, deepening my sense of empathy for the people whose remains were now behind glass.

The Mütter Museum excels in this—not just displaying medical oddities but humanizing them, making me ponder the humanity behind the glass. It's a sobering, enlightening journey through the curious corners of medical history that left me with a deep respect for the design and diversity of the human body.

Two years later, as I lay on the MRI table, waiting to be slid into the machine that might provide answers—or more questions—my thoughts drifted to the Mütter Museum. Scattered as they were, something about that place brought me comfort. It made me feel, in my quest to live, as if I were standing on the shoulders of centuries of scientists and doctors who had come before. The Mütter reminded me that I wasn't alone in my medical journey and gave me perspective on just how far medicine has come.

Einstein's contributions to the technology briefly crossed my mind, and I reflected on how the brain I had seen years earlier had made the

MRI possible. My thoughts then drifted to the cancer specimens on display at the museum. Silently, I prayed that cancer wouldn't be the outcome for me.

A few days earlier, I had received a positive result from a liquid biopsy, an advanced blood test praised by both my doctor and the testing company for its accuracy in detecting liver cancer. The first scan found a lump, and now I just had to wait to see if it grew. What followed were three additional MRIs and lingering uncertainty.

Those months were difficult, but with my mounting experiences under my belt, I was beginning to master the anxiety that popped up. But still—fucking liver cancer! When the results of my final test came back, the lesion had disappeared. No cancer! The biopsy nine months earlier had been a false positive. I'll never forget the relief I felt—it was like coming up for air after being submerged for far too long. That experience gave me a deeper appreciation for the relentless march of medical progress, despite its occasional mishaps, and an even greater empathy for the individuals whose stories fill the exhibits at the Mütter Museum. In the end, I figured, at least it wasn't a false negative.

New Orleans Pharmacy Museum

Tucked away in the French Quarter, the New Orleans Pharmacy Museum offers a fascinating glimpse into the history of medicine. Housed in a historic townhouse once owned by America's first licensed pharmacist, it takes visitors on a journey through the evolution of treatments from the 19th century to today.

When I stepped inside, I was greeted by beautiful wooden shelves lined with antique medical instruments, and pharmaceutical containers filled with herbs and powders that once promised cures. But alongside these glass-encased relics of progress were darker reminders of the past. The museum doesn't shy away from showcasing medical quackery, when treatments often did more harm than good.

In true New Orleans fashion, the museum even includes a section on voodoo potions and remedies—a blend of science and superstition that reflects the city's rich cultural history. Among the more notable exhibits were amputation tools, trepanning instruments used to drill holes in skulls, and medications like mercury, opium, and cocaine. Seeing these items made me think about how far we've come—and how much further we have to go.

One particularly unusual and fascinating artifact at the museum is the 1855 Lippincott soda fountain, where customers could indulge in the flavors of cola and other sodas of the time. These fountains were a common feature in the early generations of pharmacies, often paired with the sale of perfumes and cosmetics. In my mind, it paints a scene straight out of a Norman Rockwell painting—full of nostalgia and charm. It's a reminder of the multifaceted role pharmacies played back then, a role that many continue to fulfill in our communities today.

It's only been about 30 years since the opioid epidemic began, fueled by greed and misinformation. I can't help but wonder how future generations will judge our current medical practices. Will they see this era as we see the dangerous remedies of the past? Will they marvel at how we moved from transplanting organs to cloning them, eliminating rejection risks and harsh medications? What will they think of our attempts to prolong life, and will they view them as primitive compared to what's possible in their time?

Just as some doctors once diagnosed diseases by the color, smell, and even the taste of urine, today's cutting-edge practices may one day seem like ancient history. The rapid advancement of medical knowledge is both humbling and inspiring. It leaves me with hope for a future where the incredible progress we've made continues to evolve, improving lives in ways we can only begin to imagine.

Glore Psychiatric Museum

If there's one museum that resonates deeply with me, it's the Glore Psychiatric Museum in St. Joseph, Missouri. Just as the medical field has undergone incredible transformations over the past 150 years, I've witnessed significant changes in mental health care since I started in the field in 2000. Back then, the approach was often more rigid and authoritarian—the doctor or therapist held the majority of the power, and patients were expected to follow orders without much question. Over time, I've seen a shift toward a more humanizing, collaborative relationship, where care is individualized, fostering hope and better outcomes. This shift has also helped reduce the stigma around mental illness, encouraging more people to seek help without needless shame.

The museum sits on the grounds of the former State Lunatic Asylum No. 2, established in 1874 and operational until 1997. Walking into one of its historic buildings, I found myself stepping back in time. The exhibits offer a haunting glimpse into the evolution of mental health care, showcasing theories, philosophies, and treatments that shaped the lives of the individuals who lived within these walls. The museum reflects not only the history of this institution but the broader journey of mental health care over centuries.

One of the first displays that caught my eye was a portrait of Dorothea Dix, a 19th-century nurse and one of my personal heroes. Dix's work transformed mental health care. She recognized that many incarcerated individuals were actually suffering from untreated mental illnesses, sparking a passionate crusade for reform. Thanks to her efforts, countless people were moved from the inhumane conditions of jails to the more therapeutic environments of hospitals. Her advocacy led to the construction and expansion of state hospitals across the U.S., including the very asylum that now houses the Glore Museum. Her legacy inspires me to this day.

Dorothea Dix's work also helped to shape my career. Her dedication to improving conditions for those with mental illness in the criminal justice system sparked my interest in the subject. This passion led me to focus my doctoral research on the criminalization of mental illness, which became the foundation of my first book, *The Criminalization of the Mentally Ill*. From working on mental health court initiatives to serving as a prison therapist, teaching criminal psychology, and consulting with criminal justice agencies, my career has been deeply inspired by her pioneering work.

One story that sticks with me is that of Joe, a young client I worked with years ago. Joe battled schizophrenia, haunted by relentless voices and disorganized thoughts. Despite his struggles, he was kind, though his paranoia and erratic speech made communication challenging. His story took a dark turn when he was arrested for stealing food. He was released from jail an hour from his home after being off his medication for several days. The jail released him without transportation. Determined to get back, he began walking the nearly 100 kilometers home. Hunger and exhaustion eventually overcame him, and he wandered into a random house, ate some food, and collapsed on the couch. When the homeowners returned, they found him asleep and called the police. Joe was arrested for breaking and entering and sent back to the same jail he'd just left—a tragic illustration of the cycles faced by many with serious and persistent mental illness.

As I wandered through the museum, I encountered another familiar name: Phineas Gage. His story is one most psychology students know well. In 1848, Gage survived an accident where an iron rod pierced his skull, obliterating his frontal lobe. Before the accident, he was known as a hardworking, reliable man. Afterward, his personality changed dramatically—he became impulsive, mean, and indifferent to consequences. The museum's exhibit, complete with graphic images and a replica of the iron rod, vividly brought his story to life. Gage's case became a cornerstone in our understanding of neuroscience and personality. His injury provided early evidence of the brain's role in shaping behavior, showing that damage to the frontal lobe could dramatically alter a person's personality and decision-making abilities.

One display stopped me in my tracks: a mesmerizing circular arrangement of rusty nails, pins, and buttons. At first, it looked like abstract art. But on closer inspection, I realized these were items surgically removed from the stomach of a woman after her death. She suffered from pica, a compulsive disorder that drives individuals to eat non-food items. While pica is more common in children, for an adult to be afflicted to this degree is exceptionally rare and often associated with serious mental health disorders. This haunting exhibit highlighted the severe consequences of psychological conditions.

Descending into the morgue, a chill settled over me. This part of the hospital carried a grim legacy, echoing the haunting sentiment: "They came in, but they never left." Families often sent loved ones to the asylum dressed in burial clothes, bracing for the inevitable. The morgue remains intact, with cold storage units and an autopsy table now occupied by a lifelike mannequin. Patient records and personal stories displayed throughout the space add a poignant, deeply human dimension—a bleak reminder of the lives that ended within these walls.

The museum's exhibits on early mental health treatments are both fascinating and horrifying. Displays like the human hamster wheel—a massive wooden contraption where manic and psychotic patients were forced to walk in darkness until they collapsed from exhaustion—show the extreme lengths people once went to in the name of treatment. Another exhibit detailed hydrotherapy, where patients were subjected to hot and cold baths to "cure" their conditions. The nearby operating table showcased the grim practice of removing organs and teeth, once believed to rid the body of infections causing mental illness. While some of these approaches may have provided slight benefits, their underwhelming effectiveness renders these types of treatments inhumane in the eyes of nearly all today.

The infamous lobotomy procedures were equally disturbing. One exhibit featured the notorious icepick lobotomy, in which doctors punctured the eye socket with an icepick and hammer to sever connections in the frontal lobe. It was horrifying to imagine the desperation felt by families, and even some patients, that led to such measures. Yet, even modern treatments like electroconvulsive therapy (ECT), though far more advanced and effective today, had similarly crude beginnings. The museum captured the complexity of these treatments—some barbaric, others hopeful, all part of the evolving journey of mental health care.

As I moved through these exhibits, I couldn't help but reflect on the progress that's been made and how far we still have to go. I've seen firsthand how mental illness is affected by factors like inflammation and immune responses. During my battle with autoimmune issues, I experienced how cytokines—components of the immune system—can influence mental health, a link that modern medicine is only beginning to understand.

Leaving the museum, I felt a mix of emotions—horror at the past, hope for the future, and a deep respect for how far we've come. The Glore Psychiatric Museum is a powerful reminder of the resilience of the human spirit and the ongoing journey toward compassionate, effective mental health care.

Body Worlds

When I tell people about my favorite medical museum, they often think I'm spinning a wild tale—until they see it for themselves. My journey began with a visit to a traveling exhibition called *Body Worlds* at the Science Museum of Minnesota. Drawn in by what I thought would be something dark and taboo, I instead discovered a masterfully executed anatomy exhibit. Using donated bodies and organs, the displays are artfully arranged to offer a 360-degree view of the human body's inner workings. It's a bit unsettling at first but ultimately enlightening, blending science with a touch of the eerie. After visiting multiple times, that eerie feeling has completely faded. Its connection to dark tourism lies in the face-to-face encounter with the dead—posed as if they were still alive.

Because of my complex medical history, I've often had to imagine the inside of my body. Doctors talk, I listen, and vivid images flood my brain. Thanks to *Body Worlds*, I know in much greater detail what the vascular and nervous systems look like—how a cirrhotic liver compares to a healthy one, and so much more. These aren't flat, 2D images from a book cast into my imagination. I'm talking high-definition, 3D visuals, with the ability to pan in and out—light-years beyond the tiny plastic models a doctor might pull out in their office.

These mental images have been incredibly helpful, whether during discussions with doctors about my conditions or when reading one of the numerous radiology reports that have shown up in my electronic medical charts. They've even proven useful in my work as a therapist and educator. In fact, after my first visit to *Body Worlds*, I purchased my very first rubber brain model, which has since been used in countless classrooms and appointments with clients.

Body Worlds has several traveling exhibitions and five permanent locations: Amsterdam, Berlin, Heidelberg, Guben, and San Jose, CA. I've lost count of how many I've visited over the years, but each one has been a fascinating education in what we look like beneath the surface. What intrigues me most is how the exhibits highlight our individuality—how, despite our similarities, each body tells a unique story. The same goes for the exhibitions themselves: while they share a common thread, each one differs just enough to feel fresh and engaging.

The last *Body Worlds* exhibit I saw was a traveling collection in Richmond, Virginia, focusing on mental wellness and happiness. That theme struck a chord with me, given my profession. It wasn't just about anatomy; it was about the connection between our physical and emotional well-being—something I've spent my career exploring. Each visit leaves me with a deeper appreciation for the complexity of the human body and the intricate interplay between our physical and mental health.

I've visited a similar exhibition in Las Vegas called *Bodies...The Exhibition*. However, this is shrouded in controversy. Reports suggest that the bodies on display were not donated but came from executed Chinese prisoners, allegedly used without their or their families' consent. Learning this after my last visit left me with deep regret for supporting something with such significant ethical issues.

There have always been objections to human body displays, and *Body Worlds* is no exception to the controversy. Religious groups have questioned the ethics and appropriateness of exposing young children to such exhibits. When I decided to take my son at a young age, it was something I considered carefully. Ultimately, I chose to go because I felt it was appropriate for his age, with parental guidance. At that time—and still today, more than 10 years later—I wanted to give my son every opportunity to learn in unique and engaging ways. I've always believed that schools often teach within the box, and it's up to parents to help children think outside of it. Seeds planted? Maybe. Today, he's a volunteer emergency medical technician in our hometown.

Walking through the displays feels like stepping into the pages of a real-life anatomy book. If someone has ever wondered what it's like to be a medical student, surgeon, or medical examiner, I bet this is as close as they will get without donning scrubs and a scalpel. It's a raw, unfiltered glimpse into the human body that's both mesmerizing and slightly unsettling at times. The intricate details, the layers of fiber and muscle, the delicate web of nerves—it's a visceral journey through what makes us human.

Body Worlds was founded by Dr. Gunther von Hagens, who developed a technique called plastination. This method allows donated bodies and organs to be preserved indefinitely and displayed in all their anatomical glory. His meticulous five-step process begins with anatomical dissection and the removal of body fat and water. The crux of the process, known as forced impregnation, involves submerging the specimen in a liquid polymer and creating a vacuum that ensures the polymer penetrates every cell. Once impregnated, the specimens are carefully positioned into lifelike poses before the polymer hardens, capturing the intricate details of the human (or animal) form for all to see.

The feeling upon entering the doors of a *Body Worlds* exhibition is like what one would experience from stumbling upon a secret garden. Immediately confronted by a surreal gallery that blurs the boundaries between art and science, full-sized bodies are posed in astonishing ways without their skin, making me think, "I can't believe this is real." A person hearing about *Body Worlds* might expect it to hit a 10 on the creepy scale, but it is done in such an artful and dignified way that it evokes a sense of wonder and deep appreciation for the intricacies of the human body.

Walking through these exhibitions, I began a journey through a meticulously curated tour of human anatomy, where organs, tissues, and systems are displayed with an artistry that is both enlightening and humbling. In just a few short hours, I learned more about the human body than I ever had from any textbook or classroom. It's an immersive experience that transforms the abstract into the tangible, leaving me with a deeper understanding and appreciation for the complexity and beauty of our biology. I'm not sure how religious institutions take issue with it—seeing the body presented this way only deepens my sense that something larger than evolution must be at play to create something so extraordinary.

Each full-body display, or plastinate, at *Body Worlds* carries its own identity, like characters in a play about the human body. One striking example is "The Skin Man." Here, a man walks, holding all his stripped skin high into the air with his right hand, gazing at it in wonder. What remains is a raw and vulnerable display of muscles, connective tissues, and a web of nerves, laying bare the fragility of our existence without its protective layer. The penis, like other features, appears noticeably longer due to the absence of skin, fat, and ligaments. Yet, as with all plastinates, it is tastefully presented as part of the anatomical whole, blending seamlessly into the exhibit without distraction.

Perhaps it's my profession, but I find myself particularly captivated by the displays showcasing the nervous system's intricacies. "The Chess Player" is one such plastinate—a man caught in a moment of deep contemplation, hand poised over a chess piece as if deciding its fate. The dissection reveals the brain just above the ears and the nerves running throughout his body, a glaring illustration of the complex web of thought and action. It's a humbling reminder of the intricate machinery that drives our every move, thought, and emotion, presented in a way that is both substantially educational and deeply moving.

Another remarkable plastinate I encountered is known as the "Lady of Arteries and Bones." This exhibit showcases the entire vascular system, revealing the heart and the intricate, bright-red network of arteries, veins, and capillaries contrasted against the white skeleton of the woman. If stretched out end to end, this sophisticated system would wrap around the Earth more than twice. This plastinate also includes the body's organs, illustrating how the vascular system supplies vital blood to each part, highlighting the incredible efficiency and complexity of human anatomy.

Among the many plastinates, I found a variety of figures engaged in sports, their muscular systems on full display, showcasing the human body's power and grace in motion. As I navigated through the exhibit, I eventually encountered an old man, hunched over with a wide stance, cane in hand, as if he were walking slowly. This figure stood in striking contrast to the athletic plastinates, serving as a sobering reminder of the inexorable march of time. It was a display meant to confront us with our own mortality—the ticking clock that spares no one.

For me, it brought complicated thoughts and questions: will I see old age? Will my liver disease take me before then? If I make it to that stage of life, will I have a partner, or will I face it alone? And if I'm alone, would I even care? It's incredible how a single display can bring such existential questions into sharp focus, forcing me to reflect on the uncertainties of life, the inevitability of aging, and what truly matters.

Juxtaposed with the elderly man is a poignant figure of a pregnant woman, appearing as if she is about to give birth at any moment. This plastinate evokes a whirlwind of emotions, and questions too: what led to their demise? Who did she leave behind? What might that child have become? *Body Worlds* transcends being just an anatomy exhibition; it's an unforgettable journey that is both intellectual and emotional. It offers new perspectives and a profound understanding of not only the human body but the very essence of life itself. I will visit *Body Worlds* again, probably several more times.

Museum of Death

Medical museums teach us about our bodies, health, and illness, but then there are museums that bring the next stage into sharp focus. Death will reach us all, but there are only a few museums that are solely devoted to the last stage of life. One such place is the Museum of Death. With locations in both Hollywood, CA and New Orleans, these museums provide an in-your-face experience that delivers more than a fair share of interesting moments.

Pee-wee Herman taught kids life lessons through odd entertainment that created plenty of "what the hell" moments. Similarly, the Museum of Death is like an adult macabre version of *Pee-wee's Playhouse*. It strives to amuse by offering a whimsical yet shocking experience, blending the realities of death with a bit of education sprinkled throughout.

Honestly, I don't like the Museum of Death. It's a sensory overload that sensationalizes death with virtually no discussion of the victims. I'd prefer a less dramatic and more well-rounded education on the topic. The Jack the Ripper Museum in Whitechapel, London also has a somewhat sensationalistic allure, but it balances this with thoughtful exhibits regarding the Ripper investigation and the victims. It's respectful, something I don't see much of at the Museum of Death.

I understand that the sensationalism resonates with some, so maybe it makes sense that these museums are in New Orleans's French Quarter and Hollywood, CA—two places known for their quirk. Despite my reservations, the museums still provide some good information with several interesting exhibits.

Upon stepping into the New Orleans museum, it feels cluttered and small. My first thought upon entering: "Is this it?" The second thought: "I want my money back." But if someone dove in and had an interest in the material, and could get past the glamorization of it all, they could spend a decent amount of time here. Both museums have a "theater of death" that continuously plays shockumentaries about death. The museum in Hollywood offers a larger space that feels less overwhelming.

Both museums sensationalize murder scenes and serial killers, which should never be the draw for a dark tourist approaching these sites with honor and respect. It's important to remember that behind the infamous faces of Gacy, Manson, or Richard Ramirez, the "Night Stalker," are real victims and grieving families. I even know of a certain museum gift shop where you can buy a T-shirt featuring all three of them or a grilling apron with Jeffrey Dahmer's face on it. Perhaps there should be a museum dedicated to those who purchase such items.

There are exhibits featuring pictures and letters from serial killers, offering a glimpse into their minds. It reminds me of the book *Mindhunter,* a memoir by John Douglas, one of the founding FBI profilers. The same book my son read as an adolescent when he was interested in criminal investigation. The book delves into Douglas's interactions with serial killers and explores their unique psychological makeup. For anyone familiar with his work—or that of Robert Hare or Stanton Samenow, researchers who wrote about the topic—the museum could be quite insightful, provided they can look past its obvious flaws.

I saw a variety of exhibits here, including death and murder scene photos—something I imagine most families of the victims wouldn't appreciate. There were also tools used by morticians, along with death certificates and autopsy reports of famous individuals. Many of the items were admittedly interesting, and a few were even fascinating with some educational value.

Honestly, I didn't know much about the museum going in. I was in New Orleans and figured I'd check it out. My son, a college student at the time, with a stronger interest in this sort of thing, mirrored my reaction of genuine disgust. Not the type of disgust that is amusing, like watching a horror movie, but something far more unsettling. We both felt it was simply wrong. In hindsight, recognizing that this museum caters more to voyeurs than typical museumgoers might have allowed me to approach the exhibits with a different perspective—rather than walking around thinking, *"What the fuck?"*

Upon leaving the museum, I initially felt a sense of relief, but that feeling was quickly replaced by a wave of guilt and sadness. I couldn't shake the sensation that I had been little more than a gawker, as if I were somehow deriving a twisted satisfaction from the tragic demise of others—or worse, inadvertently glorifying the lives of the perpetrators behind these horrific acts. But then I realized I wasn't celebrating death or murder at all—it was the way the museum presented these stories that evoked such a reaction. For a moment, I even felt angry at the museum for making me feel this way.

In the end, though, maybe having this reaction wasn't entirely negative. Perhaps confronting such uncomfortable emotions is necessary to truly grasp the depth of what happened. Still, I just wish the presentation could have been more respectful and that the victims themselves had a say in how their stories were told.

There are other museums focused on death that strike a more neutral and reflective tone. In Luxor, Egypt, there's a small museum dedicated to mummification. It isn't dramatic, but that doesn't diminish its value in presenting its subject matter thoughtfully.

In Bangkok, the Siriraj Medical Museum, often called the "Museum of Death," offers a clinical approach, providing a glimpse into the worlds of pathology and forensic medicine. Meanwhile, the National Museum of Funeral History in Houston delves into the cultural and historical aspects of funerals, offering a comprehensive look at how different cultures honor the departed.

In Amsterdam, the Torture Museum takes a historical and educational look at the tools and methods of torture, shedding light on the darker aspects of human history without resorting to sensationalism. Similarly, the Medieval Torture Museum in St. Augustine, Florida provides an immersive and educational exploration of torture. The museum provides context around its dark history.

Visiting medical and death museums, I can't help but reflect on the progress that's been made in health care—not just in physical health but in mental health as well. We've moved from the days of quackery, where treatments were often little more than placebos at best and harmful at worst, to an era of evidence-based medicine that improves and extends life. These museums offered me a chance to reflect on life and the inescapable reality of death. However, it was also a blunt reminder that not all museums strive to add something worthwhile to society; some are simply out to make easy money from the unfortunate demise of others, scraping the bottom of the barrel alongside ticket scalpers and pyramid scheme operators.

Chapter 6

Prison Tourism

"Prison walls do not form a barrier for my mind. My thoughts, dreams, and desires remain free."

—Mahatma Gandhi,
written during his imprisonment

DURING A SOLO FLIGHT from Northern Minnesota, where my plane was based, I felt immense gratitude just to be in the air, heading toward Kansas City. For me, flying is the ultimate freedom—a release from everything that weighs me down, both mentally and physically. Only a year earlier, I had been confined to a hospital bed, living through my own dark chapter with a severe episode of hepatic encephalopathy—a condition where the liver fails to filter toxins from the blood, poisoning the body. As the toxins built up, they inflamed my brain, causing disorientation, and if left untreated, would have led to coma and death. Just hours before being hospitalized, my son had found me sitting in bed, completely disoriented and soaked in urine.

It was during the height of the COVID pandemic, and no visitors were allowed in the hospital. I felt helplessly isolated as paranoid thoughts, fueled by my inflamed brain, twisted the words of a stressed-out nurse, making me question whether my son even existed. I wasn't sure if I was dying, and the nurse couldn't give me a straight answer, suggesting instead that I wait to speak with my doctor during rounds in the morning. All I wanted was to talk to a loved one. They gave me a phone, but I couldn't figure out how to use it. Hours into my hospitalization, I finally received a call from my parents. They informed me they were on their way back to Minnesota from their vacation in Arizona.

Upon my discharge a few days later, I was finally able to see my family. What had been only three days in the hospital felt like weeks. How does someone feel when they are reunited with their family after months of incarceration? I bet the relief they feel goes far beyond the gratitude I felt in that moment. That is, if they even have someone waiting for them on the outside—many don't.

For much of my career, I had worked closely with the criminal justice system, specializing in the treatment of offenders with serious mental illnesses. As I laid in that hospital bed, moderately delusional and feeling utterly alone despite the presence of staff, my thoughts turned to my former clients with thought disorders, many of whom had been confined in correctional institutions. I thought about my experiences working within the prison system and touring notorious prisons. Is this what it feels like to be in prison? I had only been in the hospital for a few days. How does it feel to be incarcerated for months, years, or even a lifetime? Especially under harsh prison conditions—what about those in solitary confinement?

Eventually, I was moved out of the ICU to a medical unit, but the impact of my experience lingered. After my discharge, it took much longer to recover from the isolation and certain interactions with nurses than it did to overcome the encephalopathy itself. Honestly, I was a bit surprised that this experience didn't trigger the anxiety disorder I had worked so hard to overcome just a few years earlier.

My time in the hospital gave me a deeper understanding of how fragile the mind can be under extreme stress. It also became a deeply personal reminder of how critical it is to treat those who are suffering with empathy and care. Just as I needed the support of my family and medical staff to recover, justice systems around the world need to shift from punishment to rehabilitation, especially for those with mental illness.

The Clink Prison

Just as my hospitalization allowed me to draw a connection between myself and my incarcerated clients, it also caused my mind to drift to the prisons I've toured. One of the most infamous prisons in the world, and one of the oldest found in England, is the Clink Prison. Located on the south bank of the River Thames, the Clink dates back to the 12th century. It was originally built under the control of Henry of Blois, who was the Bishop of Winchester and grandson of William the Conqueror. The bishop rather than the crown governed the area around the prison, known as the Liberty of the Clink, with the prison serving as a symbol of the Church's authority and power.

The sound of the blacksmith forging the shackles worn by inmates throughout their incarceration likely inspired the name "Clink Prison." Over time, the name became synonymous with prisons and jails worldwide. Upon entering the museum, a sign greets visitors with the words: "You are entering the original site of The Clink—the prison that gave its name to all others."

The conditions within the Clink Prison were bleak, a fact still evident to visitors of the site today. Burned down during the anti-Catholic Gordon riots of the 1780s, it was subsequently closed as a prison. Today, only a small portion of the original structure remains. It was a place of torture and neglect, housing a variety of prisoners, including political and religious dissenters, as well as common criminals convicted of crimes such as trespassing, prostitution, and debt. The prison was notorious for overcrowding, with frequent violence between inmates and abuse by guards. Dating back to medieval London, an area already rife with crime and poverty, the Clink contributed to the city's dark and gritty atmosphere. Not all individuals survived their time in the Clink; some died from violence or illness, while others were executed in public spectacles outside its walls.

Today, the area surrounding the Clink is a popular tourist destination and includes attractions such as the London Dungeon, where visitors can walk through interactive displays showcasing the city's dark history, including scenes inspired by the Clink. The prison is also situated near the replica of Shakespeare's Globe Theatre, a venue that once played out some of the most tragic stories in world history under the pen of Shakespeare, adding to the area's rich but somber past.

Touring the relatively small Clink Prison Museum was an intriguing and at times a somewhat amusing experience for me. While I'm sure it doesn't fully capture the feeling of being in the original prison—being a partial replica—it made a commendable effort to recreate its atmosphere. With its accessible educational displays, I could see how older children might find it engaging and informative. This is one of those sites that leans a bit on sensationalism to make the experience more accessible for visitors not looking for something overly serious, yet it still offers a memorable and thought-provoking experience.

The eerie setting, enhanced by the piped-in sounds of clanking chains and distant moaning, evoked mixed feelings of both fascination and unease as I walked through. Interactive exhibits let me try on shackles and handle replicas of torture devices, while the cells showcased artifacts and mannequins, offering a glimpse into the harsh conditions of centuries past.

As I walked around, I noticed severed mannequin heads on pikes—just unrealistic enough to strike a balance between being educational and sensational. It's the kind of display that keeps the museum firmly in PG-13 territory. Several plaques line the walls, offering insights into the prison's grim history. One, titled "Man in the Hole," tells the story of the dreaded "oubliette," derived from the French word meaning "to forget." Prisoners were dropped through a trapdoor into a pitch-black, windowless cellar that would flood with sewage whenever the River Thames rose, leaving them quite literally in a dire and filthy situation. Most men thrown into the oubliette never saw daylight again and perished in the squalid conditions.

Much like the museum, the prison itself was small, typically housing only a few dozen inmates at a time, and the museum today occupies just a portion of the original site. Although my tour lasted about an hour, it was a worthwhile stop while I was in the Southwark area of London. Overall, the Clink offered me a fascinating look into the life of a notoriously brutal medieval prison and the early systems that eventually evolved into modern incarceration. Unfortunately, modern incarceration, though absent of physical torture, still bears an unsettling resemblance to what it looked like hundreds of years ago.

My thoughts coming out of the museum reaffirmed what I believed going in: we need serious reform to our current punitive system. It's a system that not only traumatizes inmates but also fosters an environment of paranoia, leading to hypervigilance and fueling the fight-or-flight response. This, in turn, breeds violence inside prison walls and carries it over to the outside world, perpetuating a cycle that harms both individuals and society as a whole.

Reform must begin with improving the social service system and the way the criminal justice system, including the police, responds to crime—especially in cases involving poverty, addiction, and mental illness. Behind bars, providing access to education and rehabilitation programs can break the cycle of incarceration and improve outcomes upon release, helping individuals reintegrate into society and reducing the likelihood of reoffending. A system that focuses on rehabilitation, not punishment, not only benefits those incarcerated but also promotes safer, healthier communities for all.

Eastern State Penitentiary

Eastern State Penitentiary in Philadelphia, one of America's first major prison institutions, was conceived as a place of repentance rather than punishment—an idea heavily influenced by Pennsylvania's large, peace-loving Quaker population. Ironically, the methods of enforced repentance were far crueler than what the average prisoner experiences today, even though our prison system has made little genuine progress over the centuries. So-called "penitence" was often imposed through extreme isolation, where prisoners were left alone for a year or more, allowed only one hour per day in a tiny outdoor area attached to their cell, also in isolation. This practice left a legacy of mental and emotional torment for countless inmates.

Walking through the cellblocks, with the prison's Gothic architecture, towering brick walls, and intimidating guard towers that resemble a medieval castle as much as a prison, must have been a frightening experience for any prisoner arriving there. Eastern State Penitentiary, which closed in 1971, was once the most famous and, at the time of its construction, the most expensive prison in the world. Over its 142 years of operation, nearly 85,000 inmates were incarcerated within its walls.

As I walked through the prison and stepped inside one of the cells, I was struck by how bleak and oppressive it felt. The thought of how long people were held in such conditions resonated deeply. Many of the murderers and other convicted felons I've worked with over the years were often victims themselves, their childhoods marred by trauma and poverty—many endured physical or sexual abuse, while others suffered neglect. Of course, there were also those who were manipulative, cunning, and devoid of real empathy.

My thoughts turned to the kind ex-prisoners I've worked with over the years—many of whom were victims of their traumatic childhoods or developed serious mental illnesses that led them to commit quality-of-life crimes. In the United States, people with serious mental illnesses are incarcerated at rates up to five times higher than in the general population—a staggering statistic that underscores the urgent need for systemic reform.

Despite its historical focus, the tour offers many exhibits that powerfully highlight the need for prison and criminal justice reform. It delves into the devastating psychological toll of incarceration and solitary confinement, offering a blunt look at how these practices break down individuals. One exhibit reveals the shocking rise in incarceration rates driven by modern policies and reforms. The United States now incarcerates more people per capita than any other country in the world—an unimaginable reality for a nation built on the ideals of freedom.

As I absorbed these exhibits, my thoughts drifted back to my work in the corrections field. I reflected on Dorothea Dix, the nurse who spearheaded the decarceration movement, and how some of today's laws, like "three strikes and you're out" and zero-tolerance policies, fail to protect public safety in the long run. Even worse, the deinstitutionalization of people with serious mental illnesses has created a perfect storm, turning prisons into de facto mental health facilities. The cost is staggering—not just in dollars but in lives. The result is a vicious cycle: more crime, more incarceration, and more broken people.

Today, the Eastern State Penitentiary is in a state of decay. Several cellblocks remain visible but are off-limits to visitors. Many of the long hallways have peeling paint and rusted bars. The prison has a haunting feel, no doubt because of its evocative atmosphere and the imaginary echoes of those who suffered within its walls. Countless stories of hauntings, bolstered by its dark history and reported ghost sightings, have earned Eastern State a reputation as one of the most haunted places in the world.

The penitentiary wasn't as notorious for violence, murders, and sexual assaults as many other prisons, but it still had its share. What it became best known for, however, were a handful of successful and daring escapes. The most famous occurred in 1945, when a dozen inmates spent a year secretly digging a tunnel to the outside. Among them was the infamous Willie Sutton, who robbed over 30 banks and was often portrayed as a Robin Hood figure due to his charisma—though he never shared his loot. While their ingenuity was remarkable, authorities eventually recaptured all the escapees.

Although Eastern State Penitentiary wasn't notorious for violence, it became infamous for the favorable treatment of one of its inmates: Al Capone. His cell, located near the center of the prison in Cell Block 8, housed him for the majority of his one-year sentence for carrying an unlicensed concealed pistol. This area was more heavily guarded, likely a measure to protect Capone rather than to monitor his activities.

Capone's stay at Eastern State was reported as lavish by prison standards, and his cell, now recreated for visitors, reflects those accounts. It features an ornate rug, a writing desk, quality furniture, and a radio—comforts that were far from typical for an inmate. Capone was reportedly a model prisoner, though with such amenities it's easy to understand why. While stories of preferential treatment are often attributed to his wealth and notoriety, the prison's warden adamantly denied these claims. Interestingly, the recreation now includes a second bunk to reflect Capone's roommate, a detail that challenges the long-standing narrative of his solitary and luxurious confinement.

Favoritism, and its close cousin nepotism, have for millennia elevated people based on who they know or what they can offer, often creating a quid pro quo dynamic where favors are exchanged rather than earned. These practices not only raise eyebrows but also harm those who genuinely strive to succeed in an already difficult world. Personally, I even struggle with concepts like first-class seating, VIP access, and fast passes at amusement parks. To me, people are all equal, regardless of their status. I believe an even playing field is just as important in a capitalist society as hard work. Without fairness and equal opportunity, hard work often becomes undervalued, and success can feel predetermined by privilege rather than effort.

This ties into the broader theory of social stratification, which explores how those with less often resort to deviant means to level the playing field. Equality is a basic human desire. So why do we give more to those who already have more—even in prison? Why does a drug addict serve hard time in a dingy facility while a financial embezzler might be sent to a minimum-security prison? Is it acceptable to punish someone simply because they can't afford bail?

Eastern State Penitentiary raises these questions and many more. Visiting it is not just an exploration of prison life but an opportunity to confront the bigger, uncomfortable truths about our justice system and society as a whole. It forces us to reflect on fairness, privilege, and the true purpose of incarceration.

Alcatraz

About two years after his release from Eastern State Penitentiary, Capone was convicted of tax evasion and sent to a prison in Atlanta to serve his 11-year sentence. He enjoyed favorable conditions in Atlanta, much like he had at Eastern State, but about two years into his sentence, the government caught on. He was then transferred to the most notorious prison in the United States, and possibly the world—Alcatraz. On the infamous island, Capone spent the rest of his sentence in the general population with little to no preferential treatment. In fact, his notoriety may have made his experience even harsher than that of other inmates, not to mention that his syphilis was starting to take a serious toll on his health.

Although Capone may have been the most famous prisoner of Alcatraz, many other high-profile inmates also called this inescapable island prison home. Fellow gangster Machine Gun Kelly, a notorious bootlegger and kidnapper, earned his nickname from his favored weapon, the Thompson submachine gun. Another infamous criminal, Alvin "Creepy" Karpis, a member of the Barker-Karpis gang, served the longest sentence at the prison—26 years. Karpis gained notoriety for the kidnapping of banker Edward Bremer in St. Paul, Minnesota, a city that was a well-known safe haven for gangsters as long as they followed the local laws—a rule Karpis obviously broke.

The Birdman of Alcatraz, Robert Stroud, spent most of his 17 years at Alcatraz in isolation. A convicted murderer, Stroud gained fame for his study of birds during his time at Leavenworth Prison, where he bred canaries and published two books on avian diseases. However, his growing notoriety and increasingly violent behavior, including threats against staff and inmates, led to his transfer to Alcatraz in 1942. Ironically, the so-called Birdman of Alcatraz was not allowed to keep birds during his time there.

As the ferry I was aboard approached Alcatraz Island from Fisherman's Wharf in San Francisco, my anticipation of visiting grew with every passing moment. The infamous prison, perched atop a rocky hill, loomed larger and more imposing against the backdrop of the bay. Stepping off the dock onto the island, I looked up at the weathered, crumbling buildings clinging to the cliffs leading to the prison's main entrance. As I walked up the steep path, the stunning beauty of the San Francisco Bay and the iconic Golden Gate Bridge came into view, offering a stark contrast to the island's desolation. The isolation of the island quickly became apparent—I could only imagine the psychological torment of prisoners, constantly reminded of the vibrant city just beyond their reach. The steep climb also provided an early glimpse of the challenges anyone would face attempting to escape from what was, for many, considered impossible.

Was the prison, in fact, impossible to escape? First off, its location in the San Francisco Bay meant cold-water temperatures and strong currents made the survival of a swim unlikely at best. Therefore, a boat or raft would have been essential for escape. Any crafts nearing the island were closely monitored, making a coordinated pickup difficult. But before even reaching the steep, rocky cliffs, an escapee would first have to overcome the barbed wire and cement walls of the prison without being detected by the many guards within the facility and those stationed at posts around the island. Despite these measures, there were 36 prisoners who knowingly attempted escape. Of those, six were shot and killed, two drowned after making it to the water, and most others were caught.

In total, there are five men from two different escape attempts who have never been accounted for. Officially, they are listed as presumed drowned. In 1937, two men serving long sentences for robbery escaped through a window in the industrial building during a storm and attempted to swim toward shore. Official reports claim that the currents that day would have made the swim impossible.

Another escape attempt is more plausible, with at least some credible evidence of survival. A meticulous plan led two brothers and a mastermind to dig their way out of their cells, buying themselves time by placing fake heads on their pillows. A raft was later found on a nearby island, and personal items were discovered floating in the harbor. One crucial thing was missing: the bodies. This attempt is the subject of the critically acclaimed movie *Escape from Alcatraz* starring Clint Eastwood as the mastermind Frank Morris. Family members of the escapees claimed to have received letters from them, and there is at least one questionable photo showing the two brothers, allegedly living in Brazil. The case remains unconfirmed.

Walking through the lonely cellblocks is the main attraction of most tours at the famous federal prison, which began as a Union fort during the Civil War and later became a federal penitentiary. I focused mainly on Cell Blocks B and C, where the cells stand three stories high. Each small cell is a testament to the saying, "Crime doesn't pay."

At Capone's cell, I sat and pondered: was it worth it? He spent nearly half of his adulthood incarcerated. His fame and wealth culminated in this ominous cell, and by the time he was released, his quality of life had been all but destroyed by syphilis. I also visited similar cells that once held fellow notorious inmates Creepy Karpis and Machine Gun Kelly. The cell of the escapees features replicas of the fake heads they used in their daring escape attempt. Regardless of who occupied the cell or how famous they were on the outside, in Alcatraz they were all reduced to a number.

In the solitary confinement area, Cell Block D, I encountered the cells where men, including the Birdman of Alcatraz, spent 23 hours a day. I stepped inside one of these cells for about a minute and tried to imagine what it would have felt like to be confined there for years or even decades. Solitary confinement is a form of psychological torture, and it's troubling to think it is still commonly used today. In fact, nearly half of all prison suicides occur in solitary confinement.

Within a few short hours, I experienced the area equivalent to what an inmate at Alcatraz might have seen during their years-long stays: the dining room, the yard, and more. I also explored areas off-limits to inmates, such as the guards' quarters. Along the way, I encountered a variety of exhibits, including one about the Native American Occupation of the island from 1969 to 1971—a powerful protest that captured the nation's attention. Despite the dark history, I ended my visit with a serene boat ride back to the vibrant city of San Francisco—a liberty the inmates could only dream of for years.

When visiting prisons, I often leave wondering about the appropriateness of the punishments. Does the punishment fit the crime? Was justice truly served? I also find myself questioning the safety of inmates and whether more should be done to protect prisoners within the prison environment. Over the years, I've come to realize that in some prisons, inmates don't necessarily reform but instead learn to become better criminals. Prisons can become meeting places where men swap ideas and experiences, turning the facility into a kind of "crime school." Some former inmates have even referred to it as "Con College." Additionally, the paranoia and helplessness that prisons foster create the perfect breeding ground for criminal thinking.

Not much has changed over the years when it comes to justice. Our best option is to support people before they make decisions that lead to crime and punishment. Yet, the reality is that people in prison have done bad things—some truly awful things. Murder, rape, robbery—these acts not only harm individuals but also shake the very fabric of society and our collective sense of safety. There's no easy answer, but I believe justice lies in both treating people with dignity and holding them accountable for their actions. That's the approach I've always taken when counseling the countless offenders I've worked with over the years, no matter how terrible their crimes may have been. Exploring these grim relics of prison dark tourism serves as a reminder of how little has changed—and, more importantly, how far we have to go.

Chapter 7

Wars and Battlefields

> "I know not with what weapons World War III will be fought, but World War IV will be fought with sticks and stones."
>
> —Albert Einstein
> (though exact origin is debated)

STANDING ON A BATTLEFIELD, it's impossible not to sense the echoes of sacrifice, the tragedy of lives lost, and the haunting reminder of humanity's capacity for both destruction and resilience. These emotions are just the beginning of understanding war's significance. Its impact stretches far beyond individual lives, shaping the course of history in profound ways.

For as long as humans have walked the Earth, war has defined the boundaries of nations and redrawn the maps of the world. It has toppled empires and forged new nations. War has played a pivotal role in defeating fascism and ending institutional slavery, though these outcomes were part of larger historical movements. It has united people under shared causes and driven technological and medical innovation, though often at an unthinkable cost. Nearly every nation has a military, and most have used it in battle at some point in their history. As is often attributed to Plato, "Only the dead have seen the end of war."

This reality has held true for as long as history has been recorded, and there is no end in sight to war. This is why it's not enough to study war through facts and figures alone; we must allow it to reach us on an emotional level. When we let the horrors of war truly touch us, we gain a deeper understanding of its devastating impact and put ourselves in a better position to work toward preventing future conflicts.

Many lives have been both lost and saved on battlefields. The Center for International and Security Studies at the University of Maryland estimates that 231 million people died from armed conflict during the 20th century alone. This staggering number highlights the immense darkness of war and the weight it carries into battlefield tourism. The shadows of past battles loom large, reminding us of the human cost of war and why these places matter.

Parliament and the Churchill War Rooms

Any place with a history of significant decisions, influential speeches, or events tied to military conflict can be considered a dark tourism site. Capitals and government buildings, like the British Parliament, often embody these elements, making them powerful places to explore. Touring the British Parliament is one such experience—steeped in the rich history of the British Empire and its storied monarchy, including war-related trials and military conflict. One moment from this tour stands out vividly: I found myself standing before the imposing royal mace in the House of Commons, acutely aware of its symbolic power. Theoretically, if the reigning monarch disapproves of Parliament's direction, they retain the power to reclaim control—a thought that is both fascinating and unsettling.

As I pondered this, my attention shifted to the iconic green benches, and I imagined them filled with representatives. My mind flooded with images of passionate politicians, their voices raised in fervent debate, the room alive with the weight of decisions that shaped history. Then, my focus sharpened on the front bench.

Near the front bench, the ghost of Winston Churchill seems to linger, delivering his legendary "we shall fight on the beaches" speech. It was a time when Britain was on its knees, backed into a corner by the Third Reich. The people of Britain lived in fear for their lives, their families, and their way of life. Churchill, one of the few politicians who foresaw the true menace of the Nazi Party, was mocked for his vocal warnings. Yet, he was the right person at the right time, stepping into the role of British prime minister. Not only was he a master strategist, but he also inspired a nation to remain calm, stay alert, and fight back against overwhelming odds.

On the other side of the Parliament lies Westminster Hall, an expansive room crowned with an awe-inspiring wood-beam roof, adorned with plaques and statues of war heroes and British kings. In 1305, this historic site witnessed the trial of William Wallace, the Scottish knight who valiantly fought for independence against the British. Wallace was found guilty of high treason and subjected to a brutal sentence. Denied the chance to defend himself, he was dragged through the streets of London by horse, hanged, and, before death could claim him, cut down. His suffering didn't end there; he was disemboweled, and his genitals were cut off. Finally, he was beheaded, and his body was quartered, with his body parts displayed in various locations across England and Scotland as a grim warning to others.

A short five-minute walk from Parliament brought me to the Churchill War Rooms. During much of World War II, Winston Churchill and his closest advisers operated from this subterranean hideout, directing Britain's troops and coordinating efforts within the Allies' war strategy.

The dimly lit concrete hallways of the Churchill War Rooms bunker contain artifacts that transported me to the darkest days of World War II. Maps cover the walls, and tables and chairs are arranged in a square, allowing high-ranking government and military officials to face each other during intense strategizing sessions.

Continuing the tour, I came across the Transatlantic Telephone Room, where Churchill and President Roosevelt frequently communicated. This room is also where Churchill recorded many of his speeches that the BBC broadcast to inform troops and British citizens, bolstering the morale of all who called Britain home. Other notable locations within the War Rooms include Churchill's office and bedroom, as well as the Map Room, equipped with numerous phones and detailed maps tracking troop movements. Additionally, the adjacent museum offers in-depth information on Churchill's life and the critical decisions he made during his tenure as prime minister.

Both Churchill and Wallace were exceptional leaders who inspired their people with their unwavering vision during the most challenging times. These leaders were both unlikely heroes. Wallace of humble beginnings, and Churchill, despite growing up in a privileged family, experienced emotional neglect from his parents.

Their determination went beyond what is typically found in leaders. They evoked a sense of hope that fostered fortitude among their people, motivating them to fight for their homelands and way of life. Both men were also master military strategists who played crucial roles in leading their people through dire circumstances. While Wallace was executed several years before the Scots achieved independence, his speeches and martyrdom served as significant sources of inspiration for the Scottish cause.

Yet, in many ways, Churchill embodied the type of authority Wallace fought against. Churchill, as prime minister, was the face of the British Empire—a symbol of the monarchy and the centralized power that had long oppressed Scotland. Wallace's rebellion was aimed at breaking free from the very system Churchill represented centuries later, though Churchill himself fought for the survival of that same empire during World War II.

I try to imagine what it was like being a citizen during the tumultuous times of Churchill or Wallace. The wars of their eras were terrifying and tragic, casting long shadows over daily life. Yet, amidst the chaos and fear, the comfort and unyielding determination these leaders brought served as a beacon of hope. Their resolve and inspiring words fueled the souls of the masses, igniting a collective spirit that dared to dream of a brighter future even in the darkest of times.

When I toured Parliament, I was under the impression that Churchill once said, "If you're going through hell, keep going." Although this quote isn't directly tied to any of his speeches, he is often given credit for it. It also sounds like something he might have said, given his knack for memorable phrases. Regardless of its origins, this saying became my mantra in the grueling weeks leading up to my liver transplant. It became my own beacon of hope and perseverance.

In the aftermath of my surgery, this phrase became a lifeline. At first, it gave me the strength to sit up and get out of bed. I would mumble it to myself whenever I faced something I didn't want to do but knew was essential for my recovery. Over time, it pushed me to walk the hospital halls and later venture outside, motivating me to keep moving forward. I firmly believe this simple yet powerful mantra sped up my recovery, giving me an edge when every bit of motivation mattered. Even today, when life inevitably throws its punches, I remind myself to keep going.

Pearl Harbor

Roosevelt was right—7 December 1941 is a day that indeed lives in infamy. A tour of Pearl Harbor in Hawaii provides all the proof I need to understand the gravity of his words. The remnants of that fateful day, preserved in the still waters of the harbor, tell a story of unimaginable loss and enduring resolve. Picturing the low-flying planes of the Japanese military marked with their large red dot under each wing is a chilling reminder of the journey the United States was about to endure.

The shock, disbelief, and anger that permeated the nation in the aftermath of the surprise attack were far-reaching. How could the U.S. military have allowed such vulnerability? In the wake of the attack, the resolve of the American people soared to unprecedented heights. Patriotism skyrocketed, and enlistments into the military surged. Political affiliations became secondary as the country united under a common identity—Americans. Nearly all citizens contributed to the war effort, demonstrating unparalleled solidarity and determination.

The events at Pearl Harbor, in retrospect, gave me a better understanding of the importance of my visit. As the enormity of being at Pearl Harbor slowly set in, I took the shuttle boat over to the iconic white platform that overlooks the sunken USS *Arizona*. Being on the platform was an emotional experience that I didn't expect to hit so hard. Gazing into the water, I noticed the oil seeping to the surface, often referred to as the "black tears" of the ship and its crew. This poignant symbol represents the 1,177 crew members who perished on that fateful day. Many of these brave souls remain entombed within the ship, and several survivors who passed away later have also chosen to be interred there, joining their fallen comrades in a solemn and enduring tribute.

Pearl Harbor is filled with details and artifacts that were striking to me, providing a deep understanding of the events and emotions surrounding the infamous attack. The museum meticulously details the events leading up to the surprise attack, the battle, and the immediate aftermath, setting a somber tone for the visit. Among these historical treasures is the USS *Bowfin*, a Balao-class submarine known as the "Pearl Harbor Avenger." This highly decorated vessel sank at least 44 enemy ships between 1943 and 1945, contributing significantly to the U.S. Navy's efforts in the Pacific during World War II.

Touring the USS *Bowfin* offers a glimpse into the challenging and often perilous life of submariners. The confined quarters where sailors lived and worked are striking, highlighting the immense physical and psychological demands they faced. These men took shifts sleeping, eating, and working in warm, thin air, often without the luxury of frequent bathing. The tour provides a vivid understanding of their tenacity and dedication, underscoring the *Bowfin*'s significant role in avenging Pearl Harbor and its legacy as a symbol of bravery and sacrifice.

Another must-see ship at Pearl Harbor is the USS *Missouri*, affectionately known as the "Mighty Mo." Walking its decks was a humbling experience. The steel ship with its hardwood decks eventually led me to the exact spot where Foreign Minister Mamoru Shigemitsu and General Yoshijirō Umezu signed the formal surrender on behalf of Japan. Representing the Allies, General Douglas MacArthur and Admiral Chester Nimitz signed the document, marking the official end of World War II on 2 September 1945.

Touring Pearl Harbor allowed me to witness the full arc of America's involvement in World War II. It is the place where the conflict began for the United States, with the surprise attack on 7 December 1941, and it is also home to the ship where the war's conclusion was formalized. These tours, combined with the broader context provided by the museum, ensured that I left with a deep appreciation for the sacrifices made during World War II and the enduring spirit of those who served.

Beaches of Normandy

Two and a half years separated the attack on Pearl Harbor from the Allied invasion at Normandy, France. The meticulous preparation for "Operation Overlord" led the Nazi command to believe the invasion would occur elsewhere, prompting them to divert significant resources away from Normandy. This strategic deception, combined with extensive naval and aerial bombardments, softened the German defenses, allowing the Allied forces to land on the beaches and gain a crucial foothold in the area. Despite these efforts, the Nazi forces remaining at Normandy were still formidable, with enough firepower to potentially win the battle. However, the determination and superior firepower of the Allied forces ultimately overcame the Nazi defenses.

Because of poor weather, the invasion was initially delayed, forcing the troops to endure an additional day of anxious anticipation. I'm sure many of the soldiers found little relief in the delay and instead had to grapple with a mixture of anxiety, uncertainty, and resolve for the mission ahead. During this time, a motivating speech by General Eisenhower galvanized the soldiers, emphasizing the historic significance of their mission and bolstering their determination.

Normandy's story of courage and sacrifice spoke to me during the days my own life hung in the balance. Two weeks after being placed on the waiting list for a liver transplant, I received the call. My skin and eyes had taken on a sickly yellow hue, and fluid filled my abdomen and legs despite medications that had staved off severe symptoms for nearly two years. Lying in that hospital bed, flanked by my son and parents, I felt a cocktail of emotions: the comfort of my family's presence, the marvel of modern medicine awaiting me, the sorrow for the donor whose life had ended, and the gnawing anticipation of the impending surgery. It made for an unforgettable night.

The next morning, the news came: a delay. The donor had not yet been taken off life support, giving my surgeon the chance to run one more test on the organ. He explained that the liver was fatty but still within normal limits for donation. He wanted to use the delay to take another sample, just to be sure.

Another day passed with no word on the liver, and my family sought rest with relatives nearby. Then, just after midnight, the phone rang, jolting me awake. It was my surgeon. He told me the donor's family had refused the test, saying we had to either take the liver as it was or leave it. This made my surgeon uneasy, so he declined the donation.

I thanked him, but my heart sank. Why had the family changed their minds over what seemed like a simple request? I'm sure they had been through a lot with the passing of their family member, but this was my life. Was this my only chance? Would I die waiting for another call? The uncertainty reminded me of the troops on D-Day, facing delays and unknowns, wondering if they would make it through. In an odd way, it was comforting to think about, reminding me that I wasn't alone in facing the unknown.

In the days following that devastating setback, my thoughts often drifted to the Normandy invasion and the troops waiting for the green light to move. I thought of Eisenhower and his speech and gave myself a rallying self-talk that would have made the pioneers of psychotherapy proud.

During this time, my liver was barely holding on, and my health continued to decline. My second chance at a liver transplant came about two weeks later. At the hospital, a wheelchair arrived at my room instead of a midnight phone call. When they asked if I needed something for anxiety, I declined. "No thanks, we've got this."

As I was wheeled to the surgery floor, I noticed a man being pushed out of an adjacent elevator. He seemed to match the vague details I'd been told about my donor: middle-aged, slightly husky, and appearing as though he were being kept around for donation. Was this my guardian angel in the flesh? I have yet to find out. The sight paired with the old green tiles made me feel as if I were being wheeled into an old military hospital. I began to regret declining the benzodiazepine offered minutes before, thinking this must be similar to what some troops might feel before battle. Were these the final moments of my life?

The scene shifted dramatically, from a dated hospital corridor to a futuristic operating room. Under the bright surgical lights, surrounded by buzzing technicians and gleaming stainless-steel instruments, I felt an unexpected sense of calm. But as they extended the small platforms for my arms and began strapping them down, a sudden jolt of anxiety hit me. I quickly sat up and blurted, "Can I get that anxiety pill now?" The next thing I remembered was waking up from the surgery.

In uncertain times in the past, I often reached for a beer—or several. But in the years leading up to my transplant, I had stopped drinking, and that's when my fascination with the past began to resurface. Alcohol had always been an easy escape, but it did nothing to help me build strength or resilience—instead, it was reflections born from my experiences of honoring others that seemed to appear when I least expected them, almost as if to say thank you. That shared humanity in crisis—even when the crises were vastly different—carried me through what should have been one of the most difficult days of my life with almost no fear at all.

I never expected my trip to Normandy to resurface during such a pivotal moment in my life, but there it was. I could feel the bravery and resolve of the soldiers carrying me forward when I needed it most. The surgery was a turning point in my life, just as Normandy was a turning point in the war. I had reached the other side of my metaphorical beach and a new battle was about to commence—the fight to recover.

As the 156,000 troops approached the 80-kilometer stretch of beach, divided into five beachheads codenamed Utah, Omaha, Gold, Juno, and Sword, the fear of facing the unknown must have set in. Simultaneously, their courage and commitment to their comrades fostered a sense of hope and optimism. Many soldiers likely reflected on their families, their rigorous training, and the larger purpose of their mission, channeling their anxiety into focused determination.

Reaching the shore through the rough seas was no small feat. Many soldiers were killed before even exiting their landing crafts, while others drowned under the weight of their equipment. In these moments, the fight-or-flight mechanism took over, overriding the normal flow of information in their frontal lobes. Fueled by sheer adrenaline and rigorous training, the troops pressed forward, fully aware of the high risk of death.

Touring the beaches of the Normandy coast was an experience filled with mixed feelings. Standing on the cliffs, looking down onto the expansive beaches, I was struck by the immense scale of the battle and the overwhelming emotions the soldiers must have felt as they came ashore. Along the coast, large divots in the landscape marked the impact of Allied bombardments, alongside Nazi pillboxes that are now open to tourists. As I descended the steps into these fortified positions, I came across small apertures through which Nazi soldiers aimed their weapons, waiting for the Allied troops to advance.

Inside the now-bare pillboxes, several rooms likely once stored ammunition and housed troops. The charred wooden ceilings, possibly scorched by flamethrowers, evoked haunting images of men consumed by fire. It's a stark reminder that these were human beings—many of them young boys or elderly men—forced into combat by a regime they couldn't escape. Many of the Nazi defenders at Normandy were stationed there because the most experienced and capable German forces had been diverted elsewhere, misled by Allied deception about the invasion's true location.

As I moved toward the section of the pillbox overlooking the beach, I realized the brutal purpose of its design—to annihilate Allied soldiers attempting to land. This grim reality brought forth a troubling thought: we had to kill them to protect them. These casualties were part of a larger mission to liberate Europe from fascist regimes—a grim but essential step in preserving freedom and ending tyranny.

Before I took the train back to Paris, I stopped to pay my respects at the beautiful and humbling Normandy American Cemetery, which overlooks Omaha Beach. The cemetery's reflective atmosphere reminded me of Arlington National Cemetery. At the center of the grounds stood a semicircular colonnade featuring maps and narratives of the military operations. This iconic spot has served as the backdrop for many U.S. presidents delivering D-Day speeches. Among the nearly 10,000 graves, I saw the markers of over 300 unknown soldiers—a solemn testament to the sacrifices made during World War II.

Berlin

Few cities carry the historical weight and gritty complexity of Berlin when it comes to military conflict. Berlin has been at the epicenter of Germany's political and military upheavals, from its establishment as the capital of the German Empire in 1871, through the cataclysms of both World Wars, and into the shadowy intrigues of the Cold War. Wandering through Berlin today, it's impossible to escape the echoes of its tumultuous past. Reminders of its darker days are woven into the very fabric of the city, contrasting with the vibrant life that now pulses through its streets.

A first stop for many dark tourists in Berlin is the Topography of Terror. This powerful museum is built on the site that once housed the headquarters of the Gestapo, SS, and Reich Security. Once the nerve center of Nazi oppression, it now stands as a place of education and remembrance. The museum features extensive photo panels with detailed text descriptions in a grand hall, as well as a large outdoor exhibit along the remnants of the building's former wall. These panels meticulously document the rise of the Nazi Party, the political climate, the mechanisms of repression, the battles, the Holocaust, and the eventual liberation of countries under the Third Reich's grip. From the haunting imagery of book burnings to the chilling purge of political and academic elites, the Topography of Terror is a bleak reminder of the catastrophic consequences of unchecked leadership driven by a nightmarish agenda.

The Berlin Story Bunker museum, located not far from the Topography of Terror, offers a more immersive, multimedia experience that covers much of the same historical material. Its unique setting: an actual air raid bunker. The museum's extensive exhibits span hundreds of years and are housed within a multi-floor concrete bunker, interconnected by seemingly endless hallways and rooms. One of the most interesting exhibits provides information on Adolf Hitler's youth and young adulthood and how it influenced him in later years. I left thinking that there were many opportunities to influence his trajectory, which may have prevented his rise to power.

As I navigated the bunker, my thoughts oscillated between the detailed information presented in the exhibits and the haunting reality of the space itself, where thousands of Berliners huddled together to escape Allied bombings. I imagined the sheer terror they must have felt as bombs exploded above, the ground shaking beneath them, and the dark halls echoing with the cries of children. Holding their bladders and desperately hoping for the "all clear" signal must have been a horrific ordeal. This visceral connection to history made the Berlin Story Bunker a deeply meaningful stop during my time in Berlin.

The final section of the Berlin Story Bunker vividly recounts the last days of Adolf Hitler in his Führerbunker. Among its features is an exact replica of Hitler's office, where he and his wife, Eva Braun, committed suicide in 1945.

Upon exiting the bunker, I walked a short distance to a nondescript apartment parking lot near the large and solemn Memorial to the Murdered Jews of Europe. At first glance, it seemed like just an ordinary parking lot. I wandered around until I found the information sign I had been searching for. The sign detailed the layout and history of the Führerbunker, which once lay beneath this very spot—the place where Hitler spent his final days before taking his own life in April 1945.

Here, Hitler took cyanide and shot himself, ordering his body to be burned to prevent the Allies from using his corpse as a trophy. A few days later, Russian troops discovered his charred remains outside the bunker and buried him in an anonymous grave. Eventually, his body was exhumed, and his jawbone was definitively identified by comparing his unique dental work with X-rays from his dentist. This confirmation largely put to rest conspiracy theories about his survival.

The Cold War

After the Allies defeated the Nazis, Berlin was divided into four sectors, each controlled by a different country: the United States, the Soviet Union, the United Kingdom, and France. The contrasting political ideologies between the Western Allies (capitalist democracies) and the Soviet Union (communism) created a rift that tore Germany into two separate states. The Western Allies controlled the Federal Republic of Germany, known as West Germany, while the German Democratic Republic, or East Germany, was established in the Soviet sector.

The term "cold" signifies the absence of direct military conflict, yet the Cold War brought with it a significant arms race, extensive espionage, and widespread paranoia. It carried the potential for casualties far surpassing those of World War II, with the constant threat of nuclear Armageddon looming over the world. Walking through Berlin's historic neighborhoods, with their mix of restored historic buildings and modern, utilitarian architecture, I could catch a glimpse of what life might have felt like during the Cold War.

The vibrant, modern sections of Berlin reflect the city's reunification, while the large, plain buildings in certain areas evoke the Soviet-era architecture of East Germany. Immersing myself in the Cold War mindset—imagining the spies, the tension, and the constant feeling of being watched—made it the perfect time to tour the Berlin Wall and Checkpoint Charlie.

The Berlin Wall was constructed by East Germany to prevent its citizens from fleeing to West Germany. Visiting the Berlin Wall Memorial gave me a deeper understanding of its construction and the far-reaching impact it had on all Germans. The outdoor exhibit includes a substantial section of the original wall, showcasing both the inner and outer barriers. The area between these two walls, known as the "death strip," ranged from nine to 45 meters in width and was designed to create a clear shooting lane for guards to target anyone attempting to escape to freedom.

While the exact number of those killed trying to cross the Wall is debated, estimates suggest that between 140 and 200 people lost their lives in the attempt. Located on the former death strip, the Chapel of Reconciliation serves as a quiet place for reflection and remembrance—honoring those who were killed while trying to cross the Wall and offering a space to contemplate the broader implications of the Cold War and the Wall's enduring legacy.

About three kilometers from the Berlin Wall Memorial was a section of the Berlin Wall with a much lighter atmosphere. The East Side Gallery featured over 100 spray-painted murals stretching across 1.5 kilometers, making it the longest intact section of the Wall still standing. The graffiti conveyed powerful themes of freedom and hope, with the most famous mural depicting a kiss on the lips between Soviet leader Leonid Brezhnev and East German leader Erich Honecker, commemorating the 30th anniversary of the German Democratic Republic (East Germany). This mural poignantly captured the complexities and absurdities of the relationship between the Soviet Union and East Germany.

I left the gallery with a sense of optimism, offering a glimpse into how the world might have felt when the Wall fell in 1989. I was 11 at the time and had only vague memories of that momentous event.

As an American, one spot I knew I had to visit while in Berlin was Checkpoint Charlie. The reconstructed checkpoint stands in the middle of a busy street at the actual site where it once operated. It features a small guard booth surrounded by protective sandbags and the iconic sign: "YOU ARE LEAVING THE AMERICAN SECTOR." Standing there, I was instantly transported back to a tense and fearful period in world history. It seemed like that era had ended, but in recent years, I'm not so sure. Perhaps it wasn't truly over—just dormant for a while.

As a therapist, I often work with clients grappling with the ambivalence of making significant changes—whether it's deciding to change jobs, move to a new town, get sober, or end a relationship.

When counseling people on the verge of change, I sometimes think back to my visit to Berlin and my reflections on the Cold War. In one such case, a woman I was working with was trying to decide whether to leave an abusive husband. She recognized the toxicity of the relationship and knew that leaving was the logical thing to do, but several factors complicated her decision. She still felt love for her abuser, shared a home with children, and worried about her safety if she chose to leave.

I imagine some East Germans faced similar dilemmas during the Cold War. If they attempted to escape, would they be harmed? Would they succeed, or would they fail? And if they made it, would there be retaliation against their loved ones left behind? These choices are rarely straightforward, and the best we can do is provide resources and support—no matter what decision they make.

Hiroshima

As an American, touring Pearl Harbor evoked a deep sense of honor and reverence. With the benefit of hindsight, we know how the war concluded—two atomic bombs dropped on Japan, approximately three months after the European Theater brought an end to the Nazi regime. Touring the other side of the war, however, is equally, if not more, emotional. For me, visiting Hiroshima was an experience filled with somber reflections, compassion, and moral contemplation.

The first nuclear bomb ever used in combat, nicknamed "Little Boy," was dropped on Hiroshima on 6 August 1945. It was carried by the B-29 bomber *Enola Gay*, which departed from Tinian Island. The unprecedented destruction it caused marked a turning point in human history, leaving an indelible impact on the world's conscience.

A complex chain of events set Japan on the path to war. Admiral Yamamoto, the mastermind behind the attack on Pearl Harbor, described the decision to strike as a difficult one. He recognized that a prolonged war would likely favor the Allies and expressed doubts about Japan's ability to sustain such a conflict. Despite his concerns, the attack was approved by Japan's government and military leadership, initiating a war that dragged on for years, with the Japanese fighting fiercely.

The "way of the samurai," rooted in the Bushido code, played a significant role in this resistance. This traditional code of honor, emphasizing loyalty, sacrifice, and discipline, discouraged surrender and inspired unwavering determination among Japanese forces. During the war, this ethos was adapted and amplified by propaganda, reinforcing the idea that dying for the emperor was the ultimate act of loyalty. Coupled with a deep fear of Allied occupation—exacerbated by state propaganda—this mindset galvanized Japan's military and civilian population to continue fighting, even as the prospect of victory slipped further away. These cultural values, combined with strategic decisions and political dynamics, explain why Japan fought so long and so fiercely during the war.

The decision to use the first nuclear bomb against a civilian population remains one of the most debated in military history. It was made with the belief that the bomb would bring a swift end to the war against a Japanese force determined to resist. To prevent further Allied casualties and avoid the devastation of a costly ground invasion, the decision to deploy nuclear weaponry was authorized. While it is difficult to comprehend the immense moral weight borne by those responsible for this decision, the consequences for civilians were catastrophic and undeniable. Had such a mentality been applied in conflicts since World War II, the use of nuclear weapons could have led to devastating global consequences, pushing the world to the brink of Armageddon.

After the bomb was dropped, the United States government awaited a surrender from Japan that did not come. After passionate debate, the Japanese government decided against unconditional surrender, largely due to the U.S. demand that Emperor Hirohito's power be diminished. Just three days later, the U.S. decided to unleash another round of unimaginable devastation upon the Japanese civilians. A second bomb was dropped, this time on the city of Nagasaki. It killed indiscriminately, much as the first bomb did, and nearly the same number of people died. Would there have been a third bomb, or even more? Would the bombs have become more powerful? Fortunately, the world never needed to find out, as Japan surrendered shortly after the second bomb was dropped.

Much like touring Pearl Harbor, the Hiroshima Peace Memorial Museum honors victims and educates visitors on the horrors of war while avoiding an overt assignment of blame. Both sites are respectful in their presentation, but as a human—and especially as an American—

every turn at Hiroshima delivered a sickening gut punch. Right or wrong, my people did this to their people—emphasis on people. Civilians: women, children, parents, grandparents, schoolteachers, bankers, and bus drivers—lives lost in the blink of an eye. The bomb instantly killed 80,000 people, with countless others succumbing to nuclear exposure in the days, weeks, and years that followed. Between Hiroshima and Nagasaki, well over 200,000 people died by the end of 1945.

The beginning of the Hiroshima museum took me through the story of pre-bomb Hiroshima, a peaceful town with little military activity. Then, abruptly, everything changed. One mural shows the town from above before the bombing, and another reveals the aftermath of inconceivable devastation.

At the same time I was there, a group of schoolchildren was walking through the exhibits. There's a large photographic mural next to a clock that is stopped at the exact moment the bomb exploded over the city. The mural shows life-sized schoolchildren posing for a photo in their uniforms alongside what appears to be their teacher. As I watched the actual children standing next to it, it almost felt like a mirror image spanning across time. It was very likely that all the schoolchildren in the photo died as a result of the bomb.

In the next room, I joined a larger group of students gathered around a circular video screen raised about a meter off the floor. The film depicted the moment the plane released the atomic bomb over Hiroshima, followed by the explosion. As the smoke slowly cleared, it revealed total annihilation. As I moved on from the video alongside the children, I knew this was not going to be just another museum. I knew it had the potential to significantly change my worldview.

Throughout the museum, there are numerous artifacts that bear witness to the destruction and lives lost. Scorched clothing, including uniforms similar to those worn by the children walking through with me, along with a variety of personal items that somehow survived the blast tell the stories of countless individuals. Other artifacts, such as twisted and melted metal, vividly illustrate the destructive power of nuclear weaponry. One exhibit, almost hard to believe, shows the shadow of a man who was sitting on the steps of a local bank, his silhouette permanently seared into the stone—a haunting reminder of the bomb's catastrophic force.

As I moved through the museum, I was confronted with story after story of personal devastation. The black rain that fell after the bomb, which survivors drank in desperation to quench their unbearable thirst, likely contributed to the massive death toll. In the weeks and months that followed, the nuclear fallout—something few outside military circles fully understood at the time—wreaked havoc.

The exhibits didn't shy away from the horrors, depicting not only the immediate effects of burnt skin and mangled bodies but also the long-term consequences: full-body rashes, hair loss, and, over time, incurable cancers. Field hospitals were set up in the most atrocious conditions due to the complete destruction of anything resembling a legitimate medical facility. The sheer scale of suffering was overwhelming, a horrifying reminder of the indiscriminate destruction unleashed by the bomb.

What stood out most were the countless stories of the survivors. Many lost their entire families, and some were the sole remaining member. One well-known story that touched me deeply, though not the most horrifying, was that of Sadako Sasaki. She was just two years old when the atomic bomb was dropped and, 10 years later, she developed leukemia as a result of the exposure. Sadako believed in the Japanese tradition that folding 1,000 paper cranes would grant her a wish from the gods.

Throughout her hospital stay, she went out of her way to remain cheerful and optimistic, not wanting to burden her parents or worry others. Her concern for others seemed to be her primary motivator, and I couldn't help but wonder if her wish was to save others rather than herself. Despite her worsening symptoms, she managed to fold 644 cranes, according to one personal account. After her death, her fellow hospital patients completed the remaining cranes. Today, she is immortalized atop the Children's Peace Memorial, holding a large crane in the adjacent park.

As I moved through the museum, I kept hoping that stories of resilience and hope would somehow overpower the somber, sickened state I was in.

But with each turn, I encountered more devastating accounts, with only a few moments of resilience sprinkled throughout. The truth is there's no definitive happy ending—the ending is still unwritten. And perhaps that's the point. We must rely on diplomacy to avoid war, and when wars do occur, we cannot resort to nuclear weaponry or any means that indiscriminately takes innocent lives.

Eventually, I reached a section of the museum that offered a reprieve from the constant emotional weight of the exhibits. The focus abruptly shifted to how the bomb was created, beginning with a letter from Albert Einstein to President Franklin D. Roosevelt urging the development of nuclear weapons in response to Nazi Germany. The displays then moved through the decision to drop the bomb, its aftermath, the Cold War, and into modern times.

One part that gave me a slight sense of reassurance, as an American, was a panel highlighting President Obama's efforts. It showcased how the U.S. has played a leading role in negotiating treaties to reduce the number of nuclear weapons and limit how they are tested. However, it also made me wonder if we can maintain that leadership. Has the U.S. lost credibility on the global stage? It certainly feels that way. I couldn't help but reflect on how divided our nation is politically and what that division might mean for the rest of the world.

In today's world, would we be so forgiving if Japan had wiped out an entire city like Fort Worth, Texas—roughly 160,000 people during World War II—the same way we did in Hiroshima? Could we forgive them as they've somehow managed to forgive us? Have they truly forgiven us? I'm sure many still haven't. There are still people alive today who were deeply affected by the bomb, and its impact will echo through generations to come.

In all honesty, I did not leave this museum feeling good or overly optimistic, but I think that's the point. It put me in the perfect frame of mind to explore the Peace Memorial Park, home to the Eternal Peace Flame and the Atomic Bomb Dome—a structure that partially withstood the blast at ground zero. The ruins stand as a haunting testament to the devastation. When I approached the Children's Peace Memorial, with

Sadako Sasaki's story fresh in my mind, a lump formed in my throat. I shed the sincerest tear of sorrow I have ever shed. We did this to them.

In the days that followed, these images lingered in my mind. As I observed the city of Hiroshima, I couldn't help but notice how its modern architecture no longer reflected its ancient history. The city, once steeped in tradition, is now filled with buildings seemingly constructed with urgency, lacking the intricate designs seen in other historic Japanese cities.

Over time, this experience both upset and inspired me. It served as a powerful reminder of our shared responsibility to prevent such tragedies from ever happening again—whether through voting, protesting, or educating others. Yet, it also offers hope. Hiroshima, once completely devastated, now stands as a symbol of renewal and rebirth. The city thrives as a beacon of peace, reminding us that while we cannot change the past, we hold the power to shape a better future.

As I write this, I came across an article about the Japanese organization Nihon Hidankyo, a group of atomic bomb survivors from Hiroshima and Nagasaki. They were recently awarded the Nobel Peace Prize for their efforts to educate the world and achieve a future free of nuclear weapons. This group is credited with helping to foster a global climate of nuclear taboo.

However, soon there will be no more survivors to provide firsthand testimony of these tragedies. We must ensure their voices are never lost to history, or these events will likely be repeated—and with today's advanced technology, the consequences would likely be even worse. In recent years, not only have the world's major powers strengthened their nuclear capabilities, but smaller nations have also pursued them.

This is why places like the Hiroshima Peace Memorial Park and Museum are so crucial. They stand as enduring reminders of the devastating consequences of nuclear weapons and the importance of pursuing a peaceful world.

The journey from destruction to renewal is ongoing, and we all have a role to play. As the T-shirts in the museum's store proclaim, "No more Hiroshimas"—both on a global scale and within our own lives. On that, I couldn't agree more.

Chapter 8

Shadows of the Holocaust

*"For the dead and the living,
we must bear witness."*

—Elie Wiesel

THERE MAY BE NO SINGLE WORD that stirs a more intense emotional reaction than Auschwitz. It is not simply a location on a map; it represents the depths of human cruelty. The name itself stands as a chilling reminder of torture, death, genocide, and one of the darkest chapters in history.

Auschwitz came into existence as part of Nazi Germany's network of concentration and extermination camps. Following the Nazi invasion of Poland, a former Polish army base was converted into a prison for political detainees. The city of Oświęcim was chosen for its strategic location: it lay on a major railway line and was isolated from densely populated areas.

As the Nazis' racist agenda escalated and their so-called "Final Solution to the Jewish Problem" unfolded, the adjacent Birkenau extermination camp was constructed. Its sole purpose was chillingly clear: to exterminate Jews and others the Nazi regime deemed undesirable in their vision of Aryan supremacy.

While Auschwitz stands out in its infamy, it is not the only place where the scars of genocide demand acknowledgment and reflection. Across the world, similar sites bear witness to immense human suffering. In Cambodia, the Killing Fields, where over one million people were executed by the Khmer Rouge between 1975 and 1979, include Choeung Ek, a site marked by a stupa filled with victims' skulls. Rwanda's genocide memorials, such as the Kigali Memorial, honor more than 800,000 Tutsi and moderate Hutu who were killed during the 1994 genocide. The Armenian Genocide Memorial Complex in Yerevan remembers the 1.5 million Armenians systematically killed by the Ottoman Empire between 1915 and 1923, with a striking monument and museum documenting this atrocity.

Each of these sites serves as a solemn reminder of humanity's capacity for both unimaginable cruelty and extraordinary resilience. By opening these places to visitors, they invite remembrance and reflection. Some, like Auschwitz, even offer guided tours through the very facilities where the devastation took place, confronting visitors with the grim reality of history.

Why would anyone choose to go to such a place? And why would I?

These places of genocide demand to be remembered. Bearing witness to the atrocities ensures they are never lost to history. As long as these sites—and those who suffered and died there—are remembered, their deaths will not be in vain. Visiting these solemn spaces changes people when they go with the intention of remembering and honoring the victims with the reverence they deserve.

My visit to Auschwitz has stayed with me and always will. I will remember what happened, where it happened, and I will continue to speak out against injustice because of it. These visits, especially to places like Auschwitz, often resurface during my own struggles, allowing me to more easily find the strength to endure them.

Visiting places like Auschwitz transforms not only how we see history but also how we navigate our own challenges. These sites serve as reminders of humanity's capacity for both intense cruelty and extraordinary resilience. By walking through these places with reverence and an open heart, we honor the victims and carry their stories forward. In doing so, we affirm our commitment to ensuring that such atrocities are never repeated.

Auschwitz Memorial and Museum

I boarded the shuttle in Kraków for the 65-kilometer drive to Auschwitz-Birkenau, a journey of about an hour and a half. As we traveled through the quiet countryside, passing fields, small towns, and forests, the landscape felt unsettlingly peaceful—a sharp contrast to the incomprehensible atrocity that awaits us at our destination. With each passing mile, a growing sense of unease settled over me as I thought about the Nazi occupation and the battles that had scarred these lands.

Auschwitz is often recognized as the epitome of human suffering and tragedy. The site includes both Auschwitz I, the original concentration camp, and Auschwitz II-Birkenau, the massive extermination camp. Together, they are simply known as Auschwitz. Over 1.1 million Jews, along with thousands of Poles, Roma (Gypsies), Russian POWs, homosexuals, political prisoners, and others, were systematically murdered here by the Nazis.

As I entered through the main gate of Auschwitz, the infamous iron sign reading "Arbeit macht frei" greeted me. Translated into English, it means "Work sets you free." For many of the captured Jews and others, this sign initially offered a glimmer of hope, suggesting that their imprisonment might be bearable or even survivable. However, it was a cruel deception, masking the true horrors of the camp. It did not take long for those who entered to realize the devastating lie behind the words.

Over 1.3 million people were sent to Auschwitz, and only about 15 percent survived. Those who endured faced immense suffering: starvation, forced labor, disease, and physical abuse. Survivors carried deep physical and psychological scars, forever marked by their horrific experiences.

Moving deeper into the camp, I looked around at the tall barbed wire fences that seemed to stretch endlessly, interspersed with guard towers. Scattered along the fence were small signs bearing skulls and crossbones with the word "Halt!"—a grim warning of the fatal consequences for anyone attempting to escape. The plain brick buildings and bunkhouses spread across the grounds, connected by dirt roads forming a grid that resembled a regular street and avenue layout. This simple, orderly arrangement sharply contrasted with the chaos and horror that occurred within these confines.

At this early stage of the tour, I felt almost detached from my own body because I knew exactly where I was—one of the places where hell meets Earth. As the initial detachment began to fade, it was replaced by a heavy, suffocating sense of dread. Walking through the buildings that once served as barracks for the prisoners, I encountered exhibits displaying personal artifacts, photographs, and other remnants of the past. Thousands of pairs of shoes, eyeglasses, medical equipment, and suitcases taken from the prisoners illustrated the sheer scale of the atrocity. Each pair of shoes was once worn by a human being, and the dehumanization of what had happened became painfully palpable.

One horrifying display that stood out was a large mound of human hair cut from the prisoners. The sight of entire ponytails from women and girls was particularly gut-wrenching, leaving me feeling physically ill. During this part of the tour, the guide shared haunting stories about how the Nazis used much of the hair to make coats, and even bone fragments to craft buttons.

As I traveled the hallways and rooms of the next barracks, hundreds of prisoner mugshots lined the walls, showing their shaven heads and striped uniforms. Upon closer inspection, I noticed that each picture included two dates: the date they arrived at Auschwitz and the date they died. Most of these dates are separated by only days or weeks. A combination of sadness and anger began to seep into my bones. Turning a corner, I entered a room filled with pictures of children who perished, alongside displays of children and baby clothing. In this room stood a haunting near-life-sized, chiseled marble statue of a mother and child, both appearing extremely thin and exhausted, physically and mentally. Yet, despite their dire state, the visible bond of love between them is overwhelming.

As I moved through the buildings with the group, we came across Block 11, a structure with a façade that blended in with the others. However, what lay inside was nothing short of bone-chilling and sinister.

Upon entering, I noticed a room with a long table where members of the Gestapo met to determine sentences for those who had committed camp offenses, such as attempting to escape, conversing with civilians, or acts of sabotage. The most common sentence was death by shooting at the infamous execution wall. Those who managed to evade the death penalty were often moved to other parts of the building, which housed various types of cells. These included standard cells, other cells that barely allowed room to stand, and dark cells with windows covered and tiny air holes drilled into them. The dark cells were often used to imprison inmates condemned to death by starvation for escape attempts.

Just when I thought this building couldn't get any more horrifying, I descended a narrow, dark stairway into a dungeon-like basement. This dimly lit space contained the majority of the cells, including the notorious "dark room." Similar to the dark cells, the dark room was designed for psychological torture, but it was larger and could accommodate several prisoners at once. The concrete walls blocked out any ambient noise, deepening the prisoners' sense of isolation and despair. The cells were rarely, if ever, cleaned, intensifying the suffering as inmates were forced to relieve themselves in their confines and were unable to bathe. Most endured these inhumane conditions for days or even weeks at a time.

Walking outside, I felt a brief wave of relief, escaping from a building where I had never been confined but still felt imprisoned during those intense 15 minutes. The reflections on those who suffered and died within Block 11 left me with a sickening feeling. Then, I was confronted by a small, ominous wall that stood out distinctly from the rest. It was the highly feared execution wall. In front of it, dozens of flowers, wreaths, and candles served as a solemn memorial for the hundreds of souls executed by gunshot at this very spot. The wall's sole purpose was to catch the bullets that passed through the bodies of those who fell here. It became a meaningful place to pause, reflect, and mourn the victims.

As we walked to the next spot on the tour, reflecting on the trauma I had just been confronted with, I found myself thinking about the concept of avoidance in those suffering from post-traumatic stress disorder (PTSD). Auschwitz had a way of drawing out emotions that I rarely, if ever, experience—something that, as a therapist, speaks volumes. The depth of feelings it provoked pushed me far outside my usual emotional range.

When people endure trauma, they often go to great lengths to avoid places that remind them of it. I once worked with a woman who had been in a car accident and subsequently avoided the intersection where it happened. She would take long detours to steer clear of it, but when she had no choice but to drive near it, she was overwhelmed with vivid images of the accident. The experience brought on intense fear and panic, a reaction that illustrates how powerful the connection between place and trauma can be.

Though I've never been incarcerated or tortured—and can only imagine what it would be like to endure a place like Auschwitz—I found myself confronting emotions that might feel similar to what my PTSD clients feel when they face their triggers. This gave me a glimpse into their experience. Many people in our lives have endured trauma, and this realization underscored the critical importance of empathy and understanding in helping them heal.

As humans, we have a fundamental need to be understood. This is the essence of therapy, and it's also something we must offer one another. I've counseled many people who struggle with their pain because they believe others have it worse. Yet their pain is their reality, and it's unfair to compare. Every person's struggle is valid, and recognizing that truth is essential for healing.

During our walk, I noticed a long rail a couple of meters off the ground, suspended by posts. This, I learned, was the Auschwitz gallows. The SS conducted public hangings here, right in front of the camp kitchen, as a means of intimidating the prisoners. A bit further along, we came upon a much smaller, wooden gallows. This one struck a different tone—one of justice. It stands as a memorial to the fallen Jews; it was the very structure used to hang the Commander of Auschwitz, Rudolf Höss, after he was tried by the Polish National Tribunal.

Right next to the Höss gallows is an odd-looking, half-underground building with few windows and a large smokestack. Before entering, I noticed a sign explaining the building's history, ending with a solemn message: "You are entering a building where the SS murdered thousands of people. Please maintain silence here: remember their suffering and show respect for their memory." We were about to enter a place I dreaded, even though I knew it was part of the tour—the gas chamber and crematorium.

Descending the steps into the building provided a fleeting moment to brace for what lay ahead, but nothing could truly prepare me for the reality. Thousands of people had walked down these very steps, most unaware they were taking their final ones. My mind struggled to comprehend the enormity of it all, perhaps as a defense mechanism against the crushing weight of the trauma and death that filled this place. I was entering a space that felt like the closest one can come to hell on Earth.

Standing in the large, dimly lit room with its cold cement and brick walls was deeply solemn and felt isolating. Sadness seemed to seep from every crack. I let my tour group move ahead, taking a few moments to stand alone. I imagined the Zyklon B pellets being poured through vents and openings in the ceiling, releasing the toxic gas that claimed their lives. I allowed myself to try and imagine the weight of their suffering.

That moment changed me. Despite my divorce and illness, I had at times taken life and relationships for granted. But in that instant, I emerged with a renewed commitment to never squander another moment. Life can change in an instant—I already knew that—but standing there, reflecting on their suffering, I truly felt it.

It taught me to love with greater intention and to communicate my deepest thoughts and feelings honestly, without fear of judgment. Life is too short to live any other way. I also came to terms more deeply with my illness and the possibility of a darker fate, learning to accept it without fear. All my travels to historically dark places have shaped me, but this moment had the most profound impact on my life.

I left with a more stoic mindset, resolved to change what I could and to release my fear of what I couldn't. That room and the lives lost within it left an indelible mark on my perspective, reminding me to live fully, love deeply, and cherish every moment. It was a profoundly cathartic memento mori—a reminder of my own mortality—and a moment in time that will stay with me forever.

Upon leaving the gas chamber, I stepped into another dimly lit room and was confronted by three large, brick oven-like furnaces. Small rail tracks led directly to each furnace, and I quickly realized these were connected to the smokestack I had seen outside. This room was the crematory, a grim assembly line designed for the efficient disposal of bodies. The tragedy of what transpired here was almost impossible to comprehend.

I knew that the people forced to drag bodies from the gas chambers to the rail carts were often Jewish prisoners. These individuals, known as the Sonderkommando, were forced to perform this horrific task under threat of death. To conceal the extent of their atrocities, the Nazis frequently executed members of the Sonderkommando after a few months, ensuring their secrets never left the camp.

As I exited the building, a sense of relief washed over me, but the haunting reality of what I had experienced will undoubtedly stay with me for the rest of my life.

I then boarded a bus with my group to a parking lot just a short walk from the Auschwitz II-Birkenau site. As we approached the camp, the first thing I noticed was the large train station. This infamous station was built to look welcoming, designed to prevent panic among the new arrivals. Trains passed through the archway in the middle of the station before coming to a stop. On the opposite side of the tracks stood rows of barracks lined up in neat, symmetrical order. The captive people exited into a field where families were immediately separated by SS officers barking orders.

Then came the horrific selection process, led by Nazi doctors. Those deemed fit for work were sent to the right, while those deemed unfit—the sick, disabled, elderly, pregnant women, and children—were sent to the left. The left line rarely lived more than a few hours, as they were marched directly to the gas chambers just a few hundred meters away. We followed the same path they would have taken to the gas chambers.

Upon arriving, I saw that the gas chambers were no longer standing. What remains are basements with crumbled roofs, destroyed by the

Nazis in a desperate attempt to cover their crimes before the arrival of Russian troops near the end of the war. These piles of rubble now serve as haunting memorials to the more than one million people who perished at Auschwitz.

From here, we made our way back to the parking lot through the rows of bunkhouses. Entering a bunkhouse, the oppressive atmosphere hit me immediately. Rows of wooden bunks, stacked three tiers high, were cramped and overcrowded. Beds meant for one often held several prisoners, their emaciated bodies pressed together for warmth. The sight conjured images of starving humans in their blue-and-white striped clothing, and I couldn't help but wonder what stories these walls would tell if they could speak.

Touring the bunkhouse, I recalled the famous psychiatrist Viktor Frankl, who wrote about his experiences in Auschwitz. He observed that those who found meaning and purpose in their suffering were more likely to survive. Despite the dire circumstances, those who maintained hope and viewed their suffering as a test of inner strength could endure the unimaginable. I had always agreed with this view, but it wasn't until I faced my own suffering that I truly understood it. There is strength in suffering, and Frankl discovered how to tap into it.

Here, in this bunkhouse, I felt a deeper connection to Frankl than ever before. Standing where he once stood, I realized how profoundly his philosophy resonated in this place of indescribable despair. It reminded me that resilience, even in the darkest moments, is not just a theory—it's a lifeline.

One of the most rewarding aspects of working in mental health is witnessing people navigate their darkest hours and emerge stronger. I once worked with a woman diagnosed with breast cancer. She allowed herself a weekend to grieve her diagnosis and then resolved to fight back with unwavering optimism. Initially skeptical, I encouraged her to stick to her plan. Against the odds, she achieved just that and, with the help of her physicians, she made a miraculous recovery.

Experiences like these, both personal and professional, highlight the incredible strength of the human spirit—even in the darkest times.

Auschwitz is a stark reminder of humanity's capacity for both evil and resilience. As I reflect on my journey, I carry with me the lessons learned from those who suffered here and those who found the strength to survive.

On the van ride back to Kraków, I was silent; in fact, everyone in the van was silent. The landscapes passing by no longer held our attention. I imagine I looked as though I were staring into space, lost in thought. Auschwitz changes you.

Kraków and Oskar Schindler's Factory

Many tours of Auschwitz begin in the historic city of Kraków, a major Polish city with a heartbreaking narrative from World War II. To immerse myself in the city's heart of its history and culture, I headed to the large medieval square called the Old Town. Though this square now exudes charm and majesty, I imagined a time when the city was under Nazi occupation, with soldiers patrolling its streets and instilling fear in the hearts of the local population. My hotel overlooked the square, and as I gazed upon its beauty, I couldn't help but wonder what it was like to witness the Nazis marching below and the fear that must have gripped the people of Kraków during those dark times. This area is close to Wawel Castle, the historic Polish royal palace, which remained a potent symbol of Polish heritage even during the Nazi occupation—another meaningful area for solemn reflection.

From Old Town, I took a 10-minute cab ride to the former Jewish Ghetto, where thousands of Jews were confined under the brutal conditions of Nazi rule. Overcrowding, starvation, and forced labor defined life here until the ghetto's liquidation in 1943, when most residents were deported to concentration camps or killed. This was also where Roman Polanski, the controversial filmmaker, was smuggled out as a child and hidden by non-Jewish families, narrowly escaping the fate of his parents. His mother was captured and sent to Auschwitz, where she perished, while his father was deported to Mauthausen concentration camp but survived and was reunited with Roman after the war.

Polanski later channeled his own Holocaust experiences into *The Pianist*, an Academy Award-winning film about a survivor. However, his legacy is overshadowed by his fugitive status following a 1977 conviction for the sexual assault of a 13-year-old girl, after which he fled to Europe. This layered part of history brings to mind the saying, *hurt people, hurt people.*

Walking through the former ghetto, the gravity of history is heavy, especially when standing before the memorial of empty chairs in Ghetto Heroes Square or tracing the remnants of the ghetto wall. These sites serve as solemn reminders of the loss of identity, dignity, and countless lives.

Just outside the Ghetto is a place that continues to explore the horrors of the Holocaust, but it also leaves visitors with as much hope and optimism as it does somber reflection. This highly educational museum is located inside Oskar Schindler's Enamel Factory. Despite putting his own life and family in danger of retaliation, Schindler was able to help save over 1,200 Jews from almost certain death by employing them in his factory.

Schindler himself is not without controversy. A member of the Nazi Party, he was initially motivated by profit in employing Jews at his factory. However, over time, he came to understand the horrors of the Holocaust and made a concerted effort to persuade Nazi officials to allow Jews to work for him, ultimately saving their lives. In this museum, I walked into his secretary's office, the space where many of his lifesaving strategies were carried out. Moving through another doorway, I entered a room filled with period artifacts, including a wooden desk and a world map on the wall—this was Oskar Schindler's office. It was here that he often worked on his famous list, a document that ensured many lives were spared by transferring individuals to his factory rather than the death camps.

In his office, a memorial structure stands, bearing the names of those he saved—a solemn and powerful reminder of the impact of Schindler's choices and the countless lives spared as a result.

In addition to Schindler's life and factory, the museum provides an in-depth look at the experiences of those in Kraków during the war, particularly focusing on the harsh realities of daily existence in the ghettos. This stands in sharp contrast to the beautiful, historic city of Kraków as it exists today.

Oskar Schindler was not the only person who put himself on the line so deeply to save the lives of Jews during World War II. Two other examples include Raoul Wallenberg, a Swedish diplomat who issued protective passports and provided shelter to thousands of Hungarian Jews, and Chiune Sugihara, a Japanese diplomat in Lithuania who defied his government's orders by issuing transit visas that allowed over 6,000 Jews to escape to safety. Both of these individuals, like Schindler, displayed extraordinary courage and humanity, risking their lives to save others from the horrors of the Holocaust.

It takes a certain type of heroism to risk one's own life for the greater good of society. Many soldiers and emergency personnel do this daily, while others rise to the occasion in the face of unexpected tragedy. It makes me think of those who have shown extraordinary courage and love for humanity—figures like Mahatma Gandhi, Nelson Mandela, and Martin Luther King Jr. These men were all committed to non-violent reconciliation in their struggles for justice, and their legacies are honored at sites dedicated to their memory, much like Schindler's. One such site is Robben Island, the infamous prison where Mandela was incarcerated for 18 of his 27 years.

It is not only men who have made significant contributions to humanity through their sacrifices. Mother Teresa worked among the challenging and impoverished conditions of Kolkata, India, and her efforts grew into a major organization that has helped millions around the world. Then there's Harriet Tubman, an escaped slave who became the "conductor" of the Underground Railroad, leading hundreds of slaves to freedom. She also served as a spy, nurse, and scout for the Union forces, risking her life to gain invaluable information for the anti-slavery cause.

Holocaust Museums and Memorials

Arguably one of the most significant Holocaust museums in the world is the United States Holocaust Memorial Museum in Washington, D.C.

Located near the Washington Mall and the Capitol building, it provides a broad, comprehensive view of the Holocaust, offering a deep and multifaceted perspective on its history. This museum stands as a powerful reminder of our moral responsibility to confront all forms of hate and genocide. Its mission is to educate, inform, and prevent future atrocities while preserving an extensive collection of documents for researchers.

Walking through the main exhibit, I experienced its powerful narrative spread across three floors, each representing a distinct phase of the Holocaust. It begins with the rise of Hitler and the Nazi Party, along with the early persecution of Jews and other marginalized groups. It then transitions into the "Final Solution," examining life in the ghettos, and moves into the horrifying realities of the concentration and extermination camps. The final floor covers liberation—what the troops saw and felt as they entered the camps and what liberation meant for the survivors. As I exited the main exhibit, I was struck by a mix of emotions: anger, sadness, and even pride at seeing my country's role in liberating those under Nazi control. Questions raced through my mind: how could humanity have let this happen? Would I or my family have survived? What must it have been like for the troops and the liberated individuals to witness such horrors?

One of the most haunting moments of my visit was standing before the mounds of leather shoes, thousands of pairs confiscated from victims before their deaths. The smell of decaying leather was grounding, making the reality of what I was seeing even more visceral. Each pair of shoes symbolized a life taken—empty reminders of lives lost to evil and hate.

Another stop on my journey was the Memorial to the Murdered Jews of Europe in Berlin, which I visited shortly after my time at Auschwitz and in Washington. These earlier visits gave my time at the memorial a bit more context and greater meaning. The site is just steps away from the Brandenburg Gate and across from the bunker where Hitler took his own life. This sprawling site, covering 19,000 square meters, is filled with 2,711 concrete slabs, or stelae, arranged in symmetrical rows. Walking through the narrow, confining paths of this concrete labyrinth, I couldn't help but feel disoriented, as if the ground beneath my feet was shifting.

It's a subtle but powerful reminder of the industrial-scale slaughter that reduced people to statistics. The disorientation echoed the confusion and terror that must have gripped those torn from their lives and loved ones. This memorial forces visitors to confront the reality of what happened and leaves a sense of loss that lingers long after.

For those looking to explore further, Jerusalem's Yad Vashem offers one of the most comprehensive collections of Holocaust documentation, including exhibits like the Hall of Names, which strives to tell the stories of every person lost in the Holocaust. Similarly, the Anne Frank House in Amsterdam provides insight into the life of one of the Holocaust's most well-known victims. Her diary, written while hiding with her family in the building's annex, continues to resonate with millions worldwide.

There are many places like these around the world, each offering unique ways to remember and reflect on the Holocaust. Visiting such sites is not only a privilege but also a responsibility—to honor the victims, bear witness, and ensure that the lessons of the past guide us in confronting hate and preserving humanity.

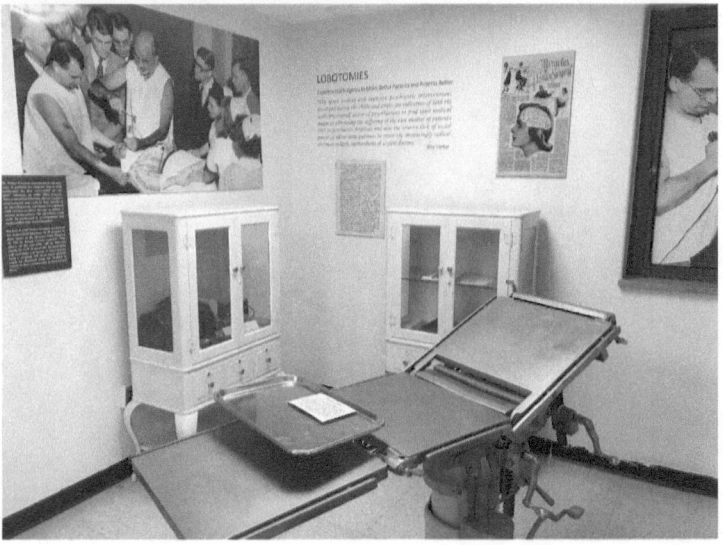

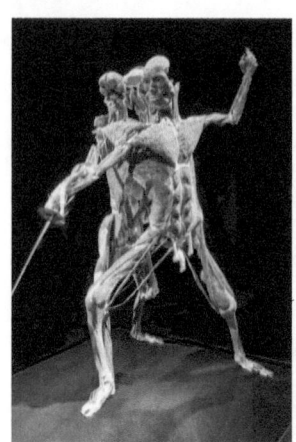

Chapter 9

Legendary Legacies

> How will our struggles and triumphs shape the legacy we leave behind, and what will they say about the lives we lived?

AS A PILOT, I have always admired pioneering aviators, especially Amelia Earhart and Charles Lindbergh. Their bravery and skill stood out in an era when aviation was still in its infancy. Both Earhart and Lindbergh represent not just triumphs of human innovation but also the darker complexities that often accompany historic figures.

Earhart shattered barriers, setting numerous aviation records at a time when women were often discouraged from stepping outside traditional gender roles. Her boldness and charisma captivated the public—sometimes sparking admiration, other times controversy. She became the first female pilot to cross the Atlantic solo and later attempted to become the first woman to fly around the world. Tragically, she and her navigator, Fred Noonan, vanished somewhere over the South Pacific. The mystery of their disappearance has inspired endless speculation. Did they perish on a remote island, or did their plane sink into the ocean's depths? While we may never know the answer, the enduring mystery continues to keep her legacy alive.

Five years before Earhart's solo transatlantic flight, Charles Lindbergh became the first person to complete the journey successfully. I've always felt a connection to Lindbergh, but my feelings about him are complicated. He was from my home state of Minnesota and lived just a few kilometers from my grandfather in the early 1920s—they likely crossed paths during their childhoods.

Lindbergh's legacy, however, is far more complex than Earhart's—or my grandfather's, for that matter. His isolationist views and alleged pro-German sympathies before World War II sparked criticism, and it was later revealed that he fathered seven children out of wedlock with three women in Europe. While initially opposed to U.S. involvement in the war, Lindbergh eventually contributed to the Allied effort by consulting with the military and even flying combat missions as a civilian.

On the darker side of his story, the kidnapping of his infant son in 1932 became known as the "crime of the century," leading to kidnapping becoming a federal crime in the United States. The tragedy began with a ransom note demanding $50,000 and ended with the heartbreaking discovery of the child's body. Bruno Richard Hauptmann was arrested after ransom money was traced to him, and handwriting analysis linked him to the notes. He was convicted and later executed.

Both Earhart and Lindbergh left behind places that preserve their legacies—not only as aviators but as monumental figures in history. I've visited Atchison, Kansas, where Earhart was born and spent part of her childhood. Her birthplace, now a museum, offers a glimpse into her early life, while another museum at the local airport celebrates her extraordinary achievements.

Lindbergh's story, meanwhile, is rooted in Little Falls, Minnesota, where his family settled after inheriting land. Today, the property is preserved as a museum. Touring the home, I imagined young Lindbergh lying on his back in the yard, staring up at the clouds, and dreaming of flight—much as I had once gazed in awe at F-14s launching from aircraft carriers in *Top Gun*.

A particularly memorable feature of the house is the three-season porch where Lindbergh slept year-round. In the bitter cold of Minnesota winters, it must have tested his fortitude—a trait that likely served him well during his 1927 solo transatlantic flight in the *Spirit of St. Louis*, now on display at the Smithsonian National Air and Space Museum.

Nearly everyone has moments of darkness in their lives. For me, it was an illness and a divorce. For others, it might be the loss of a loved one—or confronting their own mortality. When I visit sites connected to people with dark histories, I find myself reflecting on the lessons embedded in their stories. Dark tourism invites us to step into these shadows and confront the complexities of human experience.

In this chapter, I explore places connected to individuals whose darker complexities continue to intrigue. These figures left behind legacies that challenge us to confront darkness. By walking through the spaces associated with historic figures and reflecting on their stories—and those of the people impacted by their actions—we uncover lessons about resilience, morality, and the enduring impact of human choices. What insights might we gain by stepping into these shadows, and how can they shape the way we live today?

Edgar Allan Poe

Exploring sites associated with Edgar Allan Poe makes up a distinct category of literary dark tourism. One need not be a fan of Poe's writing to benefit from exploring the life of this literary giant. His life story, intertwined with his unmatched ability to evoke terror and suspense through words, defies comprehension. A poet and master of the short story, Poe pioneered the detective and horror novel genres. Strolling through his former haunts and delving into his life is a captivating journey into the depths of the literary macabre.

Poe's father abandoned the family in 1810, when Edgar was just a year old, his reasons for leaving shrouded in mystery. Within a year, he passed away—a fleeting figure in Poe's young life. Both his parents were actors and led lives filled with their own drama. His mother's death soon followed, likely because of tuberculosis. Adopted by the Allan family of Richmond, Virginia, he gained his middle name from them. However, his brother and sister were sent to live in separate homes, and he had little contact with them. While his adoptive mother provided warmth and care, his adoptive father was strict, often chastising Edgar for what he perceived as ingratitude toward his adoption.

In Richmond, at the Poe Museum, I embarked on an exploration through much of Poe's life, from birth to his mysterious death. Poe lived in Richmond during his childhood until he left to attend the University of Virginia, but his time there was short-lived, marred by debt exacerbated by gambling losses. From there, he found himself at the Military Academy at West Point, only to be court-martialed—Poe's claim was that he was trying to get kicked out. Eventually, he returned to Richmond and began writing for the struggling magazine, the *Southern Literary Messenger*. Under Poe's tenure, the magazine significantly improved because of his critiques, writing, and editing abilities.

Poe possessed more than just a flair for the dramatic; perhaps it was a gift inherited from his biological parents. His characters, like Lenore and Annabel Lee, evoke themes of deep love and devastating loss that resonate with my own experiences post-divorce. Much like music's ability to stir our souls, Poe's writing strikes emotional chords that linger. His legendary dark gothic motifs forge a penetrating connection with readers, leaving a lasting impression. For me, visiting sites associated with him became a meaningful journey into not only his life but also his mind.

When I'm driving down a quiet road and a love song comes on, it has the power to pull me back to a bittersweet memory. Sometimes, I change the station, unwilling to confront the emotions it stirs. Other times, I turn up the volume, letting the music take me wherever it wants. Sound, especially songs tied to strong emotions, has a way of triggering the brain's memory and emotional centers almost instantly. Reading works in a similar way, but it tends to resonate deeper, creating a more reflective and introspective experience. Music often hits us hard in the short term, but writing—especially Poe's kind—lingers long after we close the book. For me, "Lenore" echoes the immense grief I felt, but "Annabel Lee," with its hauntingly beautiful 238 words, resonates on an even deeper level. It speaks of an extraordinary love so immense that even angels became jealous and took Annabel Lee's life. Yet, in death, the love only grew stronger—enduring beyond mortality.

Grief is the price we pay for love, and I felt that price in the years after my divorce. Much like Poe's narrator, I wrestled with loss, haunted by memories of what once was. But through it all, "Annabel Lee" remains a poignant reminder of love's power to endure, even in the shadow of heartbreak.

When visiting dark tourism sites, they can evoke intense emotions, much like Poe's writing itself. Confronting these emotions reminds us that someone else understands our pain—an essential part of my work as a therapist. This process can help bring peace and acceptance to our losses. I never expected to think about my ex-wife while visiting Poe's sites or reading his works, but I did, and it added deeper meaning to my journey.

Poe moved to Baltimore nearly 200 years ago to live with his aunt and first cousin. I visited the small brick townhouse where he began crafting his signature stories. Despite their age difference and relation, he married his cousin, a relationship often thought to be one of convenience rather than passion. Only one person at a time can ascend the tiny staircase to Poe's room on the third floor. Standing there, I couldn't help but wonder what went through his mind as he gazed out that very window, complete with lattice and a large black bird perched upon it—a nod to his masterpiece, "The Raven." A poem that so brilliantly symbolizes unending grief, with its haunting refrain of "Nevermore" and the mournful presence of the raven, evoking the persistent sorrow of loss with Poe's trademark emotional precision.

Poe's death in 1849 was as mysterious as his writing. He traveled from Richmond to Philadelphia for an editing job, reportedly in good spirits and health. However, people discovered him a few days later in a disheveled and distressed state. Retrieved by his physician and hospitalized, Poe drifted in and out of consciousness over the next three days, but never was able to explain what happened. His last words: "Lord, help my poor soul."

They laid him to rest at Westminster Hall and Burying Ground, less than two kilometers from his Baltimore home. Initially interred toward the back of the church, his remains were later moved to the front, marked by a grand monument. He now rests beside his wife and mother-in-law. It's a serene spot, where I spent a few moments reflecting and paying my respects to one of my literary heroes. Poe's greatest legacy isn't just his words but their ability to compel us to confront the depths of our own humanity—much like visiting the sites associated with him did for me.

Jack the Ripper

Before criminals can be brought to justice, they must first be caught and prosecuted. Yet, in some cases, the perpetrator remains elusive. Advances in forensic science—from criminal profiling and enhanced surveillance in high-crime areas to ballistic analysis, DNA sequencing, and AI technology—have significantly improved our ability to apprehend criminals. However, before these advancements, solving crimes relied heavily on the analytical skills of detectives, leaving many cases unresolved for victims and their families.

One of the most infamous unsolved cases dates back to 1888 in Whitechapel, London, where a shadowy figure, later dubbed Jack the Ripper, stalked the foggy, narrow cobblestone streets. These dimly lit alleys, illuminated by gas lamps and teeming with poverty-stricken passersby, became the backdrop for a chilling reign of terror. Occurring long before the advent of modern forensic science, the case remains shrouded in mystery. Today, visitors can retrace these notorious paths on guided tours and visit a museum dedicated to the victims and the relentless manhunt that followed.

Before embarking on a tour of the Whitechapel neighborhood, I stopped at the Jack the Ripper Museum to get myself better acquainted with both the case and Victorian London. The museum offered insights into the investigation by Scotland Yard detectives, and the victims for whom they sought justice. While the museum does sensationalize the case somewhat, it's important to remember that the case itself became famous due to the sensationalism it sparked at the time. Newspapers led with stories about the murders, creating a public frenzy with their bold headlines and the printing of letters allegedly sent by the killer himself. I was able to view perfect recreations of these letters, including the chilling "From Hell" letter—a letter that was sent with half a human kidney, the other half allegedly fried and eaten by the killer, so the letter claimed.

The brutality of Jack the Ripper's crimes was rarely seen in history, as was the number of victims—five in total—a figure that was shocking for the era. The museum excels in portraying the victims, highlighting the hardships they faced long before their gruesome deaths. All were middle-aged women struggling with poverty and alcoholism. While it has long been believed that the victims all likely engaged in sex work, this assumption is now disputed. I also learned about the wide range of suspects, from a common butcher to a royal prince. Over the years, many have claimed to know the Ripper's identity, but none have been confirmed—a mystery still shrouded in fog, much like the London streets during the brutal killings.

Walking the streets of Whitechapel, where Jack the Ripper once lurked, his victims roamed, and detectives searched, guided by a voice steeped in the macabre, is an eerie experience. Many of the streets still resemble how they looked over 100 years ago. As I navigated these cobblestone alleys, I heard the stories of London at the time and can almost imagine the caped killer, top hat on, butcher knife in hand, hunting for his next victim. The guide took us to the very spots where the murders took place, including the site where Mary Ann Nichols, his first victim, was found with her throat slashed and abdomen mutilated.

With one exception, as the murders increased, so did the brutality. The second victim was found almost decapitated, and her uterus and organs removed. The third victim, however, suffered only a slashed throat, as it's believed her murder was interrupted. Later that same night, the killer struck again in a horrific attack: the victim's throat was cut, her abdomen opened, and her kidneys and uterus were removed. Her bloodied apron was found nearby, along with graffiti stating: "The Juwes are the men that will not be blamed for nothing." This misspelled phrase has long puzzled investigators but reflected the anti-Semitic tensions in Whitechapel at the time.

The last known victim, Mary Jane Kelly, marked the killer's gruesome finale. Our tour group stood outside the building where this murder took place—his only known killing indoors. In the small apartment, Jack the Ripper committed one of the most horrifying murders in history, likely because he had more time, free from the risk of being caught on the streets. The youngest victim, Kelly, was found with her throat slashed and her face mutilated beyond recognition. Her breasts, organs, and skin were removed and arranged around the room, forming a macabre display. After this murder, Jack the Ripper disappeared from Whitechapel—or at least his killings ceased. He may have moved to another town, died, been committed to an institution, or imprisoned for another crime. Some even speculate that he took his own life or moved to America, with fringe theories linking him to H.H. Holmes, often recognized as America's first serial killer. Holmes constructed a sinister "Murder Castle" in Chicago during the 1893 World's Fair.

Jack the Ripper's true identity may forever remain a mystery, despite countless theories over the years. Given the passage of time and the enduring fascination his story has inspired, solving the case might no longer hold much significance. His name will forever haunt history, a chilling reminder of his long-ago crimes. As for the victims, I hope their suffering and memory will begin to overshadow the hype surrounding the Ripper's identity.

Since the time of Jack the Ripper, sensationalizing serial killers has been a recurring phenomenon. This trend surged in the 1970s and 80s, often referred to as the "golden age" of serial killers, with figures like Ted Bundy and John Wayne Gacy, and into the 90s with Jeffrey Dahmer dominating headlines. The sheer number of films, video games, podcasts, and books on the subject underscores society's enduring fascination with these taboo figures. Today, however, mass shootings have overtaken serial killers as the focal point of sensationalized media coverage. This new form of spree violence has captured public attention and instilled fear, much as serial killers once did. The persistent media focus on these tragedies raises an unsettling question: does such coverage inadvertently inspire future acts of violence? It is a troubling possibility that continues to demand thoughtful consideration.

The Old West and Jesse James

The American Old West fascinates not just North Americans—these larger-than-life personalities, living and dying by the gun, have become legends worldwide. For some dark tourists, the draw of these infamous figures and locations is irresistible, leading them to visit the most notorious towns of the West. In Deadwood, South Dakota, I stood in the No. 10 Saloon, where Wild Bill Hickok held two aces and two eights—the dead man's hand—the last hand he ever played before being shot. In Dodge City, Bat Masterson once patrolled the streets with no-nonsense authority. But my personal favorite is Tombstone, Arizona. There, I walked through the famous Bird Cage Theatre, where rowdy cowboys and miners came to drink, gamble, and be entertained by stage performers and sex workers. Allegedly, over 25 people died here during its heyday, and the more than a hundred bullet holes still visible today serve as a testament to those wild times.

While in Tombstone, often called "the town too tough to die," I strolled through the small Boothill Graveyard, where about 300 people are buried. Each grave is marked by simple wooden headstones and crosses, with piles of rocks serving as a reminder of the harsh and often violent realities of frontier life. Nearly half of those buried there met their end through violence, as the sign at the entrance starkly proclaims, "They died with their boots on." The graveyard's rugged simplicity underscores the fleeting nature of life in the Old West.

I then walked the very dirt street where the Earps and Doc Holliday marched toward the vacant lot near the O.K. Corral—the site of the most famous gunfight in American history. Today, reenactments by modern gunslingers bring the legendary 30-second fight to life for visitors, offering a dramatic glimpse into the Wild West's violent past.

The tale of that legendary showdown echoes something universal that many of us feel when someone crosses us. Whether it's being cut off in traffic or being swindled, there's often a pull toward revenge. The Old West was all about taking justice into your own hands, but today, rather than drawing guns, we have the opportunity to solve our conflicts in more constructive, non-violent ways. The sense of personal justice still resonates, but, hopefully, we've evolved to channel that energy toward understanding and resolution, rather than perpetuating cycles of harm.

On a road trip a few years ago, my son and I found ourselves in Northfield, Minnesota. As we drove through town, I noticed the old First National Bank, now part of the Northfield Historical Society, and I couldn't help but stop. This was where Jesse James and his gang made their ill-fated attempt to rob the bank back in 1876. The townspeople fought back, killing three of the gang members, and losing three of their own, though Jesse and his brother Frank got away. Jesse lived for six more years, pulling off smaller crimes with a new gang, but he never quite reached the same level of infamy again.

What fascinates me most about Jesse James is how his legend grew, despite the reality of who he really was. He wasn't the Robin Hood figure that the sympathetic and sensationalistic press made him out to be. Jesse was a cold-blooded killer and thief, robbing hardworking people, little different from today's criminals who steal our financial security. And then there's the violence—during the Civil War, Jesse rode with Quantrill's Raiders, ambushing Union troops and murdering civilians. Later, during his robberies, lives were lost, though it's hard to say how many Jesse himself killed. It was likely several. His myth doesn't hold up against the brutal truth.

On 3 April 1882, Jesse was at his family's farmhouse in St. Joseph, Missouri with Robert Ford, a man he had mentored and was fond of, despite sensing Ford's growing jealousy of his fame. What Jesse didn't know was that Ford was after the reward money offered for his capture, dead or alive, and the fame that came with it, valuing those more than his friendship. The opportunity came when Jesse was standing on a chair, adjusting a framed picture his mother had sewn that read "God Bless Our Home." No heists, just a regular day at home. Ford slowly raised his revolver, aimed it at the back of Jesse's head, and ended the life of the notorious gunslinger.

Standing in the small, ominous room surrounded by intricately designed red-on-white wallpaper of its time, with a stove in the corner,

I could sense how ordinary the day must have seemed to Jesse James before he died. Then I looked up at the picture, and just below it, encased in a frame, was a small hole in the wall. I immediately recognized it as the bullet hole—a haunting representation of betrayal at its highest level. Jesse James was known for his paranoia, a trait that likely kept him free and alive for so many years. But even he had to trust a few people, and Robert Ford was one of them. James probably suspected Ford's jealousy, but never imagined it would lead to his death.

That evening, while sitting in my hotel room, I reflected on my experience at the James house and the two biggest takeaways from the visit: trust and betrayal. I couldn't help but think about the times in my own life when I felt betrayed. Several moments came rushing back to me.

Not long before my visit to the house, I had left an agency where I had invested nearly two decades of hard work, striving to advance my career. My progress was halted—not due to a lack of merit, but because of nepotism, when a job I had aspired to was given to a less-qualified relative of a board member. It was a devastating blow that changed the course of my career.

Instead of giving up, I struggled to find my direction again. In time, I chose to open my own practice, where I was able to help underserved people in my hometown and a nearby tribal community. Those opportunities proved far more fulfilling than the pursuit of a CEO title ever could have been. At the time, I believed success was defined by how high I could climb. However, in part due to my experiences with dark tourism, I shifted my mindset to focus on what truly drives me—helping as many people as possible improve their satisfaction with life.

But it wasn't my job that dominated my thoughts on trust and betrayal—it was what I felt was the worst betrayal of my life. Life had felt peaceful, like everything was falling into place, until I discovered someone I loved deeply had been sexually assaulted by a friend I had introduced her to. She didn't want to report it, but at the time, I felt justice had to be served.

Unable to let it happen to anyone else, I made the agonizing decision to report it to the police myself. When the police chief said, "If she doesn't report it, it didn't happen," his words left me feeling powerless. I felt I had to take justice into my own hands. When I confronted him, he didn't deny it, and I hit him until I couldn't swing any longer. The release was fleeting—the trauma lingered.

I'm certain it impacted my friend who had been assaulted far more deeply than it did me. Sadly, I couldn't see past my own pain at the time. Our friendship slowly faded, and I stopped trusting those closest to me. For years, I kept people at arm's length, too wounded to let anyone in.

Flipping through the pictures on my phone of Jesse James's home, I had another recollection—this time, one of redemption. My story had been rewritten. I had recovered from my betrayals and found close friendships again. Jesse, whose history is etched into the bloodstained floorboards of that living room, never got that chance. He didn't live to see another moment or find redemption. The ending of his story wasn't of his own making.

As they say, you live by the gun, you die by the gun. But what about Robert Ford? Immediately pardoned by the governor for murdering Jesse, Ford spent time touring the country, making money by reenacting the moment he killed James on stage. But over time, the public turned against him, and even Ford began to regret what he had done. Ten years after killing Jesse James in cold blood, Ford's life also ended by gunshot as he went about his day, working in a pop-up saloon in Colorado.

Tsavo Man-Eaters

Humans aren't typically on the menu for lions—or most animals, for that matter. However, during the era of British colonial expansion in Africa, two lions disrupted that norm, terrorizing the workers constructing the Kenya-Uganda Railway. The year was 1898, and the setting was Kenya. These lions, later known as the Tsavo Man-Eaters, were responsible for dozens of deaths. Some reports embellished the toll, claiming as many as 135 victims, though modern estimates suggest the number was closer to 40.

What drove this unusual behavior? Was it simply a case of lions defending their territory? Not exactly.

Several factors may have contributed to this unusual behavior. The depletion of their natural prey and physical issues likely played a role. It's been hypothesized that, due to the wear on their teeth with age and a severe abscess in one of the lions, they struggled to hunt their usual prey, like buffalo and zebras. Seeing humans as easier targets, the lions exploited the vulnerability of the workers, who were already battling exhaustion and disease in unforgiving conditions. In the dead of night, the lions picked off the men, one by one.

At Tsavo National Park in Kenya, nestled between Nairobi and Mombasa, visitors can stay at the very site of the infamous lion attacks. The Man-Eaters Lodge is a stunning oasis in the heart of the savannah, featuring cabanas, a restaurant, a pool, and all the amenities of a luxury hotel. It serves as an ideal base for a safari near the Tsavo River, where visitors can encounter monkeys, crocodiles, and elephants in a setting steeped in history and shadowed by a dark past.

Over 125 years ago, sleeping in this area meant living in constant terror. Today, however, visitors can embark on safaris with a good chance of spotting one of the region's famed maneless lions—a distinctive trait of the lions here and a haunting reminder of their man-eating predecessors.

A simpler way for most people to engage with a tangible piece of the Tsavo lions' story is by visiting Chicago's Field Museum. This natural history museum houses over 40 million specimens and artifacts and rivals both the Natural History Museum in London and the American Museum of Natural History in New York. As I walked through the museum's gates, I was immediately greeted by "Sue" in the lobby—the world's most complete T. rex, a magnificent beast that roamed the Earth long before the lions. After marveling at Sue, I made my way to the Mammals of Africa exhibit, where I found a stunning collection of taxidermied animals from the savannahs. Then, I came upon two seemingly ordinary lions—but their story is anything but.

Side by side behind glass, I was able to closely examine the pair of lions that stalked the railway camp in the still of the night, picking off workers as their screams echoed through the darkness. The lions were finally killed by Lieutenant Colonel John Henry Patterson, bringing an end to their reign of terror. Looking at the two maneless lions, it's hard to believe they caused so much death and horror. Yet, they are just lions—nothing magical about them. Like some humans, they didn't follow their natural order. However, unlike humans, they lack free will. They were simply adapting to their environment in order to survive.

The story of the Tsavo lions is just one example of the complex relationship between humans and animals. As the human population and innovation grow, it's critical that we not only protect habitats, but encourage biodiversity. The lions, though a cautionary tale, remind us of our responsibility to coexist with nature.

Chapter 10

Historic Cemeteries and Graveyards

"Think of yourself as dead. You have lived your life. Now, take what's left and live it properly."

—Marcus Aurelius

ONE OF THE MOST MEMORABLE CEMETERIES I've visited is a graveyard in Norway. Norwegian graveyards often have a chapel on the grounds, adding to their serene and contemplative atmosphere. It was here that I traced my roots back to my great-great-grandparents. During this journey, I discovered a church they had helped establish and learned about their son, Julius—my grandfather's father. He was a seafarer on merchant ships, often away for months, before emigrating to America, where he changed his last name from Schjoth to the more American-sounding Scott.

Meeting my great-great-grandparents through this journey felt a bit surreal, as if I were connecting with them in person while simultaneously mourning their loss. It was an experience that transcended time, blending past and present in a way that only a place steeped in history and memory can provide. While not all cemeteries and graveyards may seem remarkable, they hold deep significance to the family and friends of those buried within them. I have visited many cemeteries, each as unique as the individuals laid to rest there. Some cemeteries are even as renowned as the notable figures interred within their gates, adding to their boundless allure.

Historic cemeteries are scattered across the globe, each offering a unique glimpse into the past. A quick search for notable burials near any major city often reveals cemeteries that are as haunting as they are beautiful, rich in history and atmosphere. These places aren't just for mourning—they're spaces for remembrance, reflection, and honor. They touch us deeply, often in ways we don't fully recognize until long after we leave. Visiting them creates meaningful, lasting memories.

For me, these cemeteries are more than historical landmarks; they are places to connect with the lives and legacies of those who shaped our world. I have visited many historic cemeteries, as well as others that stand out for their unique characteristics. Some are renowned for their beauty and gothic charm (my favorite type), while others gain fame because of the notable figures buried there—war heroes, scientists, scholars, celebrities, and leaders. Historic cemeteries often blend these elements, offering a deep sense of history wrapped in architectural elegance and personal stories.

While these visits might be considered a form of dark tourism due to their association with death, much like many other forms of dark tourism I engage in, I see them in a much deeper context. To me, cemeteries are sacred places to honor, and reflect on the lives of those who have left an impression on us. They inspire a sense of reverence, though the reflections they evoke can vary greatly. Standing at the grave of an entertainer, I might find myself laughing at the memory of a beloved film or performance—a moment of connection that reminds me how their work continues to bring joy even after their passing. In contrast, standing at the grave of a young soldier, I've felt the penetrating weight of a life cut tragically short, reflecting on the sacrifices made for the greater good.

These visits aren't just about paying respects—they're opportunities to reflect on the fragility of life, the weight of legacies, and our shared humanity. Each visit leaves an indelible mark, reminding me to honor both struggles and triumphs. I often try to imagine how the departed might wish to be remembered. Sometimes, that means smiling at a shared memory or chuckling at a quirky epitaph. Other times, it's a solemn moment of gratitude—bowing my head in reverence for a life of sacrifice and service.

Historic cemeteries are more than resting places for the dead—they are sanctuaries for the living. They invite us to honor, learn, and grow. Whether through quiet reflection, a heartfelt laugh, or a solemn tear, these visits deepen our connection to history, humanity, and ourselves.

The concept of being reminded of our fragility is not new. The Latin phrase memento mori—"remember you must die"—originates from Roman times, when victorious generals were reminded of their mortality and the fleeting nature of life. During the medieval period, Christians used it as a moral teaching, encouraging the faithful to lead virtuous lives. Over centuries, it found resonance in Stoicism, urging individuals to live intentionally and focus on what truly matters.

Memento mori is often represented in art and literature, serving as a timeless reflection on life's impermanence. Skulls, bones, hourglasses, decaying objects, and wilting flowers are recurring motifs that symbolize the inevitability of death and the transience of life. These symbols often appear in vanitas paintings, juxtaposed with objects of beauty and wealth to highlight the futility of earthly pleasures. Similarly, literature—from medieval texts to modern poetry—interweaves memento mori themes, prompting readers to contemplate mortality and embrace purposeful living.

This concept is as relevant today as it was at its origins, reminding us to focus on what truly matters in an increasingly fast-paced and superficial world. Whether expressed through art, philosophy, or mindfulness practices, memento mori continues to inspire intentional living and a deeper appreciation for the present moment.

Paris: the City of the Dead

The beauty of Paris is undeniable. With its charming streets, architecture, and iconic landmarks, it is no wonder why Paris is known as the "City of Love" and that "Paris is for lovers." As I would find out, Paris is also the city of the dead and, in a sense, "Paris is for the dead." Over seven million people are buried in Paris. If we do not include the surrounding metropolitan area, the dead significantly outnumber the living within the city itself.

As I stepped off the metro at Denfert-Rochereau in Paris's Montparnasse neighborhood, I was greeted by a quintessential Parisian scene: grand white buildings with wrought-iron balconies and bustling streets lined with cafes and shops. Navigating through the lively, high-traffic area, I joined a crowd eagerly waiting their turn to explore one of the most eerie and fascinating places on Earth—the Paris Catacombs. Arriving early, I managed to beat the long lines that so often form there.

The Catacombs have a history that stretches back to Roman times. Much of Paris's architecture is built from limestone quarried from these tunnels, which extend over 300 kilometers beneath the city's surface. While only a small section is open to the public, an underground subculture of "cataphiles" ventures illegally into the labyrinth, drawn by the thrill of exploration and the allure of hidden secrets.

Today, those interested in exploring the tunnels can do so without fear of arrest when entered appropriately. I stepped into the small, foreboding pavilion building and descended a spiral staircase that seemed to transport me to another world. In the dimly lit cavern, I walked roughly 100 meters to a sign that read, "*Arrête! C'est ici l'empire de la mort.*" Translated, it declares, "Stop! Here lies the empire of death." I had arrived at the Ossuary.

In the late 1700s, Paris faced a gruesome public health crisis. Cemeteries were overflowing, exposing decaying corpses that spread illness and foul smells. This was especially true at the Cemetery of the Innocents. Poor planning for the booming population, combined with plagues and wars, left Paris with no room for its dead. The solution? Exhume the bodies and relocate them to the Catacombs. And so, the remains of six million Parisians found their final resting place in the Ossuary I was now walking into.

The skulls and bones are not hidden in cement coffins or behind walls. Instead, they are meticulously arranged in artistic patterns along the tunnels. The passageway is about 1.5 to two meters wide, with the bones stacked approximately 1.5 to two meters high and about one meter deep on each side. The macabre display is continuous for a mile that takes about 45 minutes to move through.

As I walked past the neatly arranged rows of skulls, femurs, and other bones, I couldn't help but wonder what led to their deaths. Did they fall victim to the plague? Did they die of old age, or was it an illness or violence that took them? My thoughts, especially the second time I visited, turned to more existential matters. The sheer number of bones makes it impossible not to consider the inevitable outcome waiting for us all.

We inhabit our bodies for such a brief time. Life is incredibly fragile—lights out can come at any moment. An illness or disease could suddenly end our journey, or a split-second mistake, like failing to look left before hitting the gas, could result in disaster. It's a stark reminder to wear that seatbelt, wash our hands, and prioritize health and safety—although, in the end, life remains fragile.

Each step is a story, a person's story. Every skull once had a face, a name, a family. What was their job? Did they love and laugh like I do? The questions go on and on. Skulls are lined up side by side, forming hearts and crosses in the walls of bones. I passed many inscriptions and plaques with French words on them—several are poems, others are insightful sayings and meaningful prayers. Will I be remembered in this way? Will I be remembered at all? Does it even matter? What about God, heaven, and hell?

When confronted with death up close and on such an overwhelming scale, life takes on a sharper focus. I visited the Catacombs a couple of times, and each time, as I emerged back into the world, I felt a deep gratitude for the life I have—especially for my family. Those visits inspired me to live more fully, reminding me that failing to do so risks feeling as though a part of me is already dead.

In the city of the dead, two more sites have intrigued me: Père Lachaise Cemetery and the Panthéon. While both honor the final resting places of the departed, they do so in vastly different environments. These sites provide a chance to pay tribute to some of the most distinguished individuals buried in Paris, each within its own unique setting.

During one of my visits to Père Lachaise, my mind drifted back to my 16th birthday. I watched from the house as my parents drove down our gravel driveway in a small white pickup truck. Excitement erupted when they told me it was mine. That little truck became the center of countless adventures—laughing with friends, cruising down backcountry roads, and singing our favorite songs. The CD that got the most playtime was one from The Doors, with "Light My Fire" and "Break on Through" serving as the soundtrack to our escapades.

Thinking about these good times brought to us by Jim Morrison was emotional as I stood next to his grave. For a moment, I was back in my little white truck, reliving the carefree days of old, much like Morrison did. I was 34 then; he died at 27. Despite his death in Paris, a city he greatly admired, the decision to bury him there stemmed from a desire to avoid the publicity that would have accompanied bringing him back to the United States.

To think how much Morrison accomplished by such a young age and how many lives he touched, including my own, is humbling. Layers of graffiti with personal messages and his lyrics, along with the dozens of flowers and pictures of him, cover his grave. One message in green said "The Lizard King," his nickname given to him by his friends. His legacy transcends time as new generations discover the music of The Doors.

Although Morrison's grave is the most visited at Père Lachaise today, many others buried there resonate just as deeply with many people. As I traversed the winding paths of the large historic cemetery, I passed many interesting graves. The mature trees cast a significant amount of shade, but a few rays always seemed to poke through. It gave the Gothic-style cemetery an eerie feel as I walked around the monuments, mausoleums, and headstones.

When I visited Père Lachaise, Sarah was with me. It was early in our marriage, and learning about the deep love between the 12th-century philosopher Abelard and his student Heloise seemed to echo the ideals of love and connection Sarah and I shared. Their story, however, was far more tragic. They married in secret, but when their union was discovered by Heloise's family, Abelard was brutally castrated, and the two were forced apart. Despite their physical separation, they remained profoundly connected through letters that revealed the enduring depth of their love. Centuries later, their remains were reunited here in the same tomb, now a site of pilgrimage where visitors leave letters and flowers as tributes to their timeless bond.

Two more graves here left me with lasting memories. The first was the time-tested composer from Warsaw, Frédéric Chopin, who penned some of history's most recognizable piano compositions, including the Funeral March. A statue of a weeping woman holding a lyre tops his ornate grave, symbolizing the sorrow for a legend lost. Despite Chopin being buried here, his heart is not. His sister smuggled it back to where his heart always belonged, in his beloved Warsaw. Visitors can find it enshrined in a pillar at the Church of the Holy Cross there.

The other grave that left a lasting impression was that of Oscar Wilde. The flamboyant Irish author and playwright, famously imprisoned for his homosexuality, was a man whose immense talent was overshadowed by persecution for who he loved. Upon his death in 1900, he was living in exile in France, having been forced from his homeland following his imprisonment. As a result, he was buried there. Wilde's Art Deco tomb, adorned with a sphinx and inscriptions of his work, stands defiantly in the expansive cemetery. Enclosed in a large glass case, it bears the marks of scores of admirers who, in a bizarre tribute, left red lipstick kisses on the granite. Now, the glass is smeared with lipstick—much easier to clean, I suppose, but no less a testament to Wilde's enduring legacy and the love he continues to inspire.

Across the city lies a different setting: the historic mausoleum, the Panthéon, which honors many of France's cultural, political, and academic leaders. On the main floor, I explored a variety of monuments, photographs, and exhibits about French history. Then I descended the stairs into the dim, cool crypt, with its vaulted ceilings and stone walls and floors. It was a quiet, solemn space where the only sounds were the echoes of footsteps and the hushed whispers of others also exploring the tombs.

In the crypt, I paid my respects to two legendary authors celebrated for their powerful tales of social justice and romance—Victor Hugo and Alexandre Dumas—who rest in the same chamber alongside another literary giant, Émile Zola. Zola's legacy lies in weaving science into his narratives, leaving a significant mark on academic literature. Nearby, I visited the tomb of Marie Curie, the pioneering physicist who made history as the first woman to win a Nobel Prize and the only person to earn Nobel Prizes in two distinct scientific fields. Her untimely death from a rare form of anemia was almost certainly a result of prolonged exposure to radiation, a danger not yet understood in her time.

London: Honoring Science and Royalty

Paris might be called the city of the dead, but it's far from the only place where the famous and infamous find eternal rest. London is another remarkable city to honor and reflect on lives lived and lost. Highgate Cemetery stands out as one of the world's most intriguing burial grounds. Despite its many tourists, it retains a famously unkempt appearance. It is not neglected by any means, but overgrown vegetation and scattered trees intertwine with gravesites and Gothic tombs, creating a dark, haunting atmosphere.

Opened in 1839, Highgate Cemetery quickly became a sought-after burial site during Victorian times, celebrated for its striking Gothic architecture and picturesque hillside setting. One of its most iconic features is the Egyptian Avenue, marked by a grand entrance flanked by two tall obelisks—a testament to the Victorian fascination with both death and ancient Egyptian culture. The cemetery remains the final resting place of many notable figures, most famously Karl Marx, the father of Marxist theory and socialism.

Another sacred site in London that honors prominent figures is Westminster Abbey, located adjacent to Parliament and the iconic clock tower, Big Ben. Westminster Abbey is the final resting place for several renowned scientists. Beneath its soaring vaulted ceilings and towering pointed arches lie the graves of Charles Darwin and Isaac Newton, side by side in the Scientists' Corner. The groundbreaking work of these men revolutionized science, laying the foundation for modern physics, mathematics, biology, and evolution. I still recall being captivated by Darwin's *Voyage of the Beagle* during college, as I explored the study of biology and evolution. It deepened my appreciation for the dedication and lengths scientists go to in their pursuit of knowledge.

More recently, in 2018, the ashes of astrophysicist Stephen Hawking were interred there, placing him among the great minds commemorated in this historic space. Hawking, one of the most brilliant scientists of our time, persevered despite his long battle with ALS, a disease that confined him to a wheelchair for nearly his entire adult life. His contributions to our understanding of black holes and the universe's mysteries ensure his legacy will endure for generations.

Also buried at Westminster Abbey is Queen Mary I, known as Bloody Mary due to her persecution of Protestants during her reign. She was the daughter of Henry VIII and his first wife, Catherine of Aragon. Mary is interred alongside her half-sister, Elizabeth I, the daughter of Anne Boleyn. Anne Boleyn was beheaded when Elizabeth was only two years old, a traumatic beginning that set the stage for Elizabeth's challenging ascent to the throne.

Despite this turbulent legacy and the so-called "Tudor curse" of violent and tumultuous rulers, Elizabeth I managed to break free from the shadow of her lineage, steering England into the Elizabethan Era of relative stability and cultural flourishing. The half-sisters and former queens are buried together in the Lady Chapel of Westminster Abbey under a shared epitaph that reads: "Consorts both in throne and grave, here rest we two sisters, Elizabeth and Mary, in hope of the Resurrection."

Just outside the city of London is Windsor Castle, the oldest and largest continuously occupied castle in the world. It has been around for over 900 years, since the time of its first inhabitant, William the Conqueror.

On the grounds is St. George's Chapel, which has witnessed many of the English royals' most significant events. Prince Harry and Meghan Markle were married here, and his father, King Charles, had a "blessing" of a civil marriage to Camilla Parker Bowles. A formal marriage was not allowed since they were both previously married and divorced.

The chapel itself is beautiful, with its tall, vaulted ceiling and intricate stained-glass windows wrapping around the upper walls, letting in an array of colors that reflect off the Gothic wooden structures around the benches. The black-and-white checkered marble floors have seen many caskets containing the remains of storied royals rolled along their path to the altar. This floor also contains a plaque with the inscription of royals entombed below, including Henry VIII and his third out of six wives, Jane Seymour. She was the only wife to give birth to a male heir to the throne and was often considered Henry's favorite wife.

Although I don't follow the royals closely, I respect the institution as a symbolic monarchy that, in my view, does more good than harm. For this reason, it was important for me to pay my respects to King George VI, his wife, Queen Elizabeth The Queen Mother, and their daughter, the recently deceased Queen Elizabeth II. They are buried in a small annex of St. George's Chapel at Windsor Castle, alongside Elizabeth II's husband, Prince Philip, and her sister, Princess Margaret. Even if you're not a fan of the royals, it's worth visiting—this site represents an important part of history, for better or worse.

Rome and the Pantheon

Rome is a beautiful and ancient city, where history and grandeur often intertwine to create monumental places of entombment. The Pantheon is one such masterpiece of ancient Roman architecture, steeped in rich history. Built in the second century, it features the largest unreinforced concrete dome in the world. It also serves as the final resting place for some of Italy's most historic figures, including Queen Margherita, a cultural icon during Italy's reunification and the namesake of Margherita pizza, and her husband, King Umberto I. Their son, King Victor Emmanuel III, the controversial ruler during both World Wars who handed power to the fascist Mussolini, is interred elsewhere.

Wandering around the Pantheon, I noticed the large, round open-air skylight at the center of the dome ceiling, called the oculus. It shoots rays of sunlight onto the colorful marble floors, highlighting whatever it touches. Looking at the tombs along the walls allowed me to pay homage to one of the most pivotal artists in world history, Raphael. His Renaissance paintings and design work inspired the masses and influenced many contemporaries.

Not far from the Pantheon lies Vatican City. A few months after the puff of white smoke signaled Pope Francis's election in 2013 from the small chimney atop the Sistine Chapel, Sarah and I had the privilege of listening to the new pontiff deliver an inspiring speech. He emphasized the responsibility of Christians to be good stewards of the environment. Standing in St. Peter's Square, surrounded by thousands of faithful and the marble grandeur of the Vatican, was a humbling experience that filled me with awe.

After the speech, we moved up the steps where the Pope had been speaking and past the façade, where statues of saints watched us enter St. Peter's Basilica. Upon entering, the towering bronze columns connected by a large canopy came into view. It covers the high altar, which is directly underneath the dome of the ornate cathedral. Many believe the tomb of the first pope, the Apostle St. Peter, lies directly below the altar. It's hard to miss the symbolism of keys spread around the Vatican. The keys signify the passing of the church from Jesus to St. Peter and on to all the popes that followed.

According to legend—and possibly history—Emperor Nero ordered the crucifixion of St. Peter. He requested to be nailed to the cross upside down because he felt unworthy of dying in the same way as Jesus. In the fourth century, Constantine commissioned the construction of a church next to Nero's circus, marking the spot where St. Peter was buried. In 1940, excavations beneath the altar uncovered remains believed to be those of St. Peter.

Moving toward the altar, we found the stairs and descended into the grotto. It is home to the remains of numerous popes and other notable figures in Catholic history. Pope John Paul II, who died in 2005, was buried here but was later placed in a tomb on the main floor after he was made a saint. Standing outside the tomb of St. Peter evokes a strong sense of historical reverence in the solemn setting. The tomb is marked by the "Trophy of Gaius," a small shrine built in the second century to honor St. Peter.

One of the few women buried here is Queen Christina of Sweden. She is famous for renouncing her throne in 1654 due to a combination of religious, personal, and political reasons. She converted from Lutheranism to Catholicism and moved to Rome. Another royal buried here, James Francis Edward Stuart, known as the Old Pretender, claimed the thrones of England, Scotland, and Ireland. His claims largely went unrecognized, but he continued to assert his right to the thrones until his eventual exile to Rome.

Arlington National Cemetery

Arlington National Cemetery is a place I hold as the most important and significant cemetery in the United States. As an American, its reverence is unmatched, with over 400,000 service members, other notable Americans, and their families resting here. For visitors, the sea of white gravestones, green grass and mature trees creates a contemplative setting, a meaningful and beautiful testament to the lives and sacrifices of those who served America, honoring not just the buried but all who have given for their country.

The cemetery is built on the land of Robert E. Lee's estate, which was seized by the Union Army during the Civil War. Lee's home is now a museum that explores his life and the complexities of the Civil War. After clearing security at the Welcome Center, I took a moment to view the displays explaining the cemetery's history and purpose. Opting to skip the trolley ride, I set off on foot with the National Park Service's app, which allowed me to locate and learn about those buried within its gates. This approach provided a deeper, more personal and immersive experience for me.

In addition to the commonly visited sites, I spent time at the graves of a couple of my aviation heroes. As a pilot, I have always admired individuals who combined heroism with a dedication to advancing aviation or military efforts. I first visited John Glenn, a man who flew over 100 combat missions, became the first American astronaut to orbit the Earth, and later the oldest person to journey into space. He also served as a U.S. senator for 24 years. Bowing my head before his simple white tombstone, I reflected on the awe he must have felt as he entered orbit for the first time, gazing down at the Earth. Did he feel anxious? Perhaps, but the pride he likely experienced during the height of the space race with the Russians must have far outweighed any fear. I offered a simple prayer of gratitude, as I often do at the graves of my heroes, and quietly moved on.

Another pilot I felt fortunate to honor and thank was General "Jimmy" Doolittle, who led the Doolittle Raiders on a daring mission to bomb Tokyo, creating a significant momentum shift during World War II. This bold operation demonstrated America's ability to strike back after Pearl Harbor, lifting morale on the home front. The mission required meticulous planning and immense risk, as 16 B-25 Mitchell bombers launched from an aircraft carrier without enough fuel to return. The plan was to crash-land in China, and while most crews made it, not all survived the mission—some were killed or captured by the Japanese. Despite the risks, the raid showcased the ingenuity and determination of American forces.

In January 1986, my entire second-grade class gathered in our classroom to watch a historic event unfold on live TV: the launch of the space shuttle *Challenger*. It was a special occasion, not just because it was a space mission but because on board was Christa McAuliffe, a schoolteacher selected for the "Teacher in Space" program. She was set to inspire and educate students across the country by sharing her experiences directly from space.

Our whole grade watched with eager anticipation as the shuttle ascended. But just 73 seconds into the flight, a catastrophic explosion occurred.

The shuttle disintegrated into a massive ball of smoke, sending smaller streaks of debris plummeting back to Earth. It took several moments for the realization of what had happened to sink in. I remember the teachers gasping and rushing to turn off the television. I sat there, completely stunned into silence, wanting to scream or cry but not knowing how to process what I had just witnessed. The gravity of the event unfolded before my young eyes. Much like the 9/11 attacks years later, the explosion of the *Challenger* became a moment seared forever into our collective memory, witnessed through a television screen.

On the back side of the Memorial Amphitheater, the main site for ceremonies, I visited the *Challenger* memorial—a tribute to the astronauts I had watched perish in the sky over Florida many years earlier. The memorial is a simple yet powerful bronze plaque mounted on a stone, featuring the faces of each crew member. The inscription reads: "In grateful and loving tribute to the brave crew of the United States Space Shuttle Challenger, 28 January 1986." Nearby, another plaque honors the crew of the shuttle *Columbia*, which tragically disintegrated during re-entry in 2003.

This might sound a bit out of left field, but I believe I've kept people from going to prison because the *Challenger* disaster is etched in my memory. For a number of years, I was the mental health therapist assigned to a drug court. Drug courts are special courts designed to help felony-level offenders with drug addictions stay out of prison if they successfully complete treatment. There were two occasions I remember where everyone voted to send a person to prison due to a series of violations of their conditions. Both times, it didn't fully sit right with me, so I felt the need to be a voice for the defense. "I'm just playing devil's advocate here, but I think we should give this person another try," I'd say, then proceed to make an argument. Each time, this opened the floor for further discussion and gave the offender another chance.

Before making my stance known, I recalled how "groupthink" influenced the *Challenger* disaster. Some engineers at NASA had spoken up, warning that the O-rings might fail in the cold weather. But their concerns were dismissed under the pressure to move forward. In court,

I saw a similar groupthink emerging—the "everyone votes for prison" mentality. Remembering the importance of speaking up, even when it's difficult, I voiced my dissent. Had NASA heeded those engineers, the *Challenger* might not have exploded. I spoke up and, because of that, two people didn't go to prison—they graduated the program instead.

The most significant stop for me, and likely for most others, at Arlington National Cemetery is the Tomb of the Unknown Soldier. It is a solemn place of reverence and honor for all missing and unidentified American soldiers and, by extension, all soldiers who gave their lives for American causes. Standing on the steps behind the tomb, I gazed down at the large white stone inscribed with "Here Rests In Honored Glory An American Soldier Known Only But To God," and watched as the guard marched back and forth, a silent tribute to protect and honor the fallen. From this vantage point, I could also see the U.S. Capitol in the background.

The experience was profoundly emotional and deeply solemn. At one point, I listened as one of the guards, a member of the elite "Old Guard," firmly but professionally reminded the crowd that this was a sacred space dedicated to honoring those who made the ultimate sacrifice for the United States. Their commitment to duty is unwavering, and they will not hesitate to address anyone they feel is not showing proper respect for this hallowed ground. The last time I watched the guards at the tomb, it was 42 degrees Celsius, yet they continued their vigil without pause, guarding it day and night. A testament to the respect and honor afforded to those interred at the site.

Before exiting the cemetery, I took the short walk up the hill between the Tomb of the Unknowns and the Welcome Center. Here, I found the grave of John F. Kennedy and the eternal flame, which was lit by Jacqueline Kennedy at his funeral only three days after his assassination. The flame symbolizes his vision and legacy. They buried Jacqueline next to John, along with their stillborn daughter, Arabella, and their premature son, Patrick, who lived only two days.

Another significant spot I felt compelled to visit was the 9/11 Pentagon Memorial, located just a five-minute drive from Arlington National Cemetery. This memorial honors the 184 lives lost when American

Airlines Flight 77 crashed into the Pentagon, carried out by Al-Qaeda hijackers. The site is rich with symbolism, including a large circular timeline that surrounds much of the memorial, marking the birth years of each victim—from the youngest, who was just three years old, to the oldest, who was 71.

There are 125 cantilevered benches that either face toward the Pentagon or away from it, symbolizing whether the victim was on the plane or inside the building. Etched into the granite, each bench bears a name—or names, if they were related—with a small reflecting pool beneath and shade trees overhead. The memorial becomes even more poignant at night, with the lights of the benches reflecting off the water, creating a serene and contemplative atmosphere. Some benches held personal items like a can of Pepsi, a toy car, or even a Zima—heartfelt reminders of loved ones left behind, still grieving this senseless tragedy. Much like the American heroes of Arlington, the people who died on 9/11 will always hold a place in my heart.

The Cemeteries of Hollywood: Honoring the Legends of Entertainment

About a month after living in campus housing at the University of Minnesota in Minneapolis following my transplant, I was finally able to return home. It was spring, and the weather was cold and wet. I could feel myself backsliding in my recovery. At the campus apartment, I had been walking several miles a day, but now I found myself cooped up in my house. Being a traveler at heart, I called my surgeon and asked for permission to go to California, where I had found a mental health training program and could also get some exercise in the sunny weather.

I had been to Los Angeles before and had little interest in most of the regular tourist attractions. Like many of my previous trips, I headed to a cemetery. But this time, it was different. This cemetery held the final resting places of many people who had made my childhood feel magical. These were people I had never met, and even if they were alive today, I probably still wouldn't have had the chance to meet them. I've never been much of a fan of celebrity culture, but this felt different. I wasn't going there to gawk—I was going to pay my respects.

So, instead of starting on Hollywood Boulevard, I headed to another spot, just below the famed Hollywood sign: its cemetery.

Driving onto the lot of Hollywood Forever Cemetery off the famed Hollywood Boulevard felt like arriving at an old-time movie studio. In fact, Hollywood Forever Cemetery occupies a massive city block, sharing it with the iconic Paramount Studios, which takes up the other half.

After picking up a map at the flower shop, I got back into my car and noticed the iconic Hollywood sign watching over me from a distance. The map was dotted with famous names marking their graves—a who's who of Hollywood legends. As the old saying from the silver screen goes, "If you can make it here, you can make it anywhere," but I couldn't help but think, "If you're buried here, you certainly did."

Hollywood Forever Cemetery isn't sprawling, but it's large enough that I decided to drive between sections. As I made my way to my first stop, I passed numerous graves and tombs, each beautifully manicured, with tall palm trees swaying overhead. The vibrant vegetation gave the cemetery a tropical feel, unlike any other I'd visited. My first stop was by a pond with deep blue water and a small tomb on an island. Surprisingly, it was the grave of a non-human celebrity that I was most excited to see. His name was Terry. While few recognize him by that name, everyone knows him as Toto from *The Wizard of Oz*.

A small group of animal lovers and Toto fans immortalized the little dog with a bronze statue atop a gravestone, which concisely tells the story of Terry's original resting place being destroyed by construction. On the other side, an inscription reads, "There's No Place Like Home. Rest In Peace, Dear Friend." It's a small but touching tribute to a dog that left an indelible mark on cinema history.

Reflecting on how much Toto meant to countless movie lovers, my thoughts naturally drifted to my own dogs who have passed. Pets are more than just companions; they are integral to our emotional well-being. My current dog, Duke, a Boston Terrier, isn't just a source of daily joy for me—he also plays a role in my therapeutic work. Dr. Duke often accompanies me to sessions, where he helps lift the spirits of my clients as they navigate their struggles.

As I sat there reflecting on outside a large mausoleum, reflecting on pets, I noticed a couple dozen people laying on the lawn performing slow yoga poses in unison. They were being led by a woman with a microphone. I found it a bit odd, but it didn't seem out of place either. The cemetery doesn't really have a very somber feel to it. In an odd way, it felt full of life. Even the Gothic tombs didn't seem as dark. I was in Hollywood, one of the quirkiest places on Earth. A place where the real and surreal often have blurred lines.

I headed back toward the pond across the road, framed by the stunning Hollywood Hills backdrop. Surrounding the pond are the graves of several iconic individuals. The first one that's hard to miss is that of punk rocker Johnny Ramone. A life-sized statue sits atop his large tombstone, capturing him leaning back and playing guitar—a fitting tribute to his legendary career.

Nearby is one of my favorite rockers, Chris Cornell. His music was the soundtrack to countless nights spent around a campfire with friends, beer in one hand and a cigarette in the other. Standing by his grave, I could almost hear his raw, soulful voice singing "Black Hole Sun." I found myself quietly thanking him for bringing joy to so many Friday nights with his incredible talent.

Every turn in Hollywood Forever Cemetery reveals another famous name from the past. I spent several hours wandering among the graves, reflecting on the lives and legacies of those buried there. It was not only a deeply meaningful experience but also a great way to get some exercise—a small but important victory for someone recovering from a transplant.

Also around that same pond was the quintessential leading man of the 1970s and 80s, Burt Reynolds—someone I idolized as a young boy. As an adult, I came to know about the stories of his financial troubles, tumultuous relationships, and allegations of abuse and infidelity. Despite these struggles, Reynolds faced the public with humor and a unique humility that made him admirable in ways beyond his fame. His grave is marked by a simple stone, but with a twist—his bust proudly dons a cowboy hat reminiscent of his *Smokey and the Bandit* days, a fitting tribute to his enduring legacy.

On the other side of the pond, I almost literally stumbled over the grave of a vampire. It was Maila Nurmi, better known to many as Vampira. After a power struggle with Mae West that led to her being fired from a Broadway play, she went on to achieve cult status as the star of *The Vampira Show* and other roles. Her grave is simple but features an engraved image of her as Vampira and is covered with lipstick kiss marks left by adoring fans.

On the other side of the cemetery is the Judy Garland Pavilion, where I could pay my respects to Toto's on-screen mom. Like Reynolds and many others, she was a Hollywood legend with a complex legacy. Judy Garland faced immense pressure as a young girl to maintain her "girl next door" appearance. Movie executives often shamed her, calling her fat, lazy, and ugly. They reportedly gave her amphetamines to keep up with her grueling schedule and barbiturates to help her sleep. This relentless pressure likely contributed to her struggles with anxiety, depression, and addiction later in life. Garland tragically passed away at just 47 from an accidental overdose. Her mausoleum is an elegant design that honors her timeless legacy, featuring a plaque with her name, dates, and the inscription, "I come to you through the years." It's a fitting tribute to her enduring ability to entertain and connect with generations long after her passing.

Just a few kilometers away, about a 25-minute drive, lies another cemetery of the stars—Pierce Brothers Westwood Village Memorial Park cemetery. Though much smaller, it boasts more celebrities per square meter than anywhere else in the world. It is an excellent place to honor and reflect on the lives of some of the most iconic entertainers who ever existed. Unlike Hollywood Forever Cemetery, this cemetery has more of a regular feeling to it, despite the interments of its countless celebrities. It is really a place to reflect on both the light and dark of the entertainment world.

I was pleasantly surprised to be greeted by the grave of Don Knotts, Mr. Barney Fife, at the entrance. His plaque is adorned with a variety of characters he portrayed during his heyday.

Wandering around, I recognized several names. Some of my favorite comedians are buried here. As a child of the 80s, I loved the work of Rodney Dangerfield. It was humbling to have the opportunity to thank him, and when I did, I looked up at his grave with its epitaph featuring one of his famous sayings, "There goes the neighborhood." Even standing at his grave, he gave me one last chuckle. Another laugh came when I strolled by Merv Griffin's grave, where his epitaph humorously declares, "I will not be right back after this message."

On the outside portion of the mausoleum lies true Hollywood royalty: Marilyn Monroe. She was never fully comfortable in the spotlight and tragically died at 36 from a probable suicide. This is where the cemetery took a darker turn for me. In the crypt next to hers rests Hugh Hefner, a man partly responsible for her rise to stardom as an iconic sex symbol. Hefner paid for nude photographs of Monroe and, without her consent, published them on the cover of the first issue of *Playboy* magazine years after they were taken. Monroe had expressed discomfort with her stardom, particularly the sexualization that defined much of her public image, yet felt fame was something she had to pursue.

Hefner paid a large sum to be buried next to her, a fact that angered and saddened me as I stood there. If there was one person in Hollywood who deserved to rest in peace, it was Monroe. Yet, in that moment, it felt like she wasn't truly getting it. I left with a heavy heart, wishing she could have the peace she so desperately seemed to seek in life. At least I was able to tell her I was sorry before I exited.

St. Louis Cemetery No. 1

The St. Louis Cemetery No. 1 in New Orleans is the most iconic cemetery in a city renowned for its cemeteries. In New Orleans, high water levels make traditional burials impractical, so the dead are laid to rest in distinctive above-ground crypts. Many of these crypts have two coffin-sized levels. When someone dies, they are placed in the top crypt, and after a year and a day, the remains—now reduced to bones—are placed in a bag and moved to the lower crypt. This process allows multiple family members, sometimes even hundreds over generations, to share a single tomb. Some believe this practice may have inspired the expression "bag of bones," though its exact origins remain unclear.

St. Louis Cemetery No. 1 is a haunting place in a haunting city, and the most eerie grave there belongs to the legendary Voodoo Queen, Marie Laveau. She blended her African heritage with Catholicism, creating a legacy steeped in myth and mystery. Her tomb is a must-see when touring the city's oldest cemetery. Visitors once marked an "X" on her grave, hoping she'd grant them a wish—a practice now discouraged due to the damage it caused to her final resting place.

In visiting cemeteries, I've discovered more than history or a connection to those interred there. These places compel us to confront the fragility of life and the enduring power of legacy—both the good and the ugly. They remind us that every life, no matter how brief or storied, adds to the rich tapestry of human experience. Whether standing before the ornate tomb of a historic figure or the humble gravestone of a soldier, these moments challenge us to reflect on how we live—and how we hope to be remembered.

Chapter 11

Ghosts: Hauntings and Hunts

*Are ghosts the echoes of lives once lived,
or reflections of our own psyche
in search of meaning?*

DARK TOURISM, in its broadest sense, includes destinations that range from lighthearted, entertainment-focused venues to profoundly serious sites of historical tragedy. One fascinating branch of this, ghost tourism, spans that entire spectrum. I've experienced simple ghost tours designed for a fun, spooky time—perfect for families—where a costumed guide spins ghost stories as you stroll through the heart of a bustling city. These tours are often a mix of fact and fiction, though likely leaning more toward the latter.

On the other hand, some ghost tours and investigations are rooted in historical fact, set in places where genuinely dark events unfolded. While the existence of ghosts might be up for debate, the gravity of these locations and the intention behind exploring them demand a more serious approach. These experiences aren't just about chasing thrills—they're about engaging with history and its lingering impact in a deeply meaningful way.

I often use metaphors from aviation or sports to make a point. They're incredibly helpful in counseling and in making sense of things for myself.

One metaphor I frequently use is the concept of holding patterns—when pilots are instructed to circle before safely moving to the next phase of a flight, usually landing. In ghost tourism, we visit places believed to be haunted because some say ghosts are stuck in their own holding patterns. Are they waiting for clearance to move on to the next phase? Or are they held back by unfinished business they need to resolve? Sometimes, I wonder if I'm being foolish for even pondering such questions.

The unfinished business theory reminds me of my role as a therapist. My clients come to therapy because of difficulties they're having in their lives. Many of them are struggling due to adversity they've faced in the past. They're stuck, preventing them from meeting major life goals—caught in their own sort of holding pattern until they resolve their unfinished business. Sometimes this resolution comes in a cathartic moment, but, more often, it takes time and effort from both them and me. The most satisfying moments in counseling occur when people are able to move on from this holding pattern. This is what lies at the heart of therapy—and, to a great degree, life in general. So why would the afterlife be any different? Maybe it's just one more challenge or step toward the promised land.

The belief in the afterlife is probably more common than one might think, often intertwined with the notion of ghosts. The ability of ghosts to manifest themselves to the living remains a topic of debate. Christians hold funerals and say prayers to assist the deceased on their journey. In Judaism, family members recite the Mourner's Kaddish monthly and on the anniversary of the death, guiding the soul toward the Garden of Eden. In Islam, Muslims perform the Janazah prayer, asking Allah to forgive the sins of the deceased. Both Hinduism and Buddhism have rituals to help the deceased in their journey toward liberation from the cycle of reincarnation, ultimately aiming for Moksha or Nirvana. Even some atheists believe in the possibility of ghosts.

Indigenous tribes of America also have a strong belief in and connection with spirits or ghosts. For some, like the Navajo and Apache, rituals focus on protecting themselves from malevolent spirits. The Navajo practice strict cleansing rituals to ward off harmful spirits. Meanwhile, tribes such as the Ojibwe and Sioux foster a mutually beneficial relationship with spirits, performing rituals to seek guidance and help spirits on their sacred journey to the spirit world.

I've never seen or spoken with a specter and would consider myself an open-minded skeptic. Yet, I've had one seemingly supernatural experience that involved just too many coincidences to dismiss. Does that mean I experienced a supernatural phenomenon? I can't say for sure, but it seems so. Out of all the ghost-related places I've been and shows I've watched, this single experience has given me more confidence in the afterlife than anything else.

The fog that morning was thick. The trees, lakes, and occasional buildings I normally see on my route were invisible. Driving to work felt like I was flying through a thick cloud. About 15 minutes into my trip, I heard a voice in my head: "Chad, slow down, there's a car coming at you." I was stunned. Was it an actual voice in my head? Was it a thought inserted into my mind? All I can say is that it wasn't my own voice or thought. It seemed almost divine. I immediately thought of Jesus or a guardian angel. Could it have been God himself?

A few weeks before this incident, when Sarah and I had visited the Vatican, we attended an audience where the Pope spoke and blessed the crowd. I later learned about a Catholic belief that receiving a blessing from the Pope, especially at the Vatican, provides a higher level of spiritual protection for a time. My initial reaction was, "Yeah, right!" Yet, after that visit to the Vatican, Sarah and I began attending church services more regularly.

I slowed my car as soon as I heard the voice, gripping the steering wheel and watching the fog intently. I started ascending a small hill with a short bridge on top for trains to pass underneath. Before I reached the bridge, a car came screaming directly at me in my lane. I was ready. My reaction was lightning fast—slam the brakes, swerve right. My car stopped just before the bridge, near the edge of a 10-meter drop. The car coming toward me also pulled over, as did the car behind me. I looked over to see what appeared to be a teenage boy behind the wheel, with a car full of kids—probably siblings or friends—on their way to the nearby school. We made direct eye contact for several seconds, and I drove off. I probably never felt such peace as I did in that moment. My usual self likely would have given him the bird and yelled, "You fucking idiot!" This time was different.

How does this relate to ghosts? It might not directly, but it felt supernatural—maybe. At the time, I leaned toward the "probably not" side of agnosticism. After that, I think it nudged me closer to the believer side of the coin. When people experience something they're open-minded about, it allows them to perceive things they might otherwise have dismissed. This is especially true for ghost tourism—going in with an open mind makes all the difference.

I told a few friends I was planning to go on a ghost hunt, and their advice was, "Don't just dismiss everything—keep an open mind." I couldn't help but respond, "Why would I even go if I didn't have an open mind about it?"

Ghost Tours

I've been on a small handful of ghost tours, but the one I found most fascinating was in the French Quarter of New Orleans. The vibe of the city, especially in the French Quarter, creates the perfect environment for a guided walk. The Spanish-style buildings, with their stucco exteriors, wooden shutters, and lush courtyards, set the scene, while jazz music playing in the clubs creates the perfect dark, enchanted ambience.

Before we embarked on our guided walk, our group was told about the city's dark history, filled with tales of war, murders, duels, and massacres. Stories about voodoo spells and rituals came to life as we passed one of the many voodoo shops. Then there were the legends of vampires and pirates that added to the allure.

One story we heard about was the LaLaurie Mansion, where tales of ghostly activity have circulated for decades. Madame LaLaurie, a wealthy New Orleans socialite and prominent figure in the French Quarter during the early 1800s, owned the mansion, which is often considered one of the most haunted homes in the world. The legend centers on accounts of LaLaurie locking enslaved individuals in a small room. In 1834, a fire broke out at the mansion, revealing the horrific conditions in which they were kept—some chained and severely mistreated. While many details have likely been exaggerated over time, the discovery shocked the public. Today, visitors to the house claim to hear moaning from the room and the echoes of footsteps, adding to its eerie reputation. For me, the plight of the enslaved individuals who suffered there resonated far more deeply than any ghost stories attached to the mansion.

One particularly terrifying story that adds to the mansion's lore is about a man who rented a room there and was later found brutally murdered. A detective investigating the case allegedly spoke with the man's friends, who claimed he had told them he was being harassed by ghosts and a demon. According to the tale, the demon warned him it wouldn't be satisfied until he was dead. While it certainly makes for an entertaining story, there's no way to know if it's true—or just another chilling piece of the mansion's legend.

Rose Hall, Jamaica

When I can, I prefer to take part in ghost experiences that focus on a single story or property. Many historic estates and properties offer ghost tours that, unlike city walking tours, focus exclusively on the history and hauntings of one location. Rose Hall near Montego Bay, Jamaica, for instance, was a thrilling and educational encounter with the legend of the supernatural. This beautiful plantation conceals an exceptionally horrifying history. While they offer regular day tours, the savagely dark history lesson is reserved for the evening ghost tour.

The Rose Hall plantation on Cinnamon Hill has one bit of history that stands out to me in a good way: Johnny Cash and his wife, June Carter Cash, lived part-time on the estate's property from the early 1970s until his death in 2003. The area, with its rolling hills and lush tropical trees and flowers, is stunningly beautiful. It's no wonder the Cash family cherished their time there. But while Cash was the "Man in Black," the story of Rose Hall is much darker.

As I walked up the stone walkway and steps toward the estate's Great House, surrounded by meticulous tropical landscaping, I felt like I was approaching a majestic castle. The Great House itself is a three-story stucco mansion with a grand cement veranda out front.

Annie Palmer, a woman from Haiti, married a wealthy plantation owner and became a notorious figure in Jamaican history and folklore. She was well known for her sadistic cruelty toward slaves, earning her the title "White Witch of Rose Hall." Legend has it that she had a dungeon where she practiced voodoo and tortured slaves that she didn't care for. The ones she did like, she is said to have forced into sex. When she became bored of them, she would simply just kill them.

Annie entered into three marriages, and legend has it that she killed all three husbands. She allegedly poisoned her first husband, stabbed her second, and hung her third. Her reign of terror ended in the 1830s during a slave revolt, where she was killed by those she had treated with such cruelty.

The tour guide led us around the house at night, with only a few lights on to guide our way. We could see the gorgeous furniture and opulent living spaces that only the extremely wealthy could have obtained. As the guide slowly unraveled the story and legend of Annie Palmer, I learned that the property is allegedly haunted not only by Annie but also by many of the slaves, husbands, and lovers she killed.

Then I started to notice workers in the background moving slowly. As they came closer, I realized they weren't just workers—they were actors portraying the ghosts of enslaved individuals, likely killed by Annie. These silent figures added an eerie authenticity to the experience, despite being part of a staged performance.

By the end of the tour, it was completely dark outside. The guide led us into the woods by flashlight to see the above-ground tomb of Annie Palmer. Then, the guide turned off the light, and it happened a few seconds later—a large chain loudly rattled against the ground, causing all of us to jump and let out gasps or screams.

As a therapist, we're not allowed to diagnose anyone we haven't personally examined. This safeguard helps prevent politically motivated claims about public figures having certain mental illnesses. Diagnosing someone who lived 300 years ago would be even more challenging. That said, I'll step out on a limb and suggest that Annie Palmer was not only a psychopath but a sadistic psychopath and a serial killer of the most extreme kind. To me, hearing these stories—even if only half true—places Annie's reign of terror on a level that ranks her among the most notorious murderers of all time.

Johnny Cash and June Carter Cash were acutely aware of the stories of Annie Palmer. Johnny recorded a chilling song called "The Ballad of Annie Palmer," describing her cruelty and her ghost—a song that I had never heard prior to my visit, but one that now has context and meaning.

RMS *Queen Mary*

The RMS *Queen Mary*, launched in 1934 and once the fastest ocean liner in the world, is now permanently docked in Long Beach, California. After retiring from service in 1967, the ship was transformed into a tourist attraction and hotel, offering a mix of historic and ghost tours. I joined a regular day tour to immerse myself in the ship's legendary history, but the ghost tours are where its eerie stories come to life for thrill-seeking visitors. After the day tour, guests are free to explore the massive ship on their own. I spent a total of six hours aboard and even enjoyed a time-period band featuring a flapper-style lounge singer at the main bar.

The *Queen Mary*, often compared to the *Titanic*, was a marvel of maritime engineering, dwarfing the ill-fated ship by 1.5 times. The ship boasted an extravagant first-class section, replete with lavish entertainment and fine dining that catered to the top tier of society. In contrast, the second-class passengers had access to more basic services with limited entertainment. The third-class section was congested, and passengers often entertained themselves by creating their own makeshift shows.

The likes of Judy Garland, Liberace, Frank Sinatra, and the Glenn Miller Orchestra—names that still resonate with elegance and class—treated the first-class passengers to performances. But it wasn't just the performers of its day who graced the decks of this majestic liner. Icons such as Clark Gable, Elizabeth Taylor, Audrey Hepburn, Bob Hope, Bing Crosby, Fred Astaire, and Cary Grant all sailed aboard the *Queen Mary*. Supposedly, Queen Elizabeth, then a young princess, was the first child to slide down the nursery's slide—a delightful myth that adds a touch of royal charm to the ship's storied past.

During World War II, the *Queen Mary* earned the nickname "The Grey Ghost" due to its stealthy camouflage paint. Repurposed as a troop transport, it carried up to 16,000 troops at a time, traversing nearly one million kilometers while under constant threat from German U-boats. Remarkably, the ship remained unharmed by enemy assault throughout the war. Prime Minister Winston Churchill sailed on the *Queen Mary* multiple times, relying on its remarkable ability to evade attack.

The ship was not without incident during the war. In 1942, while performing evasive zigzag maneuvers, the *Queen Mary* collided with an escort ship. The collision cut the HMS *Curacoa* in half, resulting in the loss of over half of its 430 sailors. Bound by wartime protocols, the *Queen Mary* did not stop, continuing its course as other ships rescued the survivors from the frigid North Atlantic waters. To maintain morale on the home front, they kept this terrible event a secret until after the war.

Today, touring the RMS *Queen Mary* transports visitors into the world of yesteryear. As I walked through the historic ship, I began to imagine what life might have been like during its heyday—perhaps explaining why the ship is said to attract spirits from another dimension. Moving around the decks and hallways gave me an eerie feeling, as though a specter might be roaming nearby.

In its prime, the ship was alive with the sounds of people talking and laughing, music playing, waiters serving, children running, and the crew hard at work. Where does all that energy go when the people are gone? Does it leave with them, or does it remain, manifesting in the form of spirits?

The contrast between the ship's grand first-class sections, with their elegant ballrooms and reading areas, and the simpler, more confined spaces of second- and third-class accommodations seems to add to its haunted lore. Stories often suggest that spirits tied to different parts of the ship reflect the social divide of the era, with ghostly echoes of wealthy passengers mingling uneasily with the memories of those who lived and worked below decks. Coupled with the 239 lives lost in the collision with the HMS *Curacoa* and the 49 other deaths aboard over the years, it's no wonder there are so many reports of ghosts on the ship.

The first-class swimming pool is considered a hotspot for paranormal activity. Visitors often report seeing a lady in white roaming the area and hearing the sounds of children laughing and swimming. There are even claims of ghostly figures appearing in age-appropriate swimwear. The second-class swimming pool is also said to have had its share of hauntings. As for third-class passengers, they didn't have their own pool but occasionally used the other pools when the upper classes were occupied elsewhere.

I had the chance to glimpse the first-class swimming pool. The echoing, empty room, with its brick Art Deco design, felt eerily atmospheric—almost as if it were truly haunted, if such a thing exists. Later, after watching a horror movie about the ship, I learned that this very pool is considered a paranormal hotspot.

In infamous stateroom B340, there are countless reports of hauntings. Guests who have stayed there talk about faucets turning on by themselves, bedding being pulled, and the unsettling sensation of being touched or even pushed. Being in this room reminded me of those nights when I'd notice a shadow on my wall that looked like a spooky figure. It would send shivers down my spine—until I'd realize it was just a basket of clothes. Staying in room B340 feels like that moment, but without the comforting realization that it's just a basket of clothes.

Moving down into the ship's engine room, I had heard that I might encounter the ghost of John Henry, who was reportedly crushed by a watertight door during a drill. In the nearby, eerie boiler room and cargo hold, shadows and spooky sounds—such as footsteps—are said to be associated with him or others. I had also heard that while wandering through the rest of the ship, I might catch a distinct smell of pipe tobacco, believed to signal the presence of Treasure Jones, the ship's last captain, still patrolling the halls. These are just a few of the stories that make up the *Queen Mary*'s haunting legacy. They were on my mind as I roamed the silence of its belly, acutely aware of the ship's eerie atmosphere and open to anything paranormal.

Between the famed ship's history, the alleged hauntings, and its proximity to Hollywood, it's no wonder the *Queen Mary* has inspired multiple TV shows, movies, and books that amplify its allure. However, one aspect of the tour left me uneasy: a TV hidden in the boiler room projecting a haunting blue flicker—a clear indication that the staff are leaning into theatrics to exploit the ship's haunted history. It made me wonder what other illusions or mysteries might be artificially created.

I was hoping for an authentic experience, and while I understand the entertainment value, I would have preferred to know upfront about these added effects. It prompted me to research the subject, only to find that there's no definitive public answer about how much is real and how much is staged on the *Queen Mary*. For someone genuinely searching for answers to big questions, these kinds of embellishments have the potential to blur the line between history and fiction. To me, it's a question of ethics—transparency is key, especially when it comes to something so tied to personal curiosity and belief.

Ghost Hunting

Over the years, I've heard countless stories about paranormal experiences from the people I've worked with—most of them not struggling with delusions or hallucinations. These stories often involve loved ones who have passed away, seemingly returning to spend a little more time before moving on. One woman I worked with lost her daughter in a tragic accident during the course of our therapy. The sessions that followed were heartbreaking.

A few weeks after her daughter's death, she began sharing that her daughter was visiting her, offering signs that she was okay. Over time, my client's grief started to ease. She eventually told her daughter that she was ready for her to go to heaven, reassuring her that everything would be all right. From that point on, she reported no further paranormal experiences.

Since my childhood, I viewed ghosts as figments of imagination, thinking that Slimer and the Stay-Puft Marshmallow Man of *Ghostbusters* fame were as close to actual specters as one could get. About 10 years ago, I was home on Halloween, and a show called *Ghost Hunters* was playing back-to-back episodes. I was intrigued, still skeptical, but more open to the possibility.

I've also met people over the years who have conducted their own paranormal investigations. Their stories of footsteps, voices, and shadow figures were intriguing and allowed me to be even more open to the possibility. Eventually, I had to give in and went on my first ghost hunt. I'm not experienced—I've only been on two—but both of these experiences, while not providing the evidence I sought to make me a firm believer, did prove to have several benefits.

Nopeming Sanatorium

My first ghost-hunting experience was a blend of a ghost hunt and a ghost tour at the Nopeming Sanatorium. Sadly, the building is now off-limits due to unsafe conditions. However, there are countless opportunities for ghost hunts at both well-known and local sites. While Nopeming may no longer be accessible, this is just one of my experiences, and those interested in exploring the paranormal can find many similar adventures elsewhere.

I knew the location of the Nopeming Sanatorium as it was only about 100 kilometers from my home. I drove by the large institution that is partly hidden on a hill in the wooded area outside of Duluth, MN. It wasn't until seeing an episode of *Ghost Adventures* that I learned about its haunted history. Around Halloween in 2018, I saw that they were doing tours of the old TB hospital, so I had to go check it out.

Walking down the overgrown, winding quarter-mile road at sunset with about 10 others, I couldn't help but feel a mix of eeriness and intrigue as we approached the abandoned sanatorium. Opened in 1912, this facility was a place of hope for tuberculosis patients seeking treatment. Sadly, despite the dedication of its staff and the meaningful activities provided to patients, the majority still succumbed to the disease. Around the time the sanatorium opened, the mortality rate for TB was roughly 80 percent.

At its peak, Nopeming housed up to 400 patients at a time and, over the years, more than 1,000 lives were lost within its walls. While the staff worked tirelessly to ensure these individuals could pass with dignity, one question lingers: did all their souls move on? Many believe they didn't.

By the time we stepped inside the sanatorium, it was dark. This tour did not provide us with ghost-hunting equipment, but we all did bring the required flashlight. We had to rely on our senses to sniff out the supernatural.

I think I spent more time thinking about the patients of the facility than looking for ghosts. As I strolled around the large hospital, complete with lead paint flaking off the white and green walls and the damp stale smell of abandoned building, I pondered what the experience of the patients were like. Being separated from their families, animals, friends, knowing that their illness was going to likely take their lives must have been horrifying and extremely depressing.

The feelings of loneliness and longing for loved ones must have been overwhelming despite the large number of patients and staff around. It made me ponder a thought that I still wrestle with: "Did parents in the old days keep their loved ones at a distance, knowing they were much more likely to die an untimely death?" It seems that attachment to loved ones was a bit different back then. Even today, people who worry about being hurt or abandoned by loved ones often build emotional walls.

The tour mostly stayed together, but there were times when we could investigate on our own, weaving in and out of the most significant rooms in the sanatorium. There was a stage where patients who were well enough performed for each other, a room with diagnostic machines, and a large dormitory with metal-framed beds—each more eerie than the last. Then came the opportunity to split up and take a patient's room alone. With the flashlight off, sitting there in the darkness, eyes wide open, listening for the slightest sound, and watching for the faintest movement, I was ready to embrace anything. Waiting longer and longer, but nothing came. It was time to flip the switch on the flashlight and walk back to the starting point.

Is there just a thin veil separating the living from the dead? Was I simply thrill-seeking, or is there something that lies beyond my understanding? Although the experience didn't bring me any paranormal encounters, it brought a sense of adventure, intrigue, and, most importantly, it helped generate empathy for the souls that once called this hospital home—or maybe they still do.

Gettysburg, Pennsylvania

The Battle of Gettysburg is often considered the turning point of the Civil War. It ranks among the deadliest battles in American history, with over 7,000 soldiers losing their lives. Walking down the sidewalks of the historic town, I noticed a haunting bronze statue that turned out to be that of Jennie Wade, the young civilian woman killed by the Confederate sharpshooter, discussed in an earlier chapter. The bronze statue has her looking off into the distance, holding a loaf of bread she was making for Union soldiers. The house, now a museum, is a popular stop on many ghost tours.

With all this deadly history it is no wonder that there are well over a dozen companies providing ghost tours in Gettysburg. The vast majority also offer ghost-hunting expeditions complete with the essential equipment required to locate and communicate with specters. These tours often combine historical facts with spine-chilling lore, creating an immersive experience that highlights the town's rich and haunting past.

I rolled into town on the 3rd of July, the anniversary of the battle, hoping that it would stir up some extra paranormal activity. I secured a slot for my ghost-hunting journey and decided to walk around the town a bit more.

I was drawn into one of the several buildings still standing from the battle. It had a charming yet spooky allure with its antique decor and waitresses wearing time-period clothing. Much of the downtown area is authentically from the Civil War era and full of character. Ironically, the building happened to be the Farnsworth House Inn, the location where the sharpshooter fired the shot that killed Wade. Upon researching the property, I discovered that it is considered one of the most haunted places in Gettysburg. In addition to being associated with Wade's death, the building was used as a hospital during the battle, and visitors often report eerie sounds coming from the attic as well as singing in the basement, further adding to its haunted reputation.

After reaching the meeting point for the first of two stops on our ghost hunt, we received our equipment and a few pointers and then we all went our separate ways in the McCurdy Schoolhouse. Rumor is that it once started on fire and some of the children perished. It is also adjacent to a significant part of the battlefield where Union soldiers gathered under the command of General Merritt. It is said to be haunted by soldiers and schoolchildren. A white bench on the front porch is often accompanied by a spirit that enjoys the company of women and there are multiple reports of women being touched there.

To say I felt odd and out of place during my first few minutes in the school would be an understatement. Talking to ghosts in the dark, knowing that other people could hear me, made it even more awkward. "My name is Chad, what is your name? Did you die here?" Nothing came back to me. Maybe it was because I was whispering too softly because I didn't want others to hear.

I thought to myself, "Dammit, I came here for a reason. No one knows me anyway, and if they did, it wouldn't matter because they are here to hunt ghosts too." From then on, I went full into ghost-hunter mode. I changed my spot a few times and finally got into a position where I felt there might be some action. After tossing out some military ranks and related jargon, I evoked my knowledge of President Lincoln. I said again, "My name is Chad." Then I immediately heard back in a ghostly sounding voice: "Chad."

It came out of the "spirit box," a radio-like device that quickly scans different radio frequencies. I soon dismissed it as confirmation bias, a psychological phenomenon where someone anticipates something happening and believes it occurred when it didn't. Maybe it just sounded like my name, and instead it was a radio station coming through. It reminded me of hearing a crashing sound in the woods while out hunting deer as a kid, only to find out it was a squirrel on dry leaves. In either case, my blood was pumping hard, I was ready.

Our next location was much higher on the creepy scale. It was an old farmhouse on Hospital Row, with a mass grave on the property for soldiers who had died either in the nearby battle or its aftermath. The three-story house was large and white, and it was almost completely empty of furnishings. Hearing the stories of suffering was immense and gruesome. Surgeons had cut off so many arms and legs with their bone saws that there were piles building up on the ground outside from the limbs accumulating after being tossed out the windows.

We were off on our own again to explore. I sat in a doorway, hoping a spirit would try to pass through, listening to my spirit box and watching carefully for one of my EMF (electromagnetic field) detectors to light up, indicating that there might be a ghost in the immediate area. Nothing happened, so I went out to the mass grave. It was eerie, dark, and humid, with a spooky haze in the air. I could almost picture the hundreds of soldiers lying around in agony.

Trying to talk with ghosts may have felt bizarre at first, but it really gives an extra push toward empathy. You are trying to have a conversation with someone who lived through something extremely traumatic, in the immediate aftermath of the trauma. It's a unique situation, especially when asking them about the battle, where they were from, who they were missing back home, and how they died. It made me forget about the awkwardness of the task at hand and really express genuine empathy for someone who died over 150 years ago.

After spending some time in the field, I went back into the house to explore. I eventually sat with all my devices around me, hoping for the experience of a past lifetime. After getting nothing after several minutes, I went walking again. I found a small bathroom. My EMF meter started glowing and read 4.1. The highest reading all night had been less than 1. It was highest near a medicine cabinet. My heart sped up as I pondered, "Should I open it?" Of course, I had to. I slowly opened the door to find a surprise. Unfortunately, it was another debunk. It was a medicine cabinet containing a fuse box, and the sole reason my EMF reader went off.

Getting back together as a group was interesting. I saw several of the people during the hunt but didn't talk to them until our debriefing. This was with the exception of a husband-wife team who came up to me and asked if "Bill" had come through to me. They were talking with him all night and thought they heard him over my spirit box. I didn't hear it, but did I miss it? I don't know, but during our wrap-up session, I heard the stories from the others.

Many, about half, had interesting tales. One person said a balloon kept popping up in the air on command, another saw a moving shadow person, and others had direct responses to their spirit box. I can't say I believed anything they said was overtly paranormal in my eyes, but I can't say otherwise either. I will do it again and hope to gain concrete evidence of the other side, but, until then, I will keep an open mind and be grateful for my experiences with ghost tours and hunts.

Chapter 12

A Journey's End

*When our journey ends,
is it then that our true journey begins?*

NEARLY EVERYONE has visited a site that could be considered dark tourism. Even with a conservative definition, a study of 900 American travelers found that 82 percent had engaged in dark tourism, and over half of those who hadn't were interested in visiting such a site in the future. But what truly makes someone a dark tourist? To me, it's similar to the difference between a skydiver and someone who has gone skydiving once. A dark tourist with motives similar to mine regularly seeks out places of historical significance as a way to connect with the past, ourselves, and even to the events of today.

Whether a person visits once or hundreds of times, these experiences can be transformative when approached with the right mindset. Motivational speakers might inspire us to chase our goals or see the world differently for a moment, but dark tourism challenges us to confront the depths of human experience, leaving a lasting mark on how we understand life. I firmly believe that anyone who takes the time to honor and reflect on history—regardless of whether they embrace the "dark tourist" label—will find their explorations rewarding, just as I have. Stepping into the shadows has a unique power to transform us, offering insights and understanding that no textbook, speaker, or film ever could.

No matter where I journey, my compass always points home. Yet, it often takes time to fully process my thoughts and emotions after returning from each experience. At first, I often feel as though a dark cloud of sadness hovers over me. This, at least in part, stems from the contrast between being home and emotionally processing the weight of what I experienced at dark sites. Post-vacation depression is a common phenomenon, but it seems to hit me hardest when I visit dark destinations. Settling back into my routine becomes an essential part of this process, allowing the impact of those experiences to gradually seep into my life. Over time, small realizations emerge, ultimately leading to deeper meaning and lasting change.

Visiting these sites reminds me that life can change in an instant. Yes, we all know that, but being present at these places makes you feel it. Many scholars argue that emotional intelligence is more important than intellect, and I couldn't agree more. All the intelligence in the world means little without control over our emotions. That is the power these sites hold—the ability to stir something deeply emotional and transformative.

When I learn about suffering and death at sites of tragedy, I am reminded of my own mortality. It pushes me to live with greater intention and love more deeply. Through the stories of those who endured unimaginable suffering, I strive to connect with their experiences and draw strength. This connection has a deep impact on me, giving me the courage to confront my own fears and struggles head-on. It has helped me find a resilience I never knew I had the ability to muster.

So much of this process seems to occur on a subconscious level. At the root of many of my endeavors is a constant need to learn and grow. Despite my sincere intent to honor those remembered at dark tourism sites, I sense there's something deeper happening in my mind. The lessons and emotions from these visits take time to settle, and I allow myself the space to sit with them until they do. When I feel I've stopped growing, I seek my next journey. When life is going well, I might be more inclined to head to a beach or the mountains. But when

I'm struggling, I find myself gravitating toward places that reflect my inner turmoil.

Could this be why I chose to go to Jerusalem when I needed faith or to Auschwitz when I faced the possibility of my own death? I truly believe it was. Would I have experienced meaningful change if I had visited those sites when life was going well? Perhaps—but not in the same way. The lessons might have been there, dormant, waiting for the moment I needed them most. This reminds me of Churchill's words, which resonated deeply with me during the end stages of my illness and throughout my recovery—or when I reflected on my experiences of bravery at battle sites. Those moments taught me how to move forward when all felt lost during my divorce. Standing at the graves of ordinary humans who did extraordinary things helped me gain confidence in my own endeavors.

My life has been transformed by these experiences. Without them, I might be a lonely, anxious person, lacking confidence and meaning. More likely, I wouldn't have had the strength to endure my illness and transplant. I might have been left traumatized by the experience—or perhaps I wouldn't have survived at all.

At the heart of dark tourism, for me, is the reverence I feel when standing at these sites. I never visited any of these places expecting them to help me, but they did. And I feel compelled to share that experience.

Local Dark Tourism

Not everyone has the time, resources, or ability to travel far for dark tourism, but that doesn't mean it's out of reach. I've found that within an hour of most people's homes, there are likely dark tourism-related sites that offer meaningful connections to history. Whether to stay engaged with dark tourism or simply out of curiosity for local history, countless options are often closer than you might think.

When I began exploring my local area more strategically, I drew a circle with a radius of about 100 kilometers around my home and searched for cemeteries, museums, and monuments with historical significance.

Within this range, I discovered three cemeteries rumored to be haunted: one connected to a missing teenage hitchhiker, another located near a former tuberculosis hospital, and a third where three women were reportedly executed. Cemeteries, even those close to home, often hold fascinating stories and provide reflective spaces to honor lives once lived. For me, walking through a cemetery is far more significant than a stroll through the average park—it's a chance to connect with history, reflect on life, and honor the stories of those who came before us.

Some cemeteries, especially those tied to different cultures, provide even more solemn and unique experiences. I was fortunate to visit an Ojibway cemetery, where a tribal member explained their burial traditions, including "spirit houses" that protect the graves below. That experience gave me profound insights into how different cultures memorialize the dead.

Other local sites I've explored include historical mines, such as one near my home, where visitors can tour and reflect on the dangerous conditions iron miners once faced. In Duluth, MN, I visited Glensheen Mansion, the historic estate known in part for its infamous murder and haunted lore. Downtown, I found a memorial for three African American men tragically lynched in 1920, which was both sobering and deeply moving. The maritime museum, with its stories of shipwrecks like the *Edmund Fitzgerald*, is another site that adds depth to my dark tourism experiences.

Through some research—whether online, with historical societies, or at local libraries—I've uncovered hidden history in my area. On one visit, I came across old newspaper clippings about locals who perished on the *Titanic*. These local journeys have given me powerful connections to the past and moments of reflection, all without needing to travel far. They remind me that transformation isn't confined to grand adventures but can also be found in the quieter, often overlooked corners of our own communities.

Looking to the Future

I don't know what my future holds, but I wake up every day with gratitude and purpose. Dark tourism has taught me to see life through a deeper lens and to appreciate it in ways I never imagined. Only by walking through the darkness was I able to truly see the light.

Now, when life-altering events happen—as they inevitably do—or when I wrestle with the big questions about life, I draw on the lessons dark tourism has taught me and face them with confidence and courage. These places, steeped in history and human struggle, offer lessons we cannot afford to forget. If we don't visit them—respectfully and thoughtfully—we risk losing them, along with the truths they hold. And we all know the dangers of forgotten history, both individually and as a society.

The experience may be challenging, but the most meaningful paths often are. By stepping into these spaces with open eyes and an open heart, you may uncover insights that deepen your understanding of the world—and your appreciation for your own story.

The question isn't whether these places will teach you something—it's whether you are ready to embrace what they have to offer. Thank you for walking alongside me on this path. And as we part ways, I wish you memento mori on your quest for a deeper, more meaningful life.

To My Readers,

Thank you for joining me on this journey through some of the world's most transformative places. Sharing these stories with you has been an honor, and I hope this book has sparked reflection, inspired personal growth, and offered a fresh perspective on life and history.

If this book resonated with you, I would be deeply grateful if you could take a moment to leave a review. Your thoughts and insights not only help other readers discover this book but also foster a shared connection around meaningful experiences.

Please consider spreading the word about this book with others—whether it's recommending it to a friend, mentioning it in your book club, or sharing your thoughts on social media. Your voice can inspire others to embark on their own journey of discovery and growth.

I'd also love to stay connected with you! Visit me at DrChadScott.com to sign up for my newsletter, follow me on social media, and find my personal contact information. I look forward to hearing your stories, reflections, as well as your thoughts about the book.

I wish you safe travels and a journey filled with inspiration and transformation. Thank you for joining me on mine.

With heartfelt gratitude,

Chad

Bibliography

Citations and Recommended Reading

Introduction and 1. The Making of a "Dark Tourist"
Goodall, Jane, *Reason for Hope* (New York, Warner Books, 1999).
  A deeply inspiring memoir that weaves Jane Goodall's pioneering work with chimpanzees, her spiritual journey, and her unwavering belief in the resilience of humanity and the natural world.
Sharpley, Richard and Stone, Philip R., *The Darker Side of Travel: The Theory and Practice of Dark Tourism* (Bristol, Channel View, 2009).
  An academic exploration of dark tourism, examining why people visit sites associated with death and tragedy.
Stone, Philip R., *111 Dark Places in England That You Shouldn't Miss* (Germany, Emons, 2021).
  A comprehensive guide to England's most haunted and historically significant dark tourism sites, offering rich historical context and a respectful exploration of tragedy and difficult heritage.
Feichtinger, Gail, et al., *Will to Murder: The True Story Behind the Crimes & Trials Surrounding the Glensheen Killings* (Duluth, Zenith City, 2023).
  A detailed account of the infamous Glensheen murders, offering insights from the lead prosecutor and investigator involved in the case.
9/11 Memorial & Museum – 911memorial.org
  A museum tells the story of the tragic 9/11 events and memorializes the victims.

2. America's Early Battlefields
McCullough, David, *1776* (New York, Simon & Schuster, 2005).
  A gripping account of the pivotal year in the American Revolution, focusing on George Washington and key moments in the nation's founding.
Myers, John M., *The Alamo: A History* (Lincoln, Bison Books, 1973).
  A retelling of the Battle of the Alamo and its lasting significance in American history.
Beckon Books, *Gettysburg National Military Park* (Official Guidebook) (Nashville, Beckon, 2011).
  A concise and informative guidebook offering rich historical insights, accompanied by illustrations and photographs that bring the story of Gettysburg to life.

Swanson, James L., *Manhunt: The 12-Day Chase for Lincoln's Killer* (New York, William Morrow, 2007).
  A gripping account of the manhunt following Abraham Lincoln's assassination.
Brown, Dee, *Bury My Heart at Wounded Knee* (New York, Holt, 2007).
  A heartbreaking history of Native American struggles during the westward expansion, including the Battle of Little Bighorn.
The Freedom Trail Foundation – thefreedomtrail.org
  Information on Boston's historic Freedom Trail.
The Alamo – thealamo.org
  Historical context and visitor information for the Alamo in San Antonio.
Gettysburg National Military Park – nps.gov/gett
  Official National Park Service site for Gettysburg.
Little Bighorn Battlefield National Monument – nps.gov/libi
  Information on the Battle of Little Bighorn and Native American perspectives.

3. Historic Properties

Weir, Alison, *Henry VIII: The King and His Court* (New York, Ballantine, 2008).
  Provides a detailed account of Henry VIII's reign, exploring his personal life, his six wives, and the power dynamics of his influential court, all set against the backdrop of Renaissance England.
Fraser, Antonia, *Marie Antoinette: The Journey* (New York, Vintage, 2002).
  A biography offering insight into Marie Antoinette's life and the political forces that shaped her fate.
Hopkins, Keith and Beard, Mary, *The Roman Colosseum: The Story of the World's Most Famous Stadium and Its Deadly Games* (London, Profile, 2011).
  A historical look at the Roman Colosseum, focusing on its gladiatorial games and public executions.
Historic Royal Palaces – hrp.org.uk
  Learn more about the Tower of London and its royal history.
Palace of Versailles Official Site – chateauversailles.fr
  Explore the history of Versailles, its gardens, and historical figures.
Whitney Plantation – whitneyplantation.org
  A sobering site in Louisiana that tells the stories of enslaved people.
Roman Colosseum – rome.net/colosseum
  Information on visiting the Roman Colosseum and learning about its gladiatorial history.

4. Places of Light and Darkness

Sebag Montefiore, Simon, *Jerusalem: The Biography* (New York, Vintage, 2012).

A comprehensive history of Jerusalem, spanning over 3,000 years.
Mertz, Barbara, *Temples, Tombs, and Hieroglyphs: A Popular History of Ancient Egypt* (New York, HarperCollins, 2009).
An accessible introduction to Egypt's history, this book offers a lively narrative on Egypt's rulers, monuments, and daily life, making it engaging for general readers interested in ancient Egypt.
Devlin, Tara, *Aokigahara: The Truth Behind Japan's Suicide Forest* (Orochi Press, 2019).
An exploration of Japan's infamous "Suicide Forest," uncovering its tragic history, cultural significance, and the personal stories of those drawn to its eerie silence.
Stone, Philip R., *111 Dark Places in Scotland That You Shouldn't Miss* (Germany, Emons, 2025).
A comprehensive guide to Scotland's most haunted and historically significant dark tourism sites, offering rich historical context and a respectful exploration of tragedy and difficult heritage.
Egyptian Ministry of Tourism and Antiquities – egymonuments.gov.eg
Official site for Egypt's ancient treasures, including the Pyramids of Giza and the Valley of the Kings.

5. Medical and Macabre Museums

Graf, Traci, *The Gift of Life: The Reality Behind Donor Organ Retrieval* (Richmond Hill, Firefly, 2014).
Offers a riveting, firsthand account of the challenges and emotional complexities faced by organ transplant coordinators as they work to save lives through organ donation.
Gawande, Atul, *Complications: A Surgeon's Notes on an Imperfect Science* (New York, Metropolitan, 2003).
An exploration of ethical dilemmas, complications, and uncertainties in modern medicine, written by a practicing surgeon.
Von Hagens, Gunther, *Body Worlds: The Anatomical Exhibition of Real Human Bodies* (Heidelberg, Arts & Sciences, 2006).
This book provides detailed insights into the plastination process, featuring striking images of real human specimens showcased in the *Body Worlds* exhibition.
Mütter Museum – muttermuseum.org
Official site of the Mütter Museum in Philadelphia.
New Orleans Pharmacy Museum – pharmacymuseum.org
History of pharmaceuticals in the U.S. at the New Orleans Pharmacy Museum.
Glore Psychiatric Museum – stjosephmuseum.org/glore-psychiatric-museum
Learn about the history of mental health treatment at the Glore Psychiatric Museum.
Body Worlds – bodyworlds.com

Explore Dr. Gunther von Hagens's *Body Worlds* exhibitions.

Douglas, John, *Mindhunter: Inside the FBI's Elite Serial Crime Unit* (New York, Gallery, 2017).
A memoir by an FBI profiler, offering insights into the psychology of serial killers.

6. Prison Tourism

Foucault, Michel, *Discipline and Punish: The Birth of the Prison* (New York, Vintage, 1995).
A philosophical examination of the history of prisons and punishment, analyzing the transformation of punishment from public spectacle to institutionalized control.

Brown, Dr. Amanda, *The Prison Doctor* (Glasgow, HQ, 2019).
The memoir of a doctor working within the UK prison system, offering insight into those who are incarcerated.

Clink Prison Museum – clink.co.uk
Official site of the Clink Prison Museum in London.

Eastern State Penitentiary – easternstate.org
Historical context and exhibitions at Eastern State Penitentiary in Philadelphia.

Alcatraz Island – nps.gov/alca
Visitor information and historical background on Alcatraz Island.

7. Wars and Battlefields

Churchill, Winston S., *The Second World War* (New York, Harper, 1986).
An extensive firsthand account of World War II, written by the British prime minister who led the Allies to victory.

Nelson, Craig, *Pearl Harbor: From Infamy to Greatness* (New York, Scribner, 2017).
A comprehensive overview of the events before, during, and after the Pearl Harbor attack, featuring personal stories of survivors.

Ambrose, Stephen E., *D-Day: June 6, 1944: The Climactic Battle of World War II* (New York, Simon & Schuster, 1995).
A detailed look at the D-Day invasion of Normandy, highlighting the experiences of soldiers and the event's significance.

Hersey, John, *Hiroshima* (New York, Vintage, 1989).
A moving account of six survivors of the atomic bombing of Hiroshima, offering a personal perspective on nuclear warfare.

Churchill War Rooms – iwm.org.uk/visits/churchill-war-rooms
Official website with visitor information and historical details on Winston Churchill's wartime leadership.

Pearl Harbor Historic Sites – pearlharborhistoricsites.org
Main resource for visiting Pearl Harbor, including details on key sites like the USS *Arizona* and USS *Bowfin*.

Normandy American Cemetery – abmc.gov/normandy
  Information about the cemetery and D-Day events.
Topography of Terror museum – topographie.de/en
  Berlin museum with exhibitions on Nazi repression and the Holocaust.
Berlin Wall Memorial – berliner-mauer-gedenkstaette.de/en
  Official memorial site for the Berlin Wall.
Hiroshima Peace Memorial Museum – https://hpmmuseum.jp/?lang=eng
  Information on the Hiroshima Peace Memorial Museum and the effects of the atomic bomb.

8. Shadows of the Holocaust

Frankl, Viktor, *Man's Search for Meaning* (Boston, Beacon Press, 2006).
  A profound psychological memoir in which Holocaust survivor Viktor Frankl explores the human capacity to find meaning even in the face of unimaginable suffering.
Nyiszli, Miklos, *I Was Doctor Mengele's Assistant* (Kraków, Oswiecim, 2010).
  A harrowing firsthand account from a physician forced to assist Dr. Josef Mengele in his inhumane experiments at Auschwitz.
Keneally, Thomas, *Schindler's List* (New York, Atria, 2020).
  The story of Oskar Schindler, who saved over 1,200 Jews during the Holocaust, later adapted into the film *Schindler's List*.
Frank, Anne, *The Diary of a Young Girl* (New York, Bantam, 1994).
  The poignant reflections of Anne Frank, a young Jewish girl hiding from the Nazis, offering a personal perspective on the Holocaust.
Auschwitz-Birkenau Memorial and Museum – auschwitz.org
  Official website of the Auschwitz Memorial, offering historical information and educational resources.
Kraków's Oskar Schindler Enamel Factory Museum – muzeumkrakowa.pl/branches/oskar-schindlers-enamel-factory
  Information on Schindler's factory and Kraków's history under Nazi occupation.
Anne Frank House – annefrank.org
  Official museum website with visitor information and educational resources.

9. Legendary Legacies

Meyers, Jeffrey, *Edgar Allan Poe: His Life and Legacy* (New York, Cooper Square, 2000).
  A biography exploring Poe's life, literary genius, and mysterious death.
Baker, Geoff, *Jack the Ripper: A Chilling Insight Into One of the World's Most Infamous Killers* (Sywell, Igloo, 2016).
  A gripping exploration of the Ripper murders, blending historical investigation with chilling detail to shed light on the enduring mystery.
Gardner, Mark Lee, *Shot All to Hell: Jesse James, the Northfield Raid, and the

Wild West's Greatest Escape (New York, Mariner, 2014).
　A dramatic retelling of the Northfield bank raid and Jesse James's outlaw legacy.

Patterson, Lieut.-Col. J. H., *The Man-Eaters of Tsavo* (SDE Classics, 2019).
　The tale of the infamous lions that terrorized railway workers in Kenya, as told by the man who hunted and ultimately killed them.

Poe Museum – poemuseum.org
　Delve into the life and works of Edgar Allan Poe.

The Edgar Allan Poe Society of Baltimore – eapoe.org
　A comprehensive resource on Edgar Allan Poe's life and works.

Jack the Ripper Museum – jacktherippermuseum.com
　Learn about the Whitechapel murders and the investigation into Jack the Ripper.

Northfield History Center – northfieldhistory.org
　Discover the history of Jesse James's failed bank raid.

10. Historic Cemeteries and Graveyards

Ebestein, Joanna, *Death: A Graveside Companion* (London, Thames & Hudson, 2017).
　An exploration of death's cultural, historical, and artistic representations.

Woodyard, Chris, *The Victorian Book of the Dead* (Dayton, Kestrel, 2014).
　A deep dive into Victorian-era death customs, graveyards, and cemeteries, exploring the cultural significance of burial practices.

Koudounaris, Paul, *The Empire of Death: A Cultural History of Ossuaries and Charnel Houses* (New York, Thames & Hudson, 2011).
　A detailed exploration of ossuaries and burial practices, including the Paris Catacombs.

Paris Catacombs Official Site – catacombes.paris.fr
　Explore the history of the Paris Catacombs, an ossuary that houses the remains of over six million people.

Père Lachaise Cemetery – pere-lachaise.com
　Visit the resting place of iconic figures such as Jim Morrison and Oscar Wilde.

Arlington National Cemetery – arlingtoncemetery.mil
　Explore one of America's most iconic cemeteries, home to military heroes and presidents.

11. Ghosts: Hauntings and Hunts

Dickey, Colin, *Ghostland: An American History in Haunted Places* (New York, Penguin, 2017).
　An exploration of haunted locations across the U.S., focusing on the cultural and historical significance of these sites.

Holzer, Hans, *Ghosts: True Encounters with the World Beyond* (New York, Black Dog & Leventhal, 2004).

A collection of paranormal investigations from one of the world's most famous ghost hunters.

Rose Hall Great House – rosehall.com
Learn about the history and hauntings of the Rose Hall estate in Jamaica.

RMS *Queen Mary* – queenmary.com
Explore the haunted history of the *Queen Mary* in Long Beach, California.

12. A Journey's End

Florence, Kelly, and Hafdahl, Meg, *Travels of Terror: Strange and Spooky Spots Across America* (Naperville, Sourcebooks, 2024).
A fascinating exploration of haunted and eerie destinations across the United States, blending chilling tales with historical context.

National Geographic, *Timeless Journeys: Travels to the World's Legendary Places* (Washington, D.C., 2017).
A stunning travel guide that showcases some of the world's most historic and culturally significant destinations, offering stunning photography and insights.

Atlas Obscura – atlasobscura.com
Website dedicated to uncovering the world's hidden wonders, offering a treasure trove of unique and unusual travel destinations, cultural stories, and historical curiosities.

Acknowledgments

This book would not exist without the unwavering support of many incredible people, to whom I am deeply grateful.

To my parents, who instilled in me a love for travel from an early age, and to my son, Brennan—my most frequent and cherished travel companion—thank you for inspiring my lifelong passion for exploration.

To my friends and early readers, your encouragement and thoughtful feedback made all the difference. A special thanks to Rheanne, whose dedication and tireless efforts helped bring the concise edition to new heights.

To Sarah—thank you for allowing me to share my side of our story. Our journey shaped me in ways I never could have anticipated, and I will always be grateful for the time we shared.

To Dr. Stone—your insightful foreword adds depth and resonance to this work. I am honored by your contribution.

To my doctors and healthcare providers—your care and expertise gave me a second chance at life. And to my organ donor and his family—there are no words that could ever fully express my gratitude. Your selfless gift is the reason I am here today, and I will strive to honor your generosity every single day.

To Kiana and the exceptional team at Whitefox—this book would not have reached its full potential without you. Your collaboration, along with the skilled editors and designers you brought together, transformed this work into something I am truly proud of.

And finally, to you—the reader. Thank you for walking alongside me through some of history's most transformative places. I hope this journey leaves a lasting impact on you, just as it has on me.

Picture Credits

Chapters 1–4

Photo 1: Chad and Sarah exploring Epcot's World Showcase during their first adventure together, Orlando, FL. Chad Scott (published with permission from Sarah).
Photo 2: The 9/11 Memorial beneath One World Trade Center, New York City, honoring the victims of the September 11 attacks. Chad Scott.
Photo 3: Chad walking at the University of Minnesota hospital shortly after his transplant surgery, Minneapolis, MN. Donald Scott.
Photo 4: Bronze statue of Paul Revere's Midnight Ride, with the historic Old North Church in the background, Boston, Massachusetts. Jorge Salcedo – stock.adobe.com
Photo 5: Exterior view of the historic Alamo, San Antonio, Texas. Jorge Salcedo – stock.adobe.com
Photo 6: The statue of General Warren at Little Round Top, Gettysburg Battlefield, Pennsylvania, commemorating the Union Army's defense during the Battle of Gettysburg. Chad Scott.
Photo 7: The dining room of the Confederate White House in Richmond, Virginia, featuring a portrait of George Washington prominently overlooking the space. Chad Scott (Published with permission).
Photo 8: The legendary Tower of London, United Kingdom. Mistervlad – stock.adobe.com
Photo 9: Interior view of the Colosseum in Rome, revealing the underground hypogeum where gladiators and animals awaited their fate. Paolo – stock.adobe.com
Photo 10: The Witch House in Salem, Massachusetts, one of the last standing structures with direct ties to the Salem Witch Trials. Faina Gurevich – stock.adobe.com
Photo 11: Dome of the Rock rising over Jerusalem's Old City, one of the most sacred religious sites in the world. Chad Scott.
Photo 12: Chad standing before the Pyramids of Giza, Egypt. Chad Scott.
Photo 13: Crisis counseling signs on the Golden Gate Bridge, San Francisco, California, a site known for both its architectural significance and its history of suicides. Chad Scott.
Photo 14: Mount Fuji and the Aokigahara Forest, Japan. Joshua Daniels – stock.adobe.com
Photo 15: The grand façade of the Château de Versailles, France. Aterrom – stock.adobe.com

Chapters 5–8

Photo 16: The entrance of the Mütter Museum, Philadelphia, Pennsylvania, known for its collection of medical oddities. Chad Scott.
Photo 17: The Hiroshima Peace Memorial (Atomic Bomb Dome), a preserved ruin serving as a reminder of the devastation caused by the first atomic bombing. Chad Scott.
Photo 18: A preserved section of the Berlin Wall's East Side Gallery, featuring the famous Fraternal Kiss mural of Brezhnev and Honecker. Chad Scott.
Photo 19: The Memorial to the Murdered Jews of Europe, Berlin, Germany, dedicated to the six million Jewish victims of the Holocaust. Chad Scott.
Photo 20: Oskar Schindler's Enamel Factory, now a museum in Krakow, Poland, dedicated to his efforts to save Jews during the Holocaust. Chad Scott.
Photo 21: The Holocaust train car at Yad Vashem, Jerusalem, Israel, commemorating the victims of the Nazi deportations. Damion Ryszawy – stock.adobe.com
Photo 22: The lobotomy exhibit at the Glore Psychiatric Museum, showcasing early and controversial treatments for mental illness. Chad Scott (permission courtesy of the St. Joseph Museums in St. Joseph, Missouri).
Photo 23: Famous Body Worlds anatomy exhibition displaying plastinated human specimens for

medical education. Mara Fribus – stock.adobe.com

Photo 24: A cellblock at Eastern State Penitentiary, Philadelphia, one of America's most notorious historic prisons. Chad Scott (permission courtesy of Eastern State Penitentiary Historic Site, Philadelphia, PA).

Photo 25: Statue of Winston Churchill in Parliament Square, London. Mark Pinter – stock.adobe.com

Photo 26: Alcatraz Island, San Francisco, California, once a maximum-security prison and now a historical site. f11photo – stock.adobe.com

Photo 27: USS Arizona Memorial at Pearl Harbor, Honolulu, Hawaii, honoring the lives lost in the attack on 7 December 1941. Ryan Tishken – stock.adobe.com

Photo 28: The entrance gate of Auschwitz concentration camp, Poland, featuring the phrase "Arbeit macht frei" ("Work sets you free"), a cruel deception for prisoners. Albin Marciniak – stock.adobe.com

Photo 29: Brennan standing outside a Nazi bunker overlooking Omaha Beach, Normandy, France, where D-Day landings took place. Chad Scott.

Photo 30: Statue of an enslaved boy at the Whitney Plantation, Louisiana, a memorial dedicated to honoring the lives and experiences of those who were enslaved in the United States. Chad Scott (Published with permission of Whitney Plantation).

Photo 31: The Topography of Terror museum in Berlin, built on the former site of the Gestapo and SS headquarters, documenting Nazi crimes. Chad Scott.

Chapters 9–End

Photo 32: The Edgar Allan Poe House and Museum, Baltimore, a preserved residence dedicated to the life and legacy of the legendary writer. Chad Scott.

Photo 33: The Tomb of the Unknown Soldier at Arlington National Cemetery, a solemn tribute to unidentified U.S. service members. Chad Scott.

Photo 34: Statue and mausoleum at Hollywood Forever Cemetery, California, a final resting place for many entertainment icons. Chad Scott.

Photo 35: The adjacent crypts of Marilyn Monroe and Hugh Hefner at Pierce Brothers Westwood Village Memorial Park & Mortuary, Los Angeles. Chad Scott (published with permission of Pierce Brothers Westwood Village).

Photo 36: Rose Hall Great House, Montego Bay, Jamaica, infamous for its legends of hauntings tied to the "White Witch." Debbie Ann Powell – stock.adobe.com

Photo 37: RMS Queen Mary, a retired ocean liner and historic hotel in Long Beach, California, rumored to be one of the most haunted ships in the world. Chad Scott.

Photo 38: Inside the now-closed Nopeming Sanatorium in Duluth, Minnesota, once a tuberculosis treatment facility. Chad Scott.

Photo 39: The Ten Bells pub in London, believed to have been the last known location of two of Jack the Ripper's victims before their deaths. Alex Yeung – stock.adobe.com

Photo 40: The Bird Cage Theatre in Tombstone, Arizona, a Wild West landmark with a reputation for ghostly encounters. Brian Welker – stock.adobe.com

Photo 41: Jesse James was adjusting the picture that read "God Bless Our Home" when he was shot. The preserved bullet hole remains beneath the frame. Chad Scott (Published with permission).

Photo 42: The Ossuary of the Paris Catacombs, where millions of bones are arranged in elaborate patterns beneath the city streets. Picasa – stock.adobe.com

Photo 43: The tombs of Marie and Pierre Curie in the crypt of the Panthéon, Paris, France, honoring the pioneering scientists. Petr Polak – stock.adobe.com

Photo 44: Chad discovering the gravesite of his great-great-grandparents in Drammen, Norway. Chad Scott.

Photo 45: Highgate Cemetery West, London, renowned for its Gothic tombs and famous burials. Olivier – stock.adobe.com

Photo 46: The Pantheon in Rome, Italy, a masterpiece of ancient architecture and final resting place of historical figures. Sergey Borisov – stock.adobe.com

Index

Abelard and Heloise 171–2
Adams, Samuel 24
the Alamo 30–1
Alcatraz 110–12
Amenhotep III, Pharaoh 72
American Civil War 23, 31, 32–6, 38, 161, 177, 199
  Confederate White House 35–6
American Declaration of Independence 24
American War of Independence 23–30
Amsterdam 101, 147
Amun-Ra, Egyptian deity 71, 72
ancient Rome 4, 48–51, 72
Arizona, USS 118–19
Arlington National Cemetery 124, 177–80, 181
  Tomb of the Unknown Soldier 180
Armenia 135
astronauts 178
atomic bombs 15, 128–33
Auschwitz 1, 134–43, 205
Australia 23
aviation museums 15, 154

Bangkok
  Siriraj Medical Museum 101
battlefields 13, 22–39, 114–33
Beefeaters 42–3

Berlin 12–13, 124–8
  Berlin Story Bunker museum 124–5
  Berlin Wall 126–7
  Checkpoint Charlie 126, 127
  Memorial to the Murdered Jews of Europe 125, 146–7
  Topography of Terror 124
Bodies...The Exhibition 95
Body Worlds exhibition 8, 94–8
Boleyn, Anne 43–4, 45, 174
Bond films 69
Booth, John Wilkes 36–7
Boston 23–7
  Freedom Trail 24–7
Bourdain, Anthony 71
Bowfin, USS 119
Bran Castle 40–1
Bremer, Edward 110
Brezhnev, Leonid 127
Buddhism 188
Bundy, Ted 159
Bunker Hill, battle of 27, 29–30
Burke and Hare murders 57

Cambodia 17, 135
Capone, Al 108–9, 110, 112
Carter, Howard 74–5, 76
Cash, Johnny and June Carter 191, 193
Catherine of Aragon 44, 174

cemeteries and graveyards 2–3, 7, 13, 15–16, 166–86, 206
  Arlington National Cemetery 124, 177–80
  Boston Granary Burying Ground 24
  Gettysburg National Cemetery 32–3
  historic 166–8
  Hollywood 181–5
  Key West 7
  Normandy American Cemetery 123–4
  Norwegian graveyards 166
  Paris 168–73
Challenger space shuttle 178–80
Chalmette Battlefield 58
Charles III, King 175
Chicago Field Museum 164–5
children
  enslaved 53–4
Chopin, Frédéric 172
Christianity 60, 188
Christina, Queen of Sweden 177
churches
  Jerusalem 63, 64, 65–6
Churchill, Winston 117–18, 194, 205
  Churchill War Rooms 8, 115, 116–17
Cold War 124, 132
Columbia space shuttle 179
Concord 26, 27–8

Congdon, Elisabeth 14
Corey, Giles 57
Cornell, Chris 183
Costa Rica 10
Crusades 61
Curacao, HMS 194, 195
Curie, Marie 173
Custer, George Armstrong 38, 39

Dahmer, Jeffrey 99, 159
Dangerfield, Rodney 185
Darwin, Charles 174
David, King 59, 61
Davis, Jefferson 35–6
death, museums of 98–101
Dix, Dorothea 91, 108
Doolittle, General "Jimmy" 178
Douglas, John
 Mindhunter 99–100
drug courts 179–80
Dumas, Alexandre 173

Earhart, Amelia 152, 153
Eastern State Penitentiary 106–9, 110
Eastwood, Clint 111
Edinburgh 57
Edward IV, King of England 43
Egypt, Ancient 68–77
Einstein, Albert 87, 114, 132
Eisenhower, Dwight D. 120, 121
Elizabeth I, Queen 45, 174
Elizabeth II, Queen 175, 194
Escape from Alcatraz 111–12
Everett, Edward 32

Ford, Robert 161–2, 163
Francis, Pope 176
Frankl, Viktor 2, 11–12, 142
French Revolution 45, 46

Gacy, John Wayne 99, 159
Gage, Phineas 92
Galileo Galilei 47
Gandhi, Mahatma 102, 145
Garland, Judy 184, 193
genocide 17, 23, 135
Gettysburg
 Battle of 32–5, 36, 38, 199
 ghost tours 199–202
ghost tourism 13, 14, 187–202
gladiators 4, 48, 50
Glenn, John 178
Glensheen Mansion 14, 206
Glore Psychiatric Museum 90–4
graveyards *see* cemeteries and graveyards
Grey, Lady Jane 43–4, 45
Griffin, Merv 185

Hancock, General 24, 33
Hare, Robert 100
Hauptmann, Bruno Richard 153
Hawking, Stephen 174
Hefner, Hugh 185
Heloise and Abelard 171–2
Hemingway, Ernest 7
Henry, John 195
Henry VI, King of England 74
Henry VIII, King of England 42, 44, 45, 174, 175
Herod the Great, King 59
Hickok, Wild Bill 160
Hirohito, Emperor 129
Hiroshima museum 128–33
Hirschsprung's disease 88
Hitler, Adolf 125, 146
Holliday, Doc 160
Hollywood 98, 99, 181–5

Holmes, H.H. 159
the Holocaust 134–47
Honecker, Erich 127
Höss, Rudolf 139
Hugo, Victor 173
Hyrtl Skull Collection 87–8

Indigenous Americans 22, 23, 30, 37–9, 112
 historical trauma 17–18, 38–9
 spirits and ghosts 188–9, 206
Islam 60, 61, 63, 188
Israel 61–2

Jackson, General Andrew 58
Jamaica
 Rose Hall 191–3
James, Frank 161
James, Jessie 160, 161–2, 163
Japan
 Aokigahara Forest 20, 77, 79–80
 Hiroshima 128–33
 Pearl Harbour 118–20, 128, 178
Jerusalem 58–67, 71, 147, 205
Jesus 61, 63, 64–7, 176, 189
Jews and the Holocaust 134–47
Joan of Arc 47
John Paul II, Pope 177
Jones, Treasure 196
Judaism 60, 61, 62, 188

Karnak, Temple of 71–2, 72–3
Karpis, Alvin "Creepy" 110, 112
Kelly, Machine Gun 110, 112
Kelly, Mary Jane 159
Kennedy, John F. 180

Kenya 163–5
Khufu, pharaoh 69
King, Martin Luther Jr. 145
King, Stephen 41
Knotts, Don 184

LaLaurie, Madame 190–1
Laveau, Marie 186
Leale, Charles 37
Lee, Robert E. 32, 36, 177
Lexington 26, 27–8
Lincoln, Abraham 37–8, 200
  Gettysburg Address 22, 32–3
Lindberg, Charles 152–4
lions 163–5
Little Bighorn, Battle of 37–9
lobotomy procedures 93
local dark tourism 205–6
London 173–5
  Churchill War Rooms 8, 115, 116–17
  Clink Prison 104–6
  Dungeon 105
  Globe Theatre replica 105
  Highgate Cemetery 16, 173
  Houses of Parliament 115–16, 117, 173
  Jack the Ripper Museum, Whitechapel 99, 157–9
  London Dungeon 8, 12–13
  Tower of London 8, 42–5
  Westminster Abbey 173–4
  Westminster Hall 116
Louis XIV, King of France 45
Louis XVI, King of France 46, 47
Luxor, Egypt 71, 72–3, 101

MacArthur, General Douglas 119
McAuliffe, Christa 178
Mandela, Nelson 145
Marathon, Battle of 4
Marcus Aurelius 166
Marie Antoinette, Queen of France 46–7
maritime museum, Duluth 206
Marx, Karl 16, 173
Mary I, Queen (Bloody Mary) 44, 174
Masterson, Bat 160
medical museums 85–98
Monroe, Marilyn 185
Moore, Roger 69
More, Thomas 44–5
Morrison, Jim 171
Muhammad, Prophet 60
music 155–6
Mütter Museum, Philadelphia 86–9

Nazi Germany 47–8, 120–4
  the Holocaust 1, 17, 134–47
New Orleans 58
  Battle of (1815) 58
  ghost tours 190–1
  Museum of Death 98, 99–100
  Pharmacy Museum 89–90
  St Louis Cemetery No.1 185–6
  Whitney Plantation 16–17, 51–5, 58
New York
  Ground Zero 8–9
Newton, Isaac 174
Nichols, Mary Ann 158
Nimitz, Admiral Chester 119
Noonan, Fred 152
Nopeming Sanitorium 197–9

Normandy, Allied invasion of 8, 120–4
nuclear weapons 128–33
Nurmi, Maila (Vampira) 184

Obama, Barack 132
Palmer, Annie 192–3
Paris 168–73
  Catacombs 3–4, 8, 169–70
  Napoleon's Tomb 8
  the Panthéon 8, 170, 172–3
  Père Lachaise Cemetery 170–2
Patterson, John Henry 164–5
Paul, Logan 20
Pearl Harbor 118–20, 178
Pentagon 9/11 Memorial 180–1
Peter, St 176–7
The Pianist (film) 144
pica 92
Pickett, George 34
Pietila, Velma 14
Pilate, Pontius 65
plastinates 96–8
Poe, Edgar Allan 154–7
  "Annabel Lee" 155–6
  The Pit and the Pendulum 64–5
  "The Raven" 156
Polanski, Roman 143–4
prison tourism 102–13
Pyramids of Giza 68–71

Queen Mary, RMS 193–6

Ramirez, Richard 99
Ramis, Harold 9
Ramone, Johnny 183
Ramses the Great 72, 76
Revere, Paul 24, 26, 27–8
Reynolds, Burt 183–4
Robben Island 145

Roman Colosseum 4, 48–51
Rome
　ancient 4
　the Pantheon 175–6
　St Peter's Basilica 176–7
　the Vatican 176–7, 189
Roosevelt, Franklin D. 118, 132
Rwanda 17, 135

Salem witch trials 56–7
Samenow, Stanton 100
San Francisco
　Golden Gate Bridge 77, 78–9, 80, 111
Sasaki, Sadako 131, 133
Schindler, Oskar 144–5
Seymour, Jane 175
The Shining 41
Socrates 47
South Africa 23
the Sphinx 68, 70–1
Stanley Hotel 41
Stoker, Bram
　Dracula 40–1
Stroud, Robert, Birdman of Alcatraz 110, 112
Stuart, James Francis Edward 177

Sugihara, Chiune 145
Sutton, Willie 108

Teresa, Mother 145
Titanic 193, 206
Tituba 56–7
torture museums 101
Transylvania 41
Travis, Colonel William 30–1
Tsavo Man-Eaters 163–5
Tubman, Harriet 145
Tutankhamun 74–6

United Airlines
　Flight 93 crash site 19–20

Valley of the Kings 73–7
Versailles, Palace of 45–8
Versailles, Treaty of 47–8
Vesuvius, Mount 4
Virgin Mary 63
Vlad the Impaler 40, 41
von Hagens, Dr Gunther 96

Wade, Jennie 34–5, 199, 200
Wallace, William 116, 117

Wallenberg, Raoul 145
Warren, Dr Joseph 26
Wars of the Roses 43
Washington, D.C.
　Ford's Theatre 36–7
　Holocaust Memorial Museum 145–6
　Spy Museum 14–15
Washington, George 35
West, mae 184
Westwood Village Memorial Park cemetery 184
Wiesel, Elie 134
Wilde, Oscar 172
William the Conqueror 42, 174
Windsor Castle 174–5
　St George's Chapel 175
witches 13, 56–7
The Wizard of Oz 182
World War II 48, 58, 115–24, 128–33, 153, 194
　the Holocaust 134–47

Yamamoto, Admiral 128

Zola, Émile 173

Dr. Chad Scott is a multi-category #1 Amazon bestselling author, seasoned explorer, and licensed psychotherapist with over 25 years of experience in mental health. With a Ph.D. in counseling, Dr. Scott has taught psychology at Bemidji State University and Mesabi Range College, written three impactful nonfiction books, and captivated audiences as a speaker at a variety of conferences and seminars.

Dr. Scott combines his expertise in psychology with a passion for transformative travel, focusing on dark tourism—journeys to historically significant and often tragic sites that uncover profound lessons about resilience, healing, and the human spirit. Through his work, he explores the intersections of history, humanity, and personal growth, inspiring readers to reflect on their own challenges and find hope in life's most difficult moments. Having overcome significant challenges with illness, divorce, and anxiety, Dr. Scott brings a hard-earned grit to his writing, offering readers an authentic and inspiring perspective on how adversity shapes our lives. From Hiroshima's Peace Memorial Park to Alcatraz and the Tower of London, his experiences reveal how history's darkest moments can spark transformation and renewal.

When not writing or traveling, Dr. Scott enjoys flying, outdoor adventures, cheering on local sports teams with friends, and spending time with his loyal Boston Terrier, Duke.

www.ingramcontent.com/pod-product-compliance
Lightning Source LLC
Chambersburg PA
CBHW020405080526
44584CB00014B/1182